The Symbolic Foundations of Conditioned Behavior

CHARLES R. GALLISTEL
Rutgers University

JOHN GIBBON
New York State Psychiatric Institute and
Columbia University

 LAWRENCE ERLBAUM ASSOCIATES, PUBLISHERS
2002   Mahwah, New Jersey   London

Lawrence Erlbaum Associates, Inc., Publishers
10 Industrial Avenue
Mahwah, New Jersey 07430

Cover design by Kathryn Houghtaling Lacey

0-8058-2934-2

Printed in the United States of America
10   9   8   7   6   5   4   3   2   1

Contents

Preface

As this book goes to press, there is an ongoing discussion on the Animal Learning and Behavior List Server about the decline of behaviorism in psychology and the rise of cognitivism. Most of the participants in the discussion do research and teaching in animal learning. Most of them remain to varying degrees behaviorists. They are, by and large, uncomfortable with cognitive theorizing and unhappy about the decline of behaviorism. In this book, we hope to persuade students of animal learning that cognitive theorizing is essential for an understanding of the phenomena revealed by conditioning experiments. We hope also to persuade the cognitive psychology community that conditioning phenomena offer such a strong empirical foundation for a rigorous brand of cognitive psychology that the study of animal learning should reclaim a more central place in the field of psychology.

There is, we believe, no way to achieve a coherent understanding of animal conditioning phenomena without recognizing that computational processing of information-bearing sensory signals constructs a symbolic representation of selected aspects of the animal's experience, which is stored in memory and subsequently retrieved for use in the decision processes that determine the behavior we observe. These essentially cognitive notions—information processing, computation, symbolic representation, memory storage, retrieval from memory, and decision processes—are in no sense merely metaphors. They are what the brain is doing to produce the behavior we observe. We cannot understand the phenomena revealed by conditioning experiments without understanding the structure of the underlying information-processing operations in the brain, any more than we can understand the phenomena of chemistry without understanding the structure of the underlying atoms.

We believe our analysis of the work we review also merits the attention of the cognitive science and philosophy communities because it speaks directly to a central question that separates many forms of connectionist modeling from the artificial intelligence (AI) approach to the mind. This is also a question that figures prominently in the philosophy of mind, particularly those aspects of the philosophy of mind that have been influenced by connectionist modeling and by neurobiological considerations, that is, by the argument that the explanation for how the mind works is to be sought in our current understanding of how the brain works. Here the question is whether learning is primarily a matter of *learning that* or primarily a matter of *learning to*.

In traditional AI and traditional philosophy of mind, computers and minds learn that something is true about the world. That is, they acquire beliefs. What they then do follows from what they believe together with the computer's goals or the mind's intentions. Connectionist modeling—and the philosophy of mind allied to it—rejects this account in favor of an account in which symbolic representation of properties of the world (beliefs) play no role. Learning in connectionist computers (and in the brains imagined by philosophers who base their arguments of presumptions about how the brain works) is assumed to be a matter of learning to do something—that is, to respond in a certain way to certain inputs—by means of a rewiring process. The rewiring is driven either by feedback from the consequences of previous actions (back propagation) or by statistical patterns of co-occurrence in the inputs (Hebbian or unsupervised learning mechanisms).

It is often taken for granted by both schools of thought that animals in conditioning experiments are learning *to* respond rather than learning *that* certain things are true about the environment in which they find themselves during the experiment. The question is often taken to be whether anything other than the learning *to* that we supposedly see in animal conditioning experiments is required to explain human learning. Our argument is that the behavior we see in conditioning experiments is the consequence of learning that certain things are true, rather than learning to respond in certain ways. In other words, the symbol processing nature of mental and neural activity is evident in simple conditioning, where the behavior that emerges must be seen as driven by what the animal has come to believe is true. The rabbit blinks in response to a conditioned tone, because it has come to believe that a shock to the orbit follows the tone at a half-second latency with great regularity.

One might suppose, therefore, that we are at risk of "leaving the rat lost in thought" as Guthrie is said to have remarked about Tolman's account of spatial learning. On the contrary, however, our models are built around decision processes, which are formally specified models of how what the animal knows gets translated into what it does. Our models are explicit about how what has been learned becomes manifest in what is done, whereas associative models (learning to models) are famously vague on this very point—how the rewiring caused by experience gets translated into observable behavior.

We believe that our arguments also merit the attention of the neurobiological community. What one looks for in the nervous system is strongly determined by what a behaviorally based conceptual scheme leads one to expect to find there. If you think that talk about the memory for a variable like the duration of an interval, or the magnitude of a reward, or the distance between two landmarks is just a metaphor, then you are not going to waste your time looking for its neurobiological realization, any more than the many biochemists who thought genes were just metaphors wasted their time looking for the molecular realization of the gene.

Neuroscientists interested in the neurobiology of learning and memory are not, for the most part, looking for the mechanisms of information processing. Rather they are looking for associative bonds in the nervous system, that is, changes in synaptic conductance produced by the temporal pairing of synaptic signals. This is evident in the following quotation from the abstract of an article in *Nature,* which attracted widespread attention from the press (e.g., Wade, 1999), as a possible neuroscience breakthrough:

> Hebb's rule (1949) states that learning and memory are based on modifications of synaptic strength among neurons that are simultaneously active. This implies that enhanced synaptic coincidence detection would lead to better learning and memory. If the NMDA (N-methyl-D-aspartate) receptor, a synaptic coincidence detector, acts as a graded switch for memory formation, enhanced signal detection by NMDA receptors, should enhance learning and memory. . . . (Tang et al., 1999, p. 63)

There is, we argue, little empirical foundation for the claim that coincidence detection on a time scale of a few hundred milliseconds plays any role in learning or memory, at least not in the learning and memory processes that mediate basic conditioning. As we show at some length, the behavioral data indicate that what matters in conditioning are the relative durations of the intervals in the protocol, not their absolute durations. The importance of relative durations as opposed to absolute durations is central to our suggestion that conditioning processes are *time-scale invariant.*

We argue that what neuroscientists ought to be looking for are not mechanisms of synaptic plasticity activated by narrow temporal coincidences but rather mechanisms by which variables may be stored and retrieved. Mechanisms for the storage and retrieval of variables, together with mechanisms for doing computations with those variables, are the heart and soul of a conventional computer, so there can be no question about the physical realizability of such mechanisms. How they are realized in neural tissue is another matter. Neuroscientists will not get an answer to this profoundly important question until they begin to actively look for the mechanisms of information processing.

This book is based closely on a paper in the *Psychological Review* entitled "Time, Rate, and Conditioning" (Gallistel & Gibbon, 2000). Most of the figures and much of the text first appeared there. That paper was being written at the time one of us (CRG) was asked to give the MacEachran Lectures at the University of Alberta. The lectures, of which this book is a product, were given October 6-8, 1997. CRG is grateful to our colleagues at the University of Alberta for the opportunity they provided to put this material in lecture and book form and for the many fruitful discussions during his visit. He is also grateful for their patience with the long delay in publication. We are both indebted to many colleagues for critical readings of parts or all of what appears here. We wish particularly to thank Ralph Miller for detailed and meticulous critical readings of the *Psychological Review* manuscript.

ACKNOWLEDGMENTS

We gratefully acknowledge support from the following grants during the period when these works were being written: SBR-9720410, entitled "Learning and Intelligent Systems: Learning in Complex Environments by Natural and Artificial Systems," from the National Science Foundation (Rochel Gelman, Orville Chapman, Charles R. Gallistel, Edward P. Stabler, Charles E. Taylor, Phillip J. Kellman, John R. Merriam, James W. Stigler, and Joseph A. Wise, CoPIs) and MH14649 from the National Institutes of Health to John Gibbon.

During the copyediting process, John Gibbon died. He was a scientist of the first rank, both as a theorist, and as an experimentalist. He pioneered the application of the information-processing framework to the analysis of timing behavior. He will be sorely missed by the field, to which he contributed so much. To those who knew him as a friend and collaborator, his loss is beyond the power of words to express.

—*C. R. Gallistel*

John M. MacEachran
Memorial Lecture Series

The Department of Psychology at the University of Alberta inaugurated the MacEachran Memorial Lecture Series in 1975 in honor of the late John M. MacEachran. Professor MacEachran was born in Ontario in 1877. In 1906 he received a PhD in Philosophy from Queen's University in 1905. In 1906 he left for Germany to begin more formal study in psychology, first spending just less than a year in Berlin with Stumpf, and then moving to Leipzig, where he completed a second PhD in 1908 with Wundt as his supervisor. During this period he also spent time in Paris studying under Durkheim and Henri Bergson. With these impressive qualifications the University of Alberta was particularly fortunate in attracting him to its faculty in 1909.

Professor MacEachran's impact has been significant at the university, provincial, and national levels. At the University of Alberta he offered the first courses in psychology and subsequently served as Head of the Department of Philosophy and Psychology and Provost of the University until his retirement in 1945. It was largely owing to his activities and example that several areas of academic study were established on a firm and enduring basis. In addition to playing a major role in establishing the Faculties of Medicine, Education, and Law in the Province, Professor MacEachran was also instrumental in the formative stages of the Mental Health Movement in Alberta. At a national level, he was one of the founders of the Canadian Psychological Association and also became its first Honorary President in 1939. John M. MacEachran was indeed one of the pioneers in the development of psychology in Canada.

Perhaps the most significant aspect of the MacEachran Memorial Lecture Series has been the continuing agreement that the Department of Psychology at the University of Alberta has with Lawrence Erlbaum Associates, Publishers, Inc., for the publication of each lecture series. The following is a list of the Invited Speakers and the titles of their published lectures:

1975   Frank, A. Geldard (Princeton University)
        Sensory Saltation: Metastability in the Perceptual World

1976   Benton J. Underwood (Northwestern University)
        Temporal Codes for Memories: Issues and Problems

1977   David Elkind (Rochester University)
        The Child's Reality: Three Developmental Themes

1978   Harold Kelly (University of California, Los Angeles)
        Personal Relationships: Their Structures and processes

1979   Robert Rescorla (Yale University)
        Pavlovian Second-Order Conditioning: Studies in Associative Learning

1980   Mortimer Mishkin (NIMH-Bethesda)
        Cognitive Circuits (unpublished)

1981   James Greeno (University of Pittsburgh)
        Current Cognitive Theory in Problem Solving (Unpublished)

1982   William Uttal (University of Michigan)
        Visual Form Detection in 3-Dimensional Space

1983   Jean Mandler (University of California, San Diego)
        Stories, Scripts, and Scenes: Aspects of Schema Theory

1984   George Collier and Carolyn Rovee-Collier (Rutgers University
        Learning and Motivation: Function and Mechanisms (unpublished)

1985   Alice Eagly (Purdue University)
        Sex Differences in Social Behavior: A Social-Role Interpretation

1986   Karl Pribram (Stanford University)
        Brain and Perception: Holonomy and Structure in Figural Processing

1987   Abram Amsel (University of Texas at Austin)
        Behaviorism, Neobehaviorism, and Cognitivism in Learning Theory: Historical and Contemporary Perspectives

1988   Robert S. Siegler and Eric Jenkins (Carnegie Mellon University)
        How Children Discover New Strategies

1989   Robert Efron (University of California, Martinez)
           The Decline and Fall of Hemispheric Specialization

1999   Philip N. Johnson-Laird (Princeton University)
           Human and Machine Thinking

1991   Timothy A. Salthouse (Georgia Institute of Technology)
           Mechanisms of Age–Cognition Relations in Adulthood

1992   Scott Paris (University of Michigan)
           Authentic Assessment of Children's Literacy and Learning

1993   Bryan Kolb (University of Lethbridge)
           Brain Plasticity and Behavior

1994   Max Coltheart (Maquarie University)
           Our Mental Lexicon: Empirical Evidence of the Modularity of Mind
           (unpublished)

1995   Norbert Schwarz (University of Michigan)
           Cognition and Communication: Judgmental Biases, Research Methods,
           and the Logic of Conversation

1996   Gilbert Gottlieb (University of North Carolina at Chapel Hill)
           Synthesizing Nature–Nurture: Prenatal Roots of Instinctive Behavior

1997   Charles R. Gallistel (Rutgers University) and John Gibbon (New York
           State Psychiatric Institute and Columbia University)
           The Symbolic Foundations of Conditioned Behavior

Eugene C. Lechelt, Coordinator
MacEachran Memorial Lecture Series

Sponsored by the Department of Psychology, The University of Alberta, in
memory of John M. MacEachran, pioneer in Canadian psychology.

Introduction

In this book, we present a new conceptual framework for the understanding of the learning that occurs in the Pavlovian and operant conditioning paradigms. Many of the experiments whose results we seek to explain are familiar to anyone who has taken a course in basic learning, and even to most students who have had only an introductory course in experimental psychology. We show that many of the best known results from the vast conditioning literature—particularly the quantitative results—can be more readily explained if one starts from the assumption that what happens in the course of conditioning is not the formation of associations but rather the learning of the temporal intervals in the experimental protocol. What animals acquire are not associations, but symbolic knowledge of quantifiable properties of their experience. In the final chapter, we argue that this conclusion has broad implications for cognitive science, for neurobiology, and for all those disciplines concerned with the nature of mind.

Conditioning paradigms were created to test and elaborate associative conceptions of the learning process. In these paradigms, the subject is presented with simple, unstructured, or very simply structured stimuli—tones, lights, noises, clickers, buzzers—whose temporal relations to each other and to one or more reinforcing stimuli are manipulated. The best known example comes from the work of Pavlov (1928), who repeatedly sounded a tone or noise, followed by the presentation of food to hungry dogs. He observed that in time the dogs salivated in response to the tone or noise. He originated the study of what is now called Pavlovian conditioning, and he was such an astute observer and recorder of the phenomena to be observed when animals are being conditioned that students of animal learning continue even now to read his lectures with profit.

Stimuli like food, water, puffs of air delivered to the sclera, or mildly painful shocks to the feet—stimuli that reliably motivate observable behavior—are called *reinforcers*. The terminology reflects the conceptual framework that Pavlov and almost all students of conditioning after him have applied to the understanding of this phenomenon. Pavlov thought that the food strengthened (reinforced) a connection between elements in the nervous system. The connection served as a conducting pathway over which excitation propagated from the tone-sensitive elements to the food-sensitive elements. The development of this pathway—the conditioned reflex pathway—explained how it was that the tone came in time to elicit a response similar to the response elicited by the food itself. This conception of the underlying process—that it involves the strengthening of a connection—still dominates thinking about basic learning.

Pavlov also called reinforcers unconditioned stimuli (USs). We will use the terms reinforcer and US more or less interchangeably. Following Pavlov, we will call the originally neutral stimuli (the tones, lights, etc.) conditioned stimuli (CSs for short) and the responses that develop to them conditioned responses (CRs).

Clearly, Pavlov's account of learning that occurs during conditioning is a "learning to" account; the dog learns to salivate, rather than learning that the tone predicts food. In associative models of the conditioning process, symbolic knowledge of the world is not acquired. The altered conductive connections (the associations) may mediate an adaptive response—for example, a blink that shields the eye from an impending puff of air—but they do not encode what it is about the experienced world that makes an appropriately timed blink adaptive. The connection forged by repeated experience of a tone and an air puff or a tone and food does not encode the temporal relation between CS and the US.

In contemporary discussions of associative conditioning, properties of the stimuli used are commonly assumed to be encoded in stimulus traces left behind in the nervous system by the transient activity that the CSs and USs evoke (Balleine, Garner, Ganzalez, & Dickinson, 1995; Bouton, 1993; Colwill & Rescorla, 1990; Dickinson, 1989; Dickinson & Balleine, 1994; Rescorla, 1991, 1993; Rescorla & Colwill, 1989). However, associative theories do not specify the principles governing stimulus encoding, so it is a moot question whether stimulus properties (e.g., amount, intensity, color, flavor, size, duration, tonal composition) may themselves be represented by associative strengths, and, if so, how. In associative theories, as currently elaborated, the strength of the associative bond does not specify any objectively describable property of the CS, the US, or the relation between them. That is why the associations produced by conditioning do not have symbolic content. Their strengths do not specify objective facts about the animal's conditioning experience.

The subjects in conditioning experiments do, however, learn the temporal intervals in the protocols. This conclusion, once controversial, is now widely accepted, on the basis of the kinds of experimental evidence reviewed at length in the chapters that follow. This temporal learning has been modeled quantitatively by so-called timing models (Church, Broadbent, & Gibbon, 1992; Gibbon, 1977, 1992; Gibbon, Church, & Meck, 1984; Killeen & Fetterman, 1988).

The ability of timing models to explain the timing of conditioned responses is widely recognized. It is not widely appreciated, however, how fundamentally the discovery of an interval timing capacity may alter our conception of the conditioning process itself. Timing models give us models of conditioning in which symbolic knowledge is the foundation of the observed behavior. They are models of how this knowledge is acquired and used. In this new conceptual framework, almost every aspect of basic conditioning appears in a different light. Our purpose in this book is to make clear salient features of that conceptual framework.

One feature of this conceptual framework is that the learning mechanisms that mediate conditioned behavior should not be thought of as basic to higher learning of all kinds. What is primarily manipulated in the great majority of experiments commonly discussed under the heading of classical or operant conditioning is the temporal relations among stimuli. The models we discuss are specific to this kind of learning. Our models operate in the domain of nonstationary multivariate time series analysis. They do not purport to be general theories of learning. On the contrary, they are predicated on the assumption that there can be no such thing as a general theory of learning, because learning mechanisms, like other biological mechanisms, have problem-specific structures (Gallistel, 1992b, 1999b). Mechanisms with problem-specific structure are more or less inherent in an information processing approach to the brain, because different kinds of information must be processed in different ways.

Within the account we propose, there is no important distinction—at the level of process—between instrumental and classical conditioning. The learning that occurs in both kinds of protocols depends on mechanisms for learning temporal intervals and rates and using those intervals and rates to measure contingency. On the other hand, in our framework, the acquisition of a conditioned response, the extinction of that response and the timing of the response are distinct problems, requiring distinct decisions for their solution.

In our view, different learning mechanisms may make use of a common set of elementary neurocomputational operations, such as the storage and retrieval of the values of variables (distances, intervals, intensities, etc.), and the adding, subtracting, multiplying, dividing, and ordering of these variables. However, at the level of the learning processes themselves, the processes that compute and utilize symbolic representations of the conditioning experience, different problems necessitate different computations. Thus, learning is inherently modular in this framework, and the basis of the modularity is computational: Different representations must be computed in different ways.

A modularity of processing rooted in differing computational requirements is an unusual assumption within the study of learning, but it is the ordinary assumption within sensory psychophysics. There, different decisions that the subject makes about the properties of a stimulus—whether it is red or green, moving to the left or moving to the right, and so on—depend on different decision variables, which are assumed to be computed in different cortical modules. The modularity of stimulus processing is taken for granted in contemporary sensory psychophysics. Our models make the same modularity assumption for the stimulus processing that mediates conditioned behavior.

Our focus is on the quantitative facts. This, too, is unusual. Most learning models have been content to predict only the direction of the effects of various manipulations, not the magnitude of the effects.

In the final chapter, we discuss the radical challenge that this new information processing, cognitive framework poses for the traditional associative framework. This challenge should be of broad interest to contemporary psychologists because it is one of the few areas in experimental psychology where the associative framework and the information processing framework meet head on, offering alternative ways of thinking about an extensive body of experimentally established facts. One can then ask, which way of thinking about these facts gives a clearer more rigorously formulated and more broadly applicable account? And why? What is it about one framework that makes it more powerful and more successful than the other? These are questions of enduring import for the field of psychology.

1

Response Timing

The strengthening of an associative bond through repetitive experience is the basic idea in the associative conceptual framework. That idea is seemingly most directly evidenced in acquisition, where the conditioned response (CR) appears after some number of conditioning trials, as if something had been strengthened over successive trials. Thus, associative accounts of conditioning generally begin with simple acquisition. We begin, however, by considering the timing of the CR—when it occurs in relation to the onset of a conditioned stimulus (CS). The basic idea in timing models is that the animal learns the temporal intervals, and this knowledge determines its behavior. The fact that it learns the intervals in a protocol is most directly evident in the timing of the CR.

Our model for the timing of the CR introduces many of the important concepts in the timing framework. One concept is that remembered intervals have scalar variability. This means that the trial-to-trial variability in an interval retrieved from memory is proportional to the magnitude of that interval. The bigger a magnitude read from memory, the more that magnitude varies from one reading to the next. Another broad concept is that conditioned behavior is the result of simple decisions based on the comparison of mental magnitudes, like, for example, the mental magnitudes (signals in the brain) that represent intervals. The animal responds when a decision variable exceeds a threshold. The decision variable is itself created by means of a simple arithmetic comparison, usually between a currently elapsing interval and a remembered interval. A third concept is that decision variables are ratios, not differences. For example, the decision whether to respond at a certain latency is based on the ratio of the currently elapsed interval to a remembered interval. When that ratio exceeds a threshold the animal responds. Unifying these three concepts is the concept of the time-scale invariance of the conditioning process, which is seen to be a consequence of these principles. Empirically, time-scale invariance means that conditioning data are unaffected by the time scale of the experiment. For example, the form of the distribution of CRs about the reinforcement latency does not depend on that latency; the distributions observed with different reinforcement latencies differ only by a scaling factor.

The most common elementary Pavlovian conditioning protocol is diagrammed in Fig. 1.1. A CS (typically, a tone or light) is presented for a fixed interval T, at the end of which the unconditioned stimulus (US; also known as reinforcement) occurs. The presentation of the CS is called a trial. Because the US is delivered coincident with the termination of CS presentation, the trial duration and the reinforcement latency (delay between CS onset and reinforcement) are one and the same. The interval after a trial during which nothing happens is the intertrial interval. Test trials without reinforcement are given after a certain number of training trials to probe for the strength of the CR to the CS.

If one records the distribution of conditioned responses on test trials, one generally finds that they are maximally likely toward the end of a trial, that is, the mode (peak) of the distribution is close to the reinforcement latency (see Fig. 1.4). This means that the subject generally does not react to the CS when it is first presented (see Figs. 1.2 and 1.3). It reacts only as the time of expected reinforcement approaches. The longer the duration of a trial, that is, the longer the reinforcement latency, the longer the CR is delayed.

Pavlov termed this phenomenon the *inhibition of delay*. In his conception, delay of the US inhibited the initial occurrence of the CR. As the time to reinforcement grew shorter during a trial, this inhibition was released. Although the phenomenon has been known to experimentalists since the days of Pavlov, it is seldom emphasized in standard accounts of conditioned behavior, because the associative conceptual framework does not offer a ready explanation for it. In the timing framework, in contrast, it is the first thing to be noted about conditioned behavior, because it is direct evi-

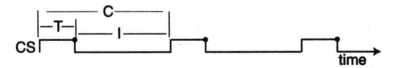

FIG. 1.1. Time line for simple classical conditioning. The duration of the CS is T, the reinforcement (dot) coincides with the offset of the CS. For reasons to be explained later, the duration of this reinforcement (the duration of the US) may be ignored. The other important interval is I, the interval between trials (CS presentations). The sum of the I and T is C, the cycle duration.

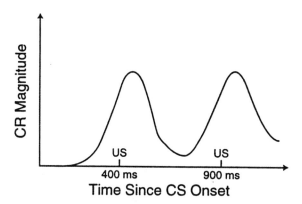

FIG. 1.2. A representative example of the conditioned eyeblink response on a single test trial in an experiment in which rabbits were conditioned to blink in response to a tone that signaled a puff of air to the sclera of the eye. The latency of reinforcement on training trials (time from CS onset to delivery of the air puff) was always either 400 ms or 900 ms, but this latency varied randomly (unpredictably) from trial to trial. The rabbit learned to blink twice on each trial, once at a latency of approximately 400 ms and once at a latency of approximately 900 ms. (Reproduced from Fig. 3, p. 289 of Kehoe, Graham-Clarke, & Schreurs, 1989. Copyright © 1989 by the American Psychological Association. Reprinted with permission.)

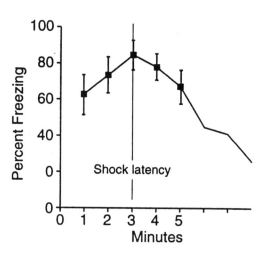

FIG. 1.3. Data from a one-trial contextual fear conditioning experiment. Rats were given a brief foot shock 3 min after being placed in an experimental chamber (the context). The next day, they were again placed in the chamber, and their freezing behavior (a manifestation of fear) was scored during an 8-min test. The percentage of rats observed to be freezing was maximal at the latency at which they had been shocked the previous day. (From Fanselow & Stote, 1995, reproduced by permission of the authors.)

dence that the animals are in fact learning at least one of the temporal intervals in the protocol, namely, the reinforcement latency.

Another property of the distribution of CRs, whose empirical generality and theoretical importance was first emphasized by Gibbon (1977) is that its standard deviation is proportional to its mode: The longer the CR is on average delayed, the more variable is its latency. Thus, the coefficient of

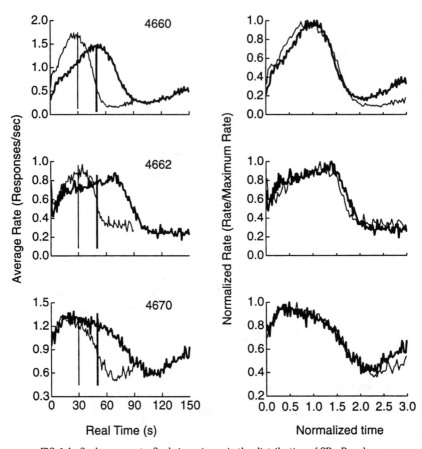

FIG. 1.4. Scalar property: Scale invariance in the distribution of CRs. Panels on left: Responding of three birds on the unreinforced trials of the peak procedure in blocked sessions at reinforcement latencies of 30 s and 50 s (unreinforced CS durations of 90 s and 150 s, respectively). Vertical bars at the reinforcement latencies have heights equal to the peaks of the corresponding distributions. Panels on right: Same functions normalized with respect to CS time and peak rate (so that vertical bars would superimpose). Note that although the distributions differ between birds, both in their shape and in whether they peak before or after the reinforcement latency (K^* error), they superimpose when normalized (rescaled). (From Gallistel & Gibbon, 2000, by permission of the publisher.)

variation, which is the ratio of the standard deviation to the mean, is constant. The fact that the mean, mode, and standard deviation of CRs all increase in proportion to the reinforcement latency means that the temporal distribution of CRs is time-scale invariant.

Time-scale invariance is a profoundly important property of the conditioning process, whose many manifestations we repeatedly call attention to. What it means, speaking somewhat loosely, is that the data from a conditioning experiment look the same regardless of the time scale of the protocol, provided that the scale factors in the graphs that display the data are adjusted to match the time scale. Thus, if one repeats a conditioning experiment using intervals twice as long as the intervals originally used, the data obtained will look just like the data originally obtained, provided one doubles the temporal units employed in analyzing and displaying the data (doubling, for example, the numbers at each tic on the temporal axis of the graph). Equivalently, the data from experiments conducted at different time scales (with different reinforcement latencies) look the same if they are plotted as a function of the fraction of the reinforcement latency elapsed. Adjusting the scale in this way is called normalization. To say that conditioning is time-scale invariant is to say that normalizing the data renders the results from experiments done on different time scales superimposable, as demonstrated in Fig. 1.4.

THE PEAK PROCEDURE

The data in Fig. 1.4 come from a conditioning procedure called the peak procedure. It is a standard conditioning protocol, modified in such a way as to reveal both the onset and the offset of conditioned responding. In this procedure, a trial begins, as usual, with the onset of the CS. When pigeons are the subjects, the CS is the illumination of a key on the wall of the pigeon's chamber. The illumination of the key is followed on some trials by reinforcement, that is, the opening of the food hopper for a few seconds. As in Fig. 1.1, when reinforcement occurs, it always occurs at a fixed latency after CS onset, provided only that the bird is pecking the key when that latency elapses. On reinforced trials, the CS terminates at the moment of reinforcement, because when the hopper opens, the bird stops its pecking in order to eat the food. However, on 50% to 75% of the trials, there is no reinforcement; the hopper fails to open. On these unreinforced trials, the CS persists for three to four times beyond the point at which the hopper should have opened. These unreinforced trials constitute the probe or test trials, the trials from which the data on the distribution of the CR are gathered. On a typical test trial, the pigeon begins to peck the illuminated key before the expected reinforcement latency and stops pecking some while after the point at which the hopper should have opened but did not.

The time at which the bird begins to peck and the time at which it stops pecking vary from test trial to test trial. The rate of pecking once it begins is fairly constant (Church, Meck, & Gibbon, 1994). However, because of the trial-to-trial variability in the onset and offset of this steady pecking, the average rate of pecking at a given point in a test trial is a smoothly increasing and subsiding function of trial duration, as may be seen in Fig. 1.4. It is important to understand, that the smooth rise and fall of the function in Fig. 1.4 is an artifact of averaging across many trials. The behavior on an individual trial does not look like that. Rather, at some latency, the subject begins abruptly to peck and it stops just as abruptly later on in that trial.

Figure 1.4 shows the data from three different pigeons, when this experiment was repeated at two different time scales. In one case, the reinforcement latency was 30 s, and in the other, it was 50 s. The unnormalized data are shown in the panels on the left. The numbers on the x axis specify the amount of time elapsed since CS onset. Notice that the curve for the 50 s data is more spread out than the curve for the 30 s data. The normalized data are shown in the panels on the right. Here, the numbers on the x axis are the time elapsed since CS onset *divided by* the reinforcement latency (normalized time). And the numbers on the y axis are the average response rate *divided by* the peak response rate (normalized rate of responding). Dividing by the reinforcement latency adjusts the units on the x axis (rescales the time axis), so that a unit (interval between ticks) represents the same fraction of the reinforcement latency in both cases. Similarly, dividing by the peak response rate scales the y axis in such a way that each unit represents the same fraction of the peak rate. These rescaling operations render the results from the experiment with a 30 s reinforcement latency and the results from the 50 s reinforcement latency superimposable. This means that the curves in the panels on the left really have the same shape, they only appear to have different shapes because of the difference in the scale factors used to plot them.

Although there are a large number of published curves demonstrating the scale invariance of CR distributions shown in Fig. 1.4 (see, for further examples, Figs. 1.6 and 1.8), we use data in Fig. 1.4 for two reasons. First, the curves from the different subjects differ noticeably in their shapes, but the data from each bird are nonetheless scale invariant. Second, if you look closely at the data, you will notice that the curves for the top and bottom birds (4660 and 4670, respectively) clearly peak somewhat before the expected reinforcement latency, whereas the curves for the middle bird (4662) clearly peak somewhat after the expected reinforcement latency.

In other words, in addition to the trial-to-trial variability in the onset and offset of conditioned responding, each subject in such an experiment has a (rather small) systematic error. Some subjects seem systematically to expect the reinforcement to occur somewhat sooner than it in fact occurs, whereas others systematically expect it to occur somewhat later than it in fact occurs. Put another way, in addition to the within subject (trial-to-trial) variability in the onset and offset of conditioned responding, there is reproducible (systematic) subject-to-subject variability in the central tendency (mean and mode) of the CR distribution. The fact that the curves superimpose when normalized means that this systematic variability is also scale invariant, that is, it is a percent error (a multiplicative or scalar error) rather than an error by a constant amount (an additive error). In chap. 7, where we discuss the neurobiological implications of the timing framework, this error figures importantly in our suggestions for how to find the neurobiological mechanism of memory.

SCALAR EXPECTANCY THEORY

Scalar Expectancy Theory was developed to account for data on the timing of the CR (Gibbon, 1977). It is a model of what we call the *when* decision, the decision that determines when the CR occurs in relation to the onset of the CS. The basic assumptions of Scalar Expectancy Theory and the components out of which the model is constructed—a timing mechanism, a memory mechanism, and a comparison mechanism (see Fig. 1.5), appear in our explanation of many other aspects of conditioned behavior.

The timing mechanism generates a signal, t_e, that grows in proportion to the increasing duration of the animal's current exposure to a CS. Its magnitude at any moment represents the duration at that moment of the interval that has elapsed since the onset of the CS. It is the magnitude of this signal that we refer to when we speak of the subjective duration of a currently elapsing interval. The timer is reset to zero by the occurrence of a reinforcement, which marks the end of the interval that began with the onset of the CS. The magnitude of t_e, at the time of reinforcement, t_T, is written to memory through a multiplicative constant, K^*, whose value is close to but not identical to one. Thus, the reinforcement latency recorded in memory, $t^* = K^* t_T$, deviates on average, from the timed value by some (generally small) percentage. The extent of this systematic deviation is determined by the deviation of K^* from 1.0. (Box 1.1 gives a list of the symbols and expressions used, together with their meanings.) As already mentioned, this error between the duration specified by the timer at the moment of reinforcement and the duration actually retrieved from memory on subsequent occasions figures importantly in our suggestions for how to use the timing framework to look for the neurobiological mechanisms of memory. (The symbols and their meaning are given in Box 1.1.)

When the CS reappears (when a new trial begins), t_e, the subjective duration of the currently elapsing interval of CS exposure, is compared to t^*, which is derived by sampling (reading) the remembered reinforcement latency in memory. The comparison takes the form of a ratio, $t_e:t^*$. We call this ratio the decision variable because when it exceeds a threshold, β, somewhat less than one, the animal responds to the CS—provided it has

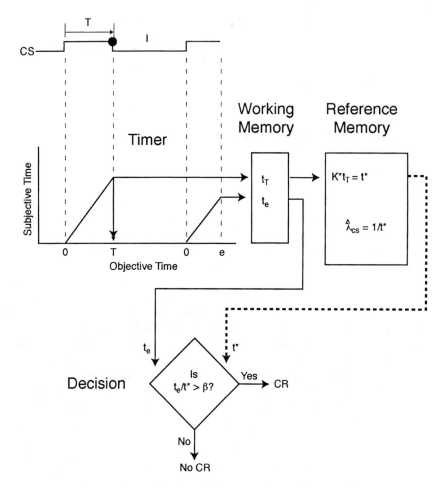

FIG. 1.5. Flow diagram for the CR timing or *when* decision. Two trials are shown, the first reinforced at T, (filled circle on time line) and the second still elapsing at e. When the first trial is reinforced, the cumulated subjective time, t_T, is stored in working memory and transferred to reference memory via the multiplicative constant, K^* ($t^* = K^*t_T$). The decision to respond is based on the ratio of the elapsing interval (in working memory) to the remembered interval (in reference memory). It occurs when this ratio exceeds a threshold (β) close to, but generally less than 1. Note that the reciprocal of t^* is equal to λ_{CS}, the estimated rate of CS reinforcement, which plays a crucial role in the acquisition and extinction decisions described in subsequent chapters.

BOX 1.1
Symbols and Expressions in Scalar Expectancy Theory

Symbol/Expression	Meaning
t_e	• the signal from the trial timer (subjective elapsed duration of the current trial)
t_T	• subjective elapsed duration of a trial at the time of reinforcement
$K*$	• constant of proportionality relating subjective elapsed duration at time of reinforcement and (average) remembered reinforcement latency
$t*$	• remembered reinforcement latency
$t_e{:}t*$	• ratio of currently elapsing trial duration to remembered reinforcement latency. The decision variable for the *when* decision
β	• decision threshold (or criterion)
T	• average duration of a trial. When trial duration is fixed, this is the reinforcement latency, also called the CS-US interval, the interstimulus interval (ISI), and the delay of reinforcement

had sufficient experience with the CS to have already decided that it is a reliable predictor of the US and to have already decided that the distribution of reinforcement latencies with respect to CS onset is not random. (Models for these two decisions are developed in chap. 2.)

The *when* decision threshold is somewhat less than 1.0, because the CR anticipates the US. If, on a given trial, reinforcement does not occur (for example, in the peak procedure, see below), then the CR ceases when this same decision ratio exceeds a second threshold, somewhat greater than 1.0. (The decision to stop responding when the reinforcement latency is past, is not diagrammed in Fig. 1.5, but see Gibbon & Church, 1990.) In short, the animal begins to respond when it estimates the currently elapsing interval to be close to the remembered latency of reinforcement. If it does not get reinforced, it stops responding when it estimates the currently elapsing interval to be past the remembered latency. Its measure of similarity between the currently elapsed interval and the remembered reinforcement interval is the ratio of its estimates for these two magnitudes. The farther this ratio is from 1.0, the less similarity between the currently elapsed interval and the remembered reinforcement latency. The decision thresholds constitute its criteria for "close enough" and "far enough past."

The interval timer in Scalar Expectancy Theory may be thought of as a stream of impulses feeding an accumulator (working memory), which continually integrates impulses over time. However, it is important to bear in mind that the essential feature of the timer—and of the accumulator analogy or metaphor—is that its output is proportional to (or, at least linearly related to) the objective duration of the interval. The output of the timer is a ramp that rises in proportion as the interval being timed gets longer. When accumulation is temporarily halted, for example, in paradigms when reinforcement is not delivered and the CS is briefly turned off and back on again after a short period (a gap), the value in the accumulator simply holds through the gap (working memory). The accumulator resumes integration when the CS comes back on. Thus, the height of the ramp represents the cumulative duration of the intervals when the CS was present.

The reference memory system, in contrast, statically preserves the values of past intervals. It carries the value of this variable forward in time, making possible subsequent comparison between a currently elapsing interval and a previously experienced reinforcement latency. When we refer to the remembered duration of an interval, it is this value we refer to. It too is a subjective variable, that is, it is a quantity in the brain of the animal.

The scalar variability in the distribution of CRs over trials is a consequence of two fundamental assumptions. The first is that the comparison mechanism uses the ratio of the two subjective durations being compared, rather than, for example, their difference. The second is that remembered subjective estimates of temporal durations, like subjective estimates of many other continuous variables (length, weight, loudness, etc.), obey Weber's law: The difference required to discriminate one subjective magnitude from another with a given degree of reliability is a fixed fraction of that magnitude (Gibbon, 1977; Killeen & Weiss, 1987). What this most likely implies—and what Scalar Expectancy Theory assumes—is that the uncertainty about the true value of a remembered magnitude (the noise in a signal read from memory) is proportional to the magnitude. These two assumptions— that the decision variable is a ratio and that estimates of duration read from memory have scalar variability—are both necessary to explain scale invariance in the distribution of onsets and offsets of CRs (Gibbon & Fairhurst, 1994).

THE FI SCALLOP

An early application of Scalar Expectancy Theory was to the explanation of the fixed interval (FI) scallop in operant conditioning. An FI schedule of reinforcement delivers reinforcement for any response made after a FI has elapsed since the delivery of the last reinforcement. When working on such a schedule, animals pause after each reinforcement, then resume responding after some interval has elapsed.

FIG. 1.6. (a) Normalized rate of responding as a function of the normalized elapsed interval, for pigeons responding on fixed interval schedules, with interreinforcement intervals, T, ranging from 30 to 3,000 s. $\overline{R}(t)$ is the average rate of responding at elapsed interval t since the last reinforcement. $\overline{R}(T)$ is the average terminal rate of responding. (Data from Dews, 1970. Plot from Gibbon, 1977. Copyright © 1977 by the American Psychological Association. Adapted with permission.)

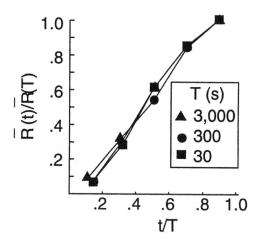

It is generally supposed that the animal's rate of responding accelerates throughout the interval leading up to reinforcement (the FI scallop). In fact, however, conditioned responding in this paradigm, as in many others, is a two-state variable (slow, sporadic pecking versus rapid, steady pecking) with one transition per interreinforcement interval (Schneider, 1969).

The average latency to the onset of the high rate state during the postreinforcement interval increases in proportion to the scheduled reinforcement interval—over a very wide range of intervals (from 30 s to at least 50 min). The variability in this onset from one interval to the next within a schedule also increases in proportion to the scheduled interval. As a result, averaging over many interreinforcement intervals results in the smooth increase in the average rate of responding that Dews (1970) termed proportional timing (see Fig. 1.6). The smooth, almost linear increase in the average rate of responding seen in Fig. 1.6 is the result of averaging across many different abrupt onsets. The figure is most appropriately read as showing the probability that the subject will have entered the high rate state as a function of the time elapsed since the last reinforcement. The data in Fig. 1.6 are another example of time-scale invariance in the distribution of CRs. In this case, the distribution in question is the distribution of response onsets following a reinforcement.

THE TIMING OF AVERSIVE CRs

Avoidance Responses

The conditioned fear that is manifest in freezing behavior and other indices of a conditioned emotional response is classically conditioned in the operational sense, because reinforcement (shock) is not contingent on the animal's response. Avoidance responses, in contrast, are instrumentally conditioned in the operational sense, because the performance of the CR forestalls the aversive reinforcement. By responding, the subject avoids the aversive stimulus. We stress the purely operational, as opposed to theoretical, distinction between classical and instrumental conditioning, because, from the perspective of timing theory, the only difference between the two paradigms is in the events that mark the beginnings of expected and elapsing intervals. In the instrumental case, the expected interval to the next shock is longest immediately after a response, and the recurrence of a response resets the shock clock. Thus, the animal's response marks the onset of the relevant interval.

The timing of instrumentally conditioned avoidance responses is as dependent on the expected time of aversive reinforcement as the timing of classically conditioned emotional reactions, and it shows the same scale invariance in the mean, and scalar variability around it (Gibbon, 1971, 1972). In shuttle box avoidance paradigms, where the animal gets shocked at either end of the box if it stays too long, the mean latency at which the animal makes the avoidance response increases in proportion to the latency of the shock that is thereby avoided, and so does the variability in this avoidance latency. A similar result is obtained in free-operant avoidance, where the rat must press a lever before a certain interval has elapsed in order to forestall for another such interval the shock that will otherwise occur (Gibbon, 1971, 1972, 1977; Libby & Church, 1974). As a result, the probability of an avoidance response at less than or equal to a given proportion of the mean latency is the same regardless of the absolute duration of the expected shock latency (see, for example, Fig. 1 in Gibbon, 1977). Scalar timing of avoidance responses is again a consequence of the central assumptions in Scalar Expectancy Theory—the use of a ratio to judge the similarity between the currently elapsed interval and the expected shock latency, and scalar variability (noise) in the shock latencies read from memory.

When an animal must respond in order to avoid a pending shock, responding appears long before the expected time of shock. One of the earliest applications of Scalar Expectancy Theory (Gibbon, 1971) showed that this early responding in avoidance procedures is nevertheless scalar in the shock delay (see Fig. 1.7). According to Scalar Expectancy Theory, the expectation of shock is maximal at the experienced latency between the onset of the warning signal and the shock, just as in other paradigms. However, a low decision threshold leads to responding at an elapsed interval equal to a small fraction of the expected shock latency. The result of course is successful avoidance on almost all trials. The low threshold compensates for trial-to-trial variability in the remembered duration of the warning interval. If the threshold were higher, the subject would more often fail to respond in time to avoid the shock. The low threshold ensures that responding almost always anticipates and thereby forestalls the shock.

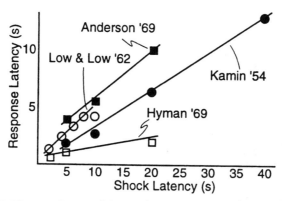

FIG. 1.7. The mean latency of the avoidance response as a function of the latency of the shock (CS–US interval) in a variety of cued avoidance experiments with rats (Anderson, 1969; Kamin, 1954; Low & Low, 1962) and monkeys (Hyman, 1969). Note that although the response latency is much shorter than the shock latency, it is nonetheless proportional to the shock latency. The straight lines are drawn by eye. (Redrawn with slight modifications from Gibbon, 1971. Copyright © 1971 by the American Psychological Association. Adapted with permission.)

The Conditioned Emotional Response

The conditioned emotional response is the suppression of appetitive responding that occurs when the subject (usually a rat) expects a mild shock to the feet (aversive reinforcement). The appetitive response is suppressed because the subject freezes in anticipation of the shock (see Fig. 1.3, p. 7). If shocks are scheduled at regular intervals, then the probability that the rat will stop its appetitive responding (pressing a bar to obtain food or licking a spout to obtain water) increases as a fraction of the intershock interval that has elapsed. Thus, the suppression measure obtained from experiments employing different intershock intervals are superimposable when they are plotted as a proportion of the intershock interval that has elapsed (La-Barbera & Church, 1974; see Fig. 1.8). Put another way, the degree to which the rat fears the impending shock is determined by how close it is to the shock. Its measure of closeness is the ratio of the interval elapsed since the last shock to the expected interval between shocks—a simple manifestation of a scalar expectancy.

The Immediate Shock Deficit

If a rat is shocked immediately after being placed in an experimental chamber (1–5 second latency), it shows very little conditioned response (freezing) in the course of an eight-minute test the next day. By contrast, if it is shocked several minutes after being placed in the chamber, it shows much

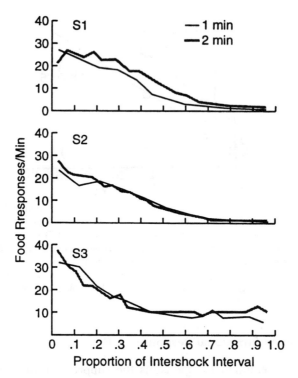

FIG. 1.8. The strength of the conditioned emotional reaction to shock is measured by the decrease in appetitive responding when shock is anticipated: data from three rats. The decrease in responding for a food reward (a measure of the average strength of the fear) is determined by the proportion of the anticipated interval that has elapsed. Thus, the data from conditions using different fixed intershock intervals (1 and 2 min) are superimposable when normalized. This is time-scale invariance in the fear response to impending shock. (Figure reproduced with slight modifications from LaBarbera and Church, 1974, by permission of the authors and publisher.)

more freezing during the subsequent test. The longer the reinforcement latency, the more total freezing is observed, up to several minutes (Fanselow, 1986). This has led to the suggestion that in contextual fear conditioning (conditioning an animal to fear the experimental apparatus), the longer the reinforcement latency, the greater the resulting strength of the association (Fanselow, DeCola, & Young, 1993; Fanselow, 1986, 1990). This explanation of the *immediate shock deficit* rests on an ad hoc assumption, made specifically in order to explain this phenomenon. It is the opposite of the usual assumption about the effect of delay on the efficacy of reinforcement, namely, that the shorter the delay the better the conditioning.

From the perspective of Scalar Expectancy Theory, the immediate shock freezing deficit is another manifestation of scalar variability in the distribution of the fear response about the expected time of shock. Bevins and Ayres (1995) varied the latency of the shock in a one-trial contextual fear conditioning paradigm and showed that the later in the training session the shock is given, the later one observes the peak in freezing behavior and the broader the distribution of this behavior throughout the session. The prediction of the immediate shock deficit follows directly from the scalar variability of the fear response about the moment of peak probability (as evidenced in Fig. 1.3 on p. 7). If the probability of freezing in a test session following training with a 3-min shock delay is given by the broad normal curve in Fig. 1.9 (compare with the freezing data in Fig. 1.3), then the distribution after a 3-s latency should be 60 times narrower (3-s curve in Fig. 1.9). Thus, the amount of freezing observed during an 8-min test session following an immediate shock should be negligible in comparison to the amount observed following a shock delayed for 3 min.

It is important to note that our explanation of the failure to see significant evidence of fear in the chamber after experiencing short latency shock does not imply that there is no fear associated with that brief delay. On the contrary, we suggest that the subjects fear the shock just as much in the short-latency conditions as in the long-latency condition. But the fear begins and ends much sooner; hence, there is much less measured evidence of fear. Because the average breadth of the interval during which the subject fears shock grows in proportion to the remembered latency of that shock, the total amount of fearful behavior (number of seconds of freezing) observed is much greater with longer shock latencies.

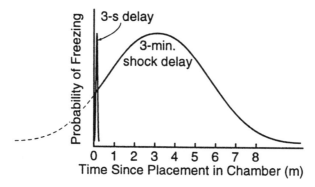

FIG. 1.9. Explanation of the immediate shock deficit by Scalar Expectancy Theory: Given the experimentally obtained probability-of-freezing curve shown for the 3-min group in Fig. 1.3, which is here approximated by the broad normal curve, the scale invariance of CR distributions predicts the very narrow curve shown for subjects shocked immediately (3 s) after placement in the box. Scoring percent freezing during the 8-min test period should show a great deal more freezing in the 3-min group than in the 3-s group (about 60 times more).

The Eye Blink

The conditioned eye blink is often regarded as a basic or primitive example of a classically conditioned response to an aversive US, but in this paradigm, too, the latency to the peak of the conditioned response approximately matches the CS–US latency. Although the response is over literally in the blink of an eye, it is so timed that the eye is closed at the moment when the aversive stimulus is expected. Figure 1.2 (p. 7) is an interesting example. In the experiment from which this representative plot of a double blink is taken, there was only one US on any given trial, but it occurred either 400 or 900 ms after CS onset, in a trial-to-trial sequence that was random (unpredictable). The rabbit learned to blink twice, once at about 400 ms and then again at 900 ms. Clearly the timing of the eye blink—the fact that longer reinforcement latencies produce longer latency blinks—cannot be explained by the idea that longer reinforcement latencies produce weaker associations. We take the fact that the blink latencies approximately match the expected latencies of the aversive stimuli to the eye as a simple indication that the learning of the temporal interval to reinforcement is the foundation of conditioned responding.

The record in Fig. 1.2 does not exhibit scalar variability, because it is a record of the blinks on a single trial. Blinks, like pecks, have, we assume, more or less fixed duration. What exhibits scalar variability from trial to trial is the time at which the CR is initiated. In cases like pigeon pecking, where the CR is repeated steadily for some while, so that there is a stop decision as well as a start decision, the duration of conditioned responding shows the scalar property of individual trials. That is, the interval between the onset of responding and its cessation increases in proportion to the midpoint of the CR interval. In the case of the eye blink, however, where there is only one CR (per expected US) per trial, the duration of the CR may be controlled by the motor system itself rather than by higher level decision processes. The distribution of these CRs (from repeated trials) does, however, exhibit scalar variability (White, Kehoe, Choi, & Moore, 2000).

TIMING THE CS: DISCRIMINATION

The acquisition and extinction models to be considered in chaps. 2 and 4 assume that the animal times the durations of the CSs and compares those durations to durations stored in memory. It is possible to directly test this assumption by presenting CSs of different duration, then asking the subject to indicate by a choice response which of two durations it has just experienced. In other words, the duration of the just experienced CS is made the basis of a discrimination in a successive discrimination paradigm, a paradigm in which the stimuli to be discriminated are presented individually on successive trials, rather than together on one trial.

In the bisection paradigm, the subject is reinforced for one choice after hearing a short duration CS (e.g., a 2 s CS) and for the other choice after hearing a long duration CS (e.g., an 8 s CS). However, as in the peak procedure, there is only partial reinforcement of correct choices. An incorrect choice never produces reinforcement, but a correct choice only produces reinforcement some of the time (typically 50% of the time). The partial reinforcement of correct choices permits the experimenter to insert unreinforced probe durations. These probe durations are intermediate between the two durations that predict which choice will be reinforced. It is essential that whatever choice the subject makes following a probe duration, it not be reinforced, because the purpose of these probes is to determine which of the two reference durations is more likely to be judged by the subject to be closer to a given probe duration. By only partially reinforcing correct choices following the reference durations, the protocol makes the lack of reinforcement following probe durations inconspicuous. The subject does not begin to withhold a response altogether on probe trials, as it would do if these probe trials were the only unreinforced trials and it could discriminate the probe duration from both reference durations.

If the subject uses ratios to compare probe durations to the reference durations in memory, then the point of indifference, the probe duration that it judges to be equidistant from the two reference durations, will be at the geometric mean of the reference durations rather than at their arithmetic mean. Scalar Expectancy Theory assumes that the decision variable in the bisection task is the ratio of the similarities of the probe to the two reference durations. The similarity of two durations, by this measure, is the ratio of the smaller to the larger. Perfect similarity is a ratio of 1:1. Thus, for example, a 5 s probe is more similar to an 8 s probe than to a 2 s probe, because 5:8 is closer to 1 than is 2:5. If, in contrast, similarity were measured by the extent to which the difference between two durations approaches 0, then a 5 s probe would be equidistant (equally similar) to a 2 and an 8 s referent, because $8 - 5 = 5 - 2$. Maximal uncertainty (indifference) should occur at the probe duration that is equally similar to 2 and 8. If similarity is measured by ratios rather than differences, then the probe is equally similar to the two anchors for T, such that $2:T = T:8$ or $T = 4$, the geometric mean of 2 and 8.

As predicted by the ratio assumption in Scalar Expectancy Theory, the probe duration at the point of indifference is in fact generally the geometric mean, the duration at which the ratio measures of similarity are equal, rather than the arithmetic mean, which is the duration at which the difference measures of similarity are equal (Church & Deluty, 1977; Gibbon et al., 1984; see Penney et al., 1998, for a review and extension to human time discrimination). Moreover, the plots of the percent choice of one referent or the other as a function of the probe duration are scale invariant, which means that the psychometric discrimination functions obtained from different pairs of reference durations superimpose when time is normalized by the geometric mean of the reference durations (Church & Deluty, 1977; Gibbon et al., 1984).

SUMMARY

The timing of the CR gives direct evidence that subjects learn the temporal intervals in conditioning protocols, because the latency of the response is proportional to the latency of reinforcement. The trial-to-trial variability in the onset of conditioned responding gives the first example of a profoundly important empirical principle: time-scale invariance. This principle asserts in essence that the results from conditioning experiments do not depend on the time scale of the experimental protocol, only on the lengths of the various intervals in the protocol relative to one another. In this case, what it means is that the shape of the distribution of CR latencies does not depend on the reinforcement latency. The test for time-scale invariance is to normalize the data from experiments performed at different time scales. If the experimental protocols are identical except for the scaling factor, then the normalized data are generally superimposable; the curves fall on top of each other when placed on the same graph. Figures 1.4, 1.6, and 1.8 are examples.

The timing of CRs is explained by Scalar Expectancy Theory. In this model, the animal is assumed to time elapsing intervals by means of an accumulator, or by any device that is like an accumulator in that its output is a ramp whose elevation is proportional to the duration of an elapsing interval. When a reinforcement is received, the contents of the accumulator (the output level at that moment) are recorded in memory—with a small scalar error. The next time the signal for reinforcement occurs (the CS), the subject compares the currently elapsing interval since signal onset to the remembered reinforcement latency. The comparison is by means of the ratio of the currently elapsing interval to the remembered interval (not, as one might suppose, the arithmetic difference between the two intervals). The remembered interval exhibits scalar variability, that is, its value varies from one trial to the next. Put another way, there is noise in the signal from memory. The noise is proportional to the remembered magnitude. The time-scale invariance in the distribution of CRs is a joint result of scalar variability in remembered reinforcement latencies and the ratio comparison process.

CHAPTER

2

Acquisition

Scalar Expectancy Theory is grounded in the decision theory framework within which most contemporary psychophysical models are elaborated. In this framework, the values of stimulus variables determine the values of one or more *decision variables* in the nervous system. By the value of a variable, we mean the strength or magnitude of a signal that represents an objectively specifiable aspect of the subject's experience, such as the duration of the CS–US interval or the ratio of two rates of reinforcement. Because the signal specifies information about the world, the processing of that signal is called *information processing*. The observer's response depends on whether the strength of the decision variable is above or below a threshold. The threshold is called the decision criterion. It is assumed to be to some extent under the subject's control, because it may vary with the *payoff matrix*, which is the set of (implicit or explicit) rewards and punishments contingent on whether the subject correctly or incorrectly judges whether the stimulus does or does not have a given property.

A psychophysical model commonly gives a *computational* (mathematical) description of the *signal processing* that intervenes between the sensory receptors and the stage at which the decision variable is compared to the threshold. Modern psychophysical models take account of the *nature and possible sources of the noise* (variability) in the decision variable. Finally, the *modularity of signal processing* is taken for granted. The processing that leads to judgments about the color of a grating stimulus is assumed to differ, at least in the later stages, from the processing that leads to judgments about the orientation of the grating. Different ways of processing the same stimulus lead to different decision variables, which control different aspects of the subject's behavior.

In the psychophysical framework, the *strength of the stimulus* is varied by varying relevant parameters. The stimulus might be, for example, a light flash, whose detectability is affected by its intensity, duration, and luminosity. The stronger the stimulus is, the more likely the decision variable is to exceed the decision threshold; hence the more likely the subject is to respond to the stimulus. The plot of the subject's response probability as a function of the strength of the stimulus is called the *psychometric function.* For example, the psychometric function for stimulus duration is the plot of the subject's response probability as a function of the duration of the stimulus.

In our approach to the analysis of conditioned behavior, the protocol is the stimulus. Its parameters determine the values of decision variables by way of computationally described signal processing operations. The conditioned response (CR) occurs or does not occur depending on whether the relevant decision variable does or does not exceed a threshold. The scalar noise in the memory signal is a critical part of the model. Finally, the protocol is processed in different ways to generate different decision variables, which govern different aspects of conditioned behavior. This is the modularity of decision processes and the computations leading to them.

The acquisition function in a conditioning experiment is the analog of the psychometric function in a experiment. Its rise (the appearance of CRs as exposure to the protocol is prolonged) reflects the growing magnitude of the decision variable. The visual stimulus in the example used above gets stronger as the duration of the flash is prolonged, because the longer a light of a given intensity continues, the more evidence (in the form of photon absorptions) there is of its presence. Similarly, the conditioning stimulus gets stronger as the duration of the subject's exposure to the protocol increases, because the continued exposure to the protocol gives stronger and stronger evidence that the CS makes a difference in the rate of reinforcement—stronger and stronger evidence of a CS–US *contingency.*

The decision variable in chap. 1 was the one on which the *when* decision was based. In this and the following two chapters, we consider the signal processing that generates the decision variables for the *whether* decisions. These are the decisions whether to respond to the CS (acquisition), ignore it (failure of acquisition), or withhold a response (extinction). In our model of conditioning, one begins to observe a CR to test CSs when the subject decides that the onset of that CS predicts a substantial change in the rate of reinforcement. Extinction occurs when the subject decides that the CS no longer predicts a change in the rate of reinforcement.

A characteristic of psychophysical modeling is the attention it pays to the quantitative results. Theorists of sensory processing try to develop models that generate curves that accurately describe the experimental data—ideally, curves that pass within the confidence limits around the data points. Moreover, they assume that subjects may differ significantly in the parameters of their signal processing and their decision processes, so they generally model the results from individual subjects.

Attention to the quantitative results from individual subjects is not a tradition in the modeling of learning, even in the operant literature. Models of learning often attempt only to predict the directions of the experimentally observed effects, not their magnitudes. And, the data on acquisition and extinction are usually presented in the form of group averages. Group averages are apt to contain misleading averaging artifacts. If acquisition is abrupt in individual subjects, but this abrupt transition occurs after a different number of reinforcements in different subjects, then the acquisition curve for the group will rise smoothly over many trials, even though for each individual subject, it was a step function. It is surprisingly difficult to find published acquisition and extinction data for individual subjects, even in the operant literature, which stresses data from individual subjects. And, well established quantitative results on the effects of basic variables like partial reinforcement, delay of reinforcement, and the intertrial interval are not as available as one might suppose, given the rich history of experimental research on conditioning and the long-recognized importance of these parameters of a conditioning protocol.

In recent years, pigeon autoshaping has been the most extensively used appetitive conditioning preparation. The most systematic and extensive data on rates of acquisition and extinction come from it. Data from other preparations, notably the rabbit nictitating membrane preparation (aversive conditioning) and rabbit jaw movement conditioning (another appetitive preparation) appear to be consistent with these data, but they do not permit as strong quantitative conclusions. For that reason, the accounts we offer of acquisition and extinction rest strongly on the data from autoshaping experiments with pigeons. It is obviously of considerable interest to know whether data on acquisition and extinction in other commonly used paradigms, such as the rabbit eye blink paradigm and the conditioned suppression of appetitive behavior in the rat, would show the same features as the autoshaping data.

Pigeon autoshaping is an automated variant of Pavlov's experimental paradigm. Pavlov conditioned dogs to salivate by sounding a buzzer (the CS) shortly before they were offered food (the US). In pigeon autoshaping, the CS is the transillumination of a round button (or key) on the wall of the experimental enclosure. The illumination of the key may or may not be followed at some latency by food reinforcement (the opening of a hopper containing grain). Instead of salivating to the stimulus that predicts food, as

Pavlov's dogs did, pigeons peck at it. The strength of the CR (the rate or probability of pecking the key) indicates the progress of the conditioning. As in Pavlov's original protocol, the CR (pecking) is the same, or nearly the same, as the UR elicited by the US.

This classical conditioning paradigm is called autoshaping because it is an automated means for teaching pigeons to peck keys in operant conditioning experiments. In operant conditioning paradigms, the learning that occurs is supposed to depend on a contingency between the CR and reinforcement, rather than a contingency between the CS and reinforcement, as in Pavlovian conditioning. In this paradigm, however, the only contingency is between the illumination of the key and the opening of the grain hopper. The hopper opens whether the pigeon pecks or not. Pigeons peck at round stimuli that predict food for the same reasons dogs salivate to stimuli that predict food: In both cases, this is unconditioned (innate) behavior.

The discovery that pigeon key pecking—the prototype of the operant response—could be so readily conditioned by a classical (Pavlovian) rather than an operant protocol has cast doubt on the traditional assumption that classical and operant protocols tap fundamentally different association-forming processes (Brown & Jenkins, 1968). In common with many contemporary associative theorists (e.g., Rescorla & Wagner, 1972), we do not distinguish sharply between these forms of conditioning. We assume that they differ only with regard to the kind of event that marks the beginning of an interval that terminates with reinforcement. The beginning of the interval leading to reinforcement is marked by a stimulus event in the case of classical conditioning (CS onset); it is marked by a response event (the instrumental response) in the case of instrumental conditioning. In either case, the conditioned behavior is a result of the learning of the intervals in the protocol and decisions based on those remembered intervals.

QUANTITATIVE RESULTS

The following quantitative results are well established for pigeon autoshaping:

The Gradual "Strengthening" of the CR. It takes a number of reinforced trials for an appetitive CR to emerge. How abruptly it emerges has not been clearly established: Acquisition curves for individual subjects are hard to find in the published literature. In pigeon autoshaping, the CR appears abruptly, attaining an asymptotic rate of occurrence soon after it first appears (unpublished observations). What has been established is the effect of several variables on the median number of trials required for the CR to reach a strength or frequency criterion in a group of pigeons.

The Effect of Partial Reinforcement on the Rate of Acquisition. Reinforcing only some of the CS presentations increases the number of trials required to reach an acquisition criterion (see Fig. 2.1B, solid lines). However, the increase is proportional to the thinning of the reinforcement schedule (S), which is the average number of trials per reinforcement. Hence, the re-

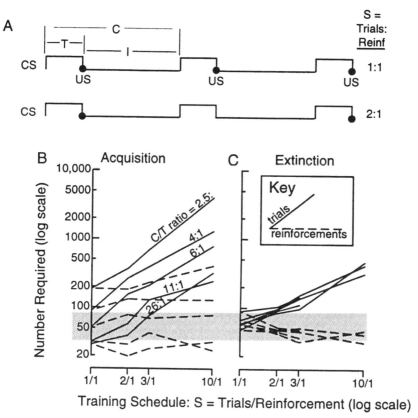

FIG. 2.1. A. Time lines showing the variables that define a basic conditioning protocol—the duration of a CS presentation (T), the duration of the intertrial interval (I), and the reinforcement schedule, S (trials/reinforcement). The US (reinforcement) is usually presented at the termination of the CS (black dots). For reasons shown in Fig. 2.5, the US may be treated as a point event, an event whose duration can be ignored. B. Trials to acquisition (solid lines) and reinforcements to acquisition (dashed lines) in pigeon autoshaping, as a function of the reinforcement schedule and the I:T ratio. The acquisition criterion was at least one peck on three out of four consecutive presentations of the CS. Notice that the pair of curves for a given I:T ratio (one solid, one dashed) join at their left end, because, with a 1:1 schedule of reinforcement, the number of reinforcements is equal to the number of trials. (Reanalysis of data in Fig. 1 of Gibbon, Farrell, Locurto, Duncan, & Terrace, 1980.)

quired number of *reinforcements* is unaffected by partial reinforcement (see Fig. 2.1B, dashed lines). Thus, partial reinforcement does not affect the *rate of acquisition*, as we define it, which is the reciprocal of the number of reinforcements required for acquisition.

The Effect of the Intertrial Interval. Increasing the average interval between trials increases the rate of acquisition, that is, it reduces the number of reinforcements required to reach an acquisition criterion (see Fig. 2.1B, dashed lines), hence, also trials to acquisition (see Fig. 2.1B, solid lines). The longer the intertrial interval relative to trial duration, the greater the $I{:}T$ ratio. The effect of the $I{:}T$ ratio on the rate of acquisition is independent of the reinforcement schedule, as may be seen from the fact that the solid lines are parallel in Fig. 2.1B, as are also, of course, the dashed lines.

More quantitatively, the rate of acquisition is approximately proportional to the $I{:}T$ ratio. The rate of acquisition is the reciprocal of the number of reinforcements required for subjects to meet an acquisition criterion. As shown in Fig. 2.2, the number of reinforcements required is approximately inversely proportional to the $I{:}T$ ratio. The higher this ratio, the more uncommon the CS intervals are relative to intervals when the CS is absent and only the background (the experimental chamber) is present. Thus, the rate of acquisition is directly proportional to the relative rarity of the CS.

It is widely recognized that spaced practice is better than massed practice (for recent review, see Barela, 1999). It is difficult, however, to find data from other paradigms comparable to the data brought together in Fig. 2.2, because the trial-spacing variable has not been varied so systematically in other paradigms. Also, as we will see, the reason that trial spacing is important in autoshaping is that increasing the trial spacing increases the amount of exposure to the experimental context (background) per reinforced trial. When trial spacing has been manipulated in other paradigms, an increase in trial spacing has not always correlated systematically with an increase in unreinforced exposure to the experimental chamber (the background), because the subjects may have been removed from the experimental environment between trials. Nonetheless, data from at least one other paradigm—rabbit eyeblink conditioning—appear to exhibit the same quantitative dependence of conditioning rate on the $I{:}T$ ratio that one sees in pigeon autoshaping. In Fig. 2.3, we have pulled together data from different experiments in which the amount of exposure to the experimental chamber per second of exposure to the CS varied. None of the studies from which we extracted these data was designed to study the effect of $I{:}T$ ratio, so the plot should be treated with caution. Studies modeled on the autoshaping experiments are clearly desirable—in this and other standard conditioning paradigms. In the autoshaping experiments, session length covaried with trial spacing.

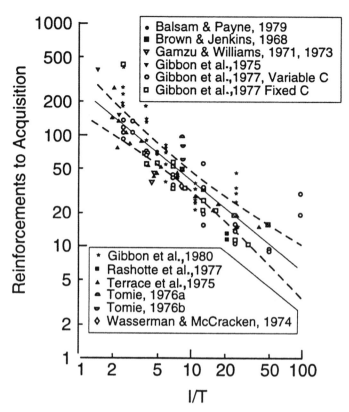

FIG. 2.2. Reinforcements to acquisition as a function of the I:T ratio (double logarithmic coordinates). The data are from the 12 experiments listed in the key. (Slightly modified from Fig. 2 in Gibbon & Balsam, 1981.) Solid line is the best fitting regression line; dashed lines are 95% confidence intervals.

The Effect of Delay of Reinforcement on the Rate of Conditioning. Increasing the delay of reinforcement while holding the intertrial interval constant, retards acquisition—in proportion to the increase in the reinforcement latency (see Fig. 2.4, solid line). Because I is held constant while T is increased, delaying reinforcement in this manner reduces the I:T ratio. In pigeon autoshaping, at least, the effect of delaying reinforcement is entirely due to the reduction in the I:T ratio. There is no effect of the delay of reinforcement per se.

The Time-Scale Invariance of Conditioning. When the intertrial interval is increased in proportion to the delay of reinforcement, delay of reinforcement has no effect on reinforcements to acquisition (see Fig. 2.4, dashed line). Increasing the intertrial interval in proportion to the increase in CS duration means that all the temporal intervals in the conditioning pro-

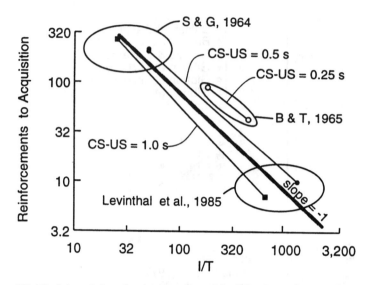

FIG. 2.3. Selected data showing the effect of the I:T ratio on the rate of eye blink conditioning in the rabbit. The quantity C in these data is our estimate of the amount of exposure to the experimental apparatus per CS trial. (Time when the subject was outside the apparatus was not counted). We used 50% CR frequency as the acquisition criterion in deriving these data from published group acquisition curves. S&G, 1964 = Schneiderman & Gormezano (1964), 70-trials per session, session length roughly half an hour, I varied randomly with mean of 25 s. B&T, 1965 = Brelsford & Theios (1965), single-session conditioning; I's of 45, 111, and 300 s; session lengths increased with I (1.25 & 2 hrs for data shown). We do not show the 300 s data from this experiment, because those sessions lasted about 7 hours. Fatigue, sleep, growing restiveness, etc. on the part of the immobilized subjects may have become an important factor. Levinthal et al., 1985 = Levinthal, Tartell, Margolin, & Fishman, 1985) one trial per 11 minute (660 s) daily session.

tocol are increased by a common scaling factor. Therefore, we call this important result the *time-scale invariance* of the acquisition process. The failure of partial reinforcement to affect rate of acquisition and the constant coefficient of variation in reinforcements to acquisition (constant vertical scatter in Fig. 2.2) are other manifestations of time-scale invariance.

Obviously, there will be limits to the range over which time-scale invariance holds, because there are critical processes in the organism with a fixed time scale—circadian processes, for example, and the duration of a lifetime, for another. Processes with a fixed time scale are bound to interact with the conditioning process in the limit. Subjects probably do not condition when they are asleep and they certainly do not condition when they are dead. Nonetheless, the data in Fig. 2.4 cover the better part of an order of magnitude, and the data in Fig. 1.6 cover two orders of magnitude, so the principle appears to hold over a surprising broad range of time scales.

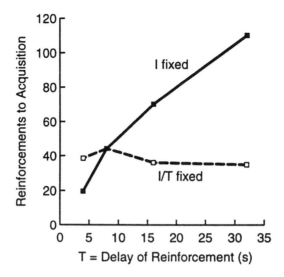

FIG. 2.4. Reinforcements to acquisition as a function of delay of reinforcement, with the (average) intertrial interval (I) fixed (solid line) or varied in proportion to the delay of reinforcement (dashed line). Replot (by interpolation) of data in (Gibbon, Baldock, Locurto, Gold, & Terrace, 1977). For the solid line, the intertrial interval was fixed at I = 48 s. For the dashed line, the I:T ratio was fixed at 6.0.

The Irrelevance of Reinforcement Magnitude. Above some threshold level, the amount of reinforcement has little or no effect on the rate of acquisition. Increasing the amount of reinforcement by increasing the duration of food-cup presentation does not reduce reinforcements to acquisition. In fact, the rate of acquisition can be dramatically increased by reducing reinforcement duration (hence, amount of reward) and adding the time thus saved to the intertrial interval (see Fig. 2.5). Clearly, the relative duration of the intertrial interval, the interval when nothing happens, matters profoundly in acquisition; but the duration or magnitude of the reinforcement does not.

We do not claim that reinforcement magnitude is unimportant in conditioning. As we emphasize in chap. 6, it is a very important determinant of preference. It is also in some cases an important determinant of the asymptotic level of performance. Furthermore, if the magnitude of reinforcement varied depending on whether the reinforcement was delivered during the CS or during the background, we would expect magnitude to affect rate of acquisition as well. A lack of effect on rate of acquisition is observed (and, on our analysis, expected) only when there are no background reinforcements (the usual case in simple conditioning) or when the magnitude of background reinforcements is the same as the magnitude of CS reinforcements (the usual case in a background conditioning protocol).

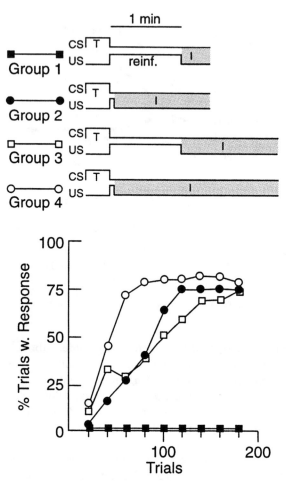

FIG. 2.5. Effect on rate of acquisition of allocating time either to reinforcement or to the intertrial interval (I). Groups 1 & 2 had the same duration of the trial cycle (T + I + reinforcement time), but Group 2 had its reinforcement duration reduced by a factor of 15 (from 60 to 4 s). The time thus saved was added to the intertrial interval. Group 2 acquired, whereas Group 1 did not. Groups 3 & 4 had longer (and equal) cycle durations. Again, a 56 s interval was used either for reinforcement (Group 3) or as part of the intertrial interval (Group 4). Group 4 acquired most rapidly. Group 3, which had the same I:T ratio as Group 2, acquired no faster than Group 2, despite getting 15 times more food per reinforcement. (Replotted from Figs. 1 & 2 in Balsam & Payne, 1979.)

Acquisition Requires Contingency. When reinforcements are delivered during the intertrial interval at the same rate as they occur during the CS conditioning does not occur. This was demonstrated by Rescorla (1968), who introduced the truly random control, a control group in which reinforcement was as frequent in the absence of the CS as in its presence (see Fig. 2.6). The reinforcers that occur when the CS is not present, that is, when the experimental chamber itself is the only stimulus, are called background reinforcers. The failure of conditioning under these conditions is not simply a performance block, as conditioned responding to the CS after random control training is not observable even with sensitive techniques (Gibbon & Balsam, 1981). Making the rate of background reinforcement equal to the rate of CS reinforcement eliminates the contingency between the CS and the US, while leaving the frequency of CS–US temporal pairings unaltered. Thus, the fact that conditioning to the CS is not observed in the truly random control group implies that conditioning is driven by CS–US contingency, not by the temporal pairing of CS and US. This very robust and well established finding has failed to have the impact that it should on thinking about the neurobiological basis of learning. If learning is basically a matter of association formation, then one thing that experiment has taught us is that association formation is driven by contingency, not by temporal pairing.

Although the best data on the quantitative properties of the acquisition process come from pigeon autoshaping, the same effects (and surprising lack of effects) are apparent in other classical conditioning paradigms. Partial reinforcement produces little or no increase in reinforcements to acqui-

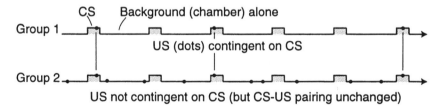

FIG. 2.6. Rescorla's (1968) experiment contrasted the effects of the upper protocol, in which the rate of background reinforcement is zero (the dots = the reinforcements = the USs only occur when the CS is present), with the effects of the lower protocol, in which the rate of background reinforcement equals the rate of reinforcement observed when the CS is present. In the first case, subjects develop a CR to the CS. In the second case, they do not, even though the CS is paired with the US equally often in both cases. This experiment established a point of fundamental importance, namely, that conditioning is produced not by the temporal pairing of CS and US but rather by the contingency between the CS and the US.

sition in a wide variety of paradigms (see citations in Table 2 of Gibbon, Farrell, Locurto, Duncan, & Terrace, 1980; also Holmes & Gormezano, 1970; Prokasy & Gormezano, 1979); whereas, lengthening the amount of exposure to the experimental apparatus per CS trial increases the rate of conditioning in the rabbit nictitating membrane preparation by almost two orders of magnitude (see Fig. 2.3; also Kehoe & Gormezano, 1974; Levinthal, Tartell, Margolin, & Fishman, 1985; Schneiderman & Gormezano, 1964). Thus, it appears to be generally true that varying the $I{:}T$ ratio has a much stronger effect on the rate of acquisition than does varying the degree of partial reinforcement. Because this is a fundamentally important result, with strong theoretical implications, it is to be hoped that the extent to which this generalization holds will be carefully tested in all the commonly used conditioning paradigms.

Increasing the magnitude of the water reinforcement in rabbit jaw-movement conditioning 20-fold has no effect on the rate of acquisition (Sheafor & Gormezano, 1972). Thus, it appears to be generally true, at least for appetitive conditioning, that the magnitude of reinforcement has little effect on rate of acquisition—provided, of course, that this magnitude exceeds some threshold of detectability or acceptability.

Turning to aversive conditioning, and Kamin (1961) examined the effect of shock intensity on the rate at which fear-induced suppression of appetitive responding is acquired. The groups receiving the three highest intensities (0.85, 1.55, & 2.91 mA) all went from negligible levels of suppression to complete suppression on the second day of training (between trials 4 & 8). The group receiving the next lower shock intensity (0.49 mA) showed less than 50% suppression asymptotically. Kamin (1969a) later examined the effect of two levels of shock intensity on the rate at which conditioned emotional responses to a light CS and a noise CS were acquired. He used 1 mA, which is the usual level in conditioned emotional response experiments, and 4 mA, which is a very intense shock. The 1 mA groups crossed the 50% median suppression criterion between Trials 4 and 5, whereas the 4 mA groups crossed this criterion between Trials 3 and 4. Thus, varying shock intensity from the minimum that sustains a vigorous fear response up to very high levels has little effect on the rate of conditioned emotional response acquisition.

The lack of an effect of US magnitude or intensity on the number of reinforcements required for acquisition is counterintuitive. It merits further investigation in a variety of paradigms. In such investigations, it will be important to show data from individual subjects to avoid averaging artifacts. For the same reason, it will be important not to bin the responses by session or number of trials, et cetera. What one wants is the real-time record of responding.

Finally, in estimating the rate of acquisition, it is important to distinguish between the asymptote of the acquisition function and the location of its rise, defined as the number of reinforcements required to produce, for example, a half-maximal rate of responding. At least from a psychophysical perspective, only the latter measure is relevant to determining the rate of acquisition. In psychophysics, it has long been recognized that it is important to distinguish between the location of the psychometric function along the x axis, on the one hand, and the asymptote of the function, on the other hand. In the present case, the x axis is reinforcements and the location of the psychometric function along this axis is the number of reinforcements at the point where the rate of conditioned responding exceeds 50% of its asymptotic value. The location of a psychometric function indicates the underlying rate or sensitivity, whereas its asymptote reflects performance factors.

The same distinction is critical in pharmacology: The location of the dose-response function along the dose axis, usually defined as the dose required to produce a half-maximal response, indicates the sensitivity to the drug (receptor affinity), whereas the asymptote of the function reflects performance factors such as the number of receptors available for binding. We propose that the number of reinforcements required to produce a half-maximal rate of conditioned responding is the appropriate measure of a subject's sensitivity to a given combination of protocol parameters (delay of reinforcement, trial spacing, magnitude of reinforcement, reinforcement schedule). The steepness with which the acquisition curve rises and the asymptote it attains are, we suggest, not appropriate measures because they are determined by performance factors, which are every bit as important a consideration in the behavioral study of learning as they are in the behavioral study of sensory processes and pharmacology.

The quantitative facts about acquisition pose a challenge to the commonly cited associative models of conditioning. We delay elaborating on this challenge to a later chapter. Here, we show that these results are predicted by a model of acquisition built on the same foundations as the model for the timing of the CR: Recall that in the model for the timing of the CR, the decision to start responding at a certain latency after CS onset depended on the ratio between the estimated interval elapsed since the onset of the CS and the remembered latency of reinforcement. Similarly, acquisition—the appearance of a reliable CR in the course of repeated conditioning trials—is the result of the decision that the CS has a large enough effect on the rate of reinforcement to make it worth responding to. This decision is also based on a ratio of two estimated temporal intervals, or equivalently, on the ratio of two estimated rates of reinforcement; the rate of reinforcement when the CS is present, and the rate of reinforcement when only the background is present. The above quantitative properties of the conditioning process follow directly from this simple assumption.

RATE ESTIMATION THEORY

From a timing perspective, acquisition and extinction are the consequences of decisions that the animal makes about whether to respond to a CS. Our models for these decisions are adapted from Gallistel's (1990, 1992a, 1992b) earlier account, married to Gibbon's Scalar Expectancy Theory. Because the essence of this model is the computation of rate estimates under multivariate conditions plus a decision rule based on those rate estimates, we call it Rate Estimation Theory. In our acquisition model, the decision to respond to the CS is based on the animal's growing certainty that the CS has a substantial and enduring effect on the rate of reinforcement. This certainty is determined jointly by the animal's estimate of the rate of reinforcement when the CS is present, which does not change systematically as conditioning progresses, and by its estimate of the maximum possible rate of background reinforcement. This latter estimate steadily decreases as conditioning progresses.

We symbolize the subject's estimate of the rate of reinforcement when the CS is present by $\hat{\lambda}_{cs} + \hat{\lambda}_b$, where $\hat{\lambda}_{cs}$ is the subject's estimate of the rate of reinforcement of the CS itself and $\hat{\lambda}_b$ is its estimate of the rate at which reinforcements occur when only the background (the experimental chamber) is present. The estimated rate of reinforcement when the CS is present is the sum of the two estimates, because the background is always present when the CS is present. Whatever rate of reinforcement is attributed to the background itself, that rate will contribute to the rate observed when the CS is present. The "hats" on the lambdas (our symbols for the subject's rate estimates) are doubly appropriate. First, a hat on a variable is commonly used by statisticians to indicate the estimated value of some parameter, as distinct from its true value. Second, the variables (quantities) that these symbols refer to are symbolic quantities in the head of the subject. That is, they are inferred neurophysiological signals whose strengths represent the subject's estimate (or perception) of the values (magnitudes) of external variables such as rates of reinforcement and durations of interevent intervals. The hats serve to distinguish the subjective values, the values in the head, from their objective counterparts, the values outside the head.

In simple conditioning with continuous reinforcement, there is one US for each T seconds of CS exposure, because there is one reinforcement per trial and there are T seconds of CS exposure per trial. Therefore, the estimate of the rate of reinforcement when the CS is present (the rate during a trial) remains constant as conditioning progresses. In the absence of any reinforcement of the background alone, the rate of background reinforcement, to which the rate when the CS is present is compared, is simply one over the cumulative unreinforced exposure to the background alone. As the unreinforced exposure to the background alone gets longer and longer, this rate estimate gets lower and lower. Therefore the ratio between the rate of CS reinforcement and the rate of background reinforcement gets steadily bigger. This ratio is the animal's measure of the contingency between the CS and the US: The greater the ratio, the greater the perceived contingency. As conditioning progresses, this estimate of the CS–US contingency grows steadily.

The estimated interval between reinforcements is the inverse of the estimated rate of reinforcement. Therefore, the ratio on which the acquisition decision is based may also be thought of as the ratio of two estimates of intervals. If one thinks of it in this way, then the interval in the numerator is the estimated interval between background reinforcements. This estimate increases steadily as the cumulative amount of unreinforced exposure to the background alone increases. The estimate in the denominator is the expected interval between reinforcements when the CS is present. This does not change as conditioning progresses, because the interval between reinforcements when the CS is present is always T seconds. One sees, then, that the functional structure of the whether decisions in Rate Estimation Theory is the same as the functional structure of the *when* decision given by Scalar Expectancy Theory. Both decisions depend on a ratio of estimated intervals that grows steadily bigger. Only the decision variables are different. The functional structure of the decision process leading to acquisition is diagrammed in Fig. 2.7.

The interval-rate duality principle means that the decision variables in both Scalar Expectancy and Rate Estimation Theories are the same kind of variables. Both decision variables are equivalent to the ratio of two estimated intervals. Rescaling time does not affect these ratios, which is why both models are time-scale invariant. Time-scale invariance is, we believe, unique to timing-based models of conditioning with decision variables that are ratios of estimated intervals. It provides a simple way of discriminating experimentally between these models and associative models. There are, for example, many associative explanations for the trial-spacing effect (Barela, 1999), which is the strong effect that lengthening the intertrial interval has on the rate of acquisition (see Figs. 2.2 & 2.3). To our knowledge, none of them is time-scale invariant. That is, in none of them is it true that the magnitude of the trial-spacing effect is determined simply by the relative amounts of exposure to the CS and to the background alone in the protocol (see Fig. 2.4).

The explanation of the trial-spacing effect given by Wagner's (1981) Sometimes Opponent Process model, for example, depends on the rates at

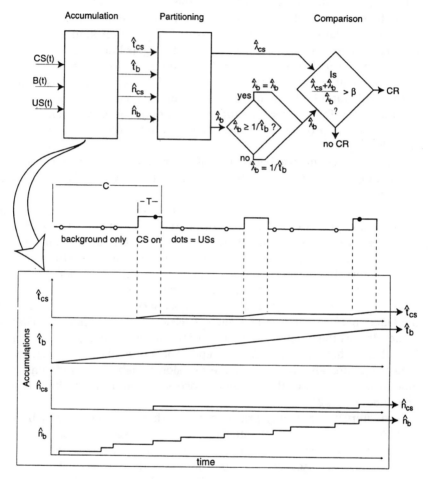

FIG. 2.7. Functional structure of the whether decision in acquisition. Three trials are shown, two of which are reinforced (black dots). There are eight reinforcements during the intertrial intervals (open dots). Subjective duration is cumulated separately for the CS ($\hat{t}_{cs}$) and for the background ($\hat{t}_b$), as are the subjective numbers of reinforcements ($\hat{n}_{cs}$ and $\hat{n}_b$). The time course of these accumulations is indicated in the expanded accumulation box at the bottom of the figure. These values in working memory enter into the partition computation to obtain estimated rates of reinforcement for the CS ($\hat{\lambda}_{cs}$) and for the background ($\hat{\lambda}_b$). (The additive partitioning process is described and diagrammed in chap. 4.) The rate estimates are continually updated and stored in reference memory. The decision to respond to the CS occurs when the ratio of ($\hat{\lambda}_{cs} + \hat{\lambda}_b$) to the estimated background rate of reinforcement ($\hat{\lambda}_b$) equals or exceeds a criterion, β.

38

which stimulus traces decay from one state of activity to another. The size of the predicted effect of trial spacing will not be the same for protocols that have the same proportion of CS exposure to intertrial interval and differ only in their time scale, because longer time scales will lead to more decay. This time-scale dependence is seen in the predictions of any model that assumes intrinsic rates of decay or any model in which experience is carved into trials with a specified duration. For example, Sutton and Barto's (1990) model, which is the most influential real-time associative model, relies heavily on stimulus traces that decay at some intrinsically determined rate; hence this model is not time-scale invariant. And the model of Rescorla and Wagner (1972), which is the most influential trial-based (ergo, not real-time) is like all trial-based models in that it carves experience into trials. These trials must have a finite duration, and their duration strongly affects the predictions of the model. Thus, this model is not time-scale invariant. Any model of the conditioning process that makes use of the notion of a window of associability, the notion of coincidence detection, or both, will also not be time-scale invariant.

Rate Estimation Theory gives a model of acquisition that is distinct from, albeit similar in inspiration to, the model proposed by Gibbon and Balsam (1981). The idea underlying both models is that the decision whether to respond to a CS in the course of acquisition depends on a comparison of the estimated rate of CS reinforcement to the estimated rate of background reinforcement. The decision to respond is based on the ratio of these rate estimates, as shown in Fig. 2.7. A somewhat similar model, called the Comparator Hypothesis, has also been suggested (Cole, Barnet, & Miller, 1995a; Miller, Barnet, & Grahame, 1992).

In our current proposal, Rate Estimation Theory incorporates scalar variability in estimating time, just as Scalar Expectancy Theory did in estimating the point within a signal (a CS) at which responding should be seen. In Rate Estimation Theory, however, two new principles are introduced: First, the relevant time intervals are cumulated across successive occurrences of the CS and across successive intervals of background alone. The total cumulated time in the CS, t_{CS}, and the cumulative exposure to the background, t_b, are integrated throughout a session and even across sessions, provided no changes in rates of reinforcement are detected. Cumulations over separated occurrences of a signal have previously been shown to be relevant to performance when no reinforcers intervene at the end of successive CSs. These are the "gap" (Meck, Church, & Gibbon, 1985) and "split trials" (Gibbon & Balsam, 1981) experiments, which show that subjects do, indeed, cumulate successive times over successive occurrences of a signal. It should be noted, however, that the gaps in these experiments were much shorter than the gaps over which Rate Estimation Theory assumes cumulation can occur.

Second, the rates that constitute the numerator and denominator of the decision ratio are not the directly experienced overall rate, and the experienced CS rate, as in Gibbon and Balsam (1981). Rather they are *attributed* rates; subjects are viewed as assigning partial credit to the CS, the background, or both, in a manner consistent with their experience. That is, they *partition* the observed rates in the CS and the intertrial interval into estimated rates for the background (the experimental chamber) by itself and for the CS(s) by itself (themselves).

Discussion of the partitioning process is postponed to chap. 4, where we consider the phenomena of cue competition. The only thing that one needs to know about the partitioning process at this point is that when there have been no reinforcements of the background alone, it attributes a zero rate of reinforcement to the background. This is equivalent to estimating the interval between background reinforcements to be infinite. However, the estimate of an infinite interval between events can never be justified by a finite period of observation. A fundamental idea in our theory of acquisition is that a failure to observe any background reinforcements during the initial exposure to a conditioning protocol should not and does not justify an estimate of zero for the rate of background reinforcement. It only justifies the conclusion that the background rate is no higher than the reciprocal of the total exposure to the background so far. Thus, Rate Estimation Theory assumes that the estimated rate of background reinforcement when no reinforcement has yet been observed during any intertrial interval is $1{:}\hat{t}_I$, where $\hat{t}_I$ is the subjective measure of the cumulative intertrial interval (the cumulative exposure to the background alone); see consistency check in Fig. 2.7. (The symbols used in Rate Estimation Theory and their meanings are given in Box 2.1.)

Correcting the background rate estimate delivered by the partitioning process in the case where there has been no background USs adapts the decision process to the objective uncertainty inherent in a finite period of observation without an observed event. Put another way, it recognizes that absence of evidence is not evidence of absence. This correction is consistent with partitioning in later examples in which reinforcements are delivered in the intertrial interval. In those cases, the estimated rate of background reinforcement, $\hat{\lambda}_b$ is always $\hat{n}_I{:}\hat{t}_I$, the cumulative number of background reinforcements divided by the cumulative exposure to the background alone.

As conditioning proceeds with no reinforcers in the intertrial intervals, $\hat{t}_I$ gets longer and longer, so $1{:}\hat{t}_I$ gets smaller and smaller. When the ratio between the rate expected during the CS and the background rate exceeds a threshold, conditioned responding appears. Thus, conditioned responding makes its appearance when

BOX 2.1
Symbols and Expressions in Rate Estimation Theory

Symbol/Expression	Meaning
n_b	• cumulative number of reinforcements delivered while background is present (equals total number of reinforcements, because background is always present)
n_{CS}	• cumulative number reinforcements delivered while CS is present
n_i	• cumulative number of reinforcements delivered during intertrial intervals $n_i = n_b - n_{CS}$
t_{CS}	• subject's cumulative exposure to the CS
t_b	• subject's cumulative exposure to the background (the experimental chamber)
t_i	• subject's cumulative exposure to the background alone (cumulative intertrial interval) $t_i = t_b - t_{CS}$
λ_{CS}	• rate of reinforcement for the CS alone (never directly observed)
$\lambda_b = n\,t_I{:}t_I$	• rate of reinforcement for the background alone = rate of reinforcement in the intertrial interval
$n_{CS}{:}t_{CS}$	• rate of reinforcement when the CS and the background are present
$\dfrac{\hat{\lambda}_{CS} + \hat{\lambda}_b}{\hat{\lambda}_b} = \dfrac{\hat{I}_b}{\hat{I}_{CS}}$	• the ratio of the estimated rate of reinforcement when the CS is present to the estimated rate of background reinforcement, which is equal to the ratio of the estimated interval between background reinforcements to the estimated interval between reinforcements when the CS is present; the decision variable in acquisition

Note. The subjective variable corresponding to an objective variable—the variable in the nervous system that represents a given objective aspect of the animal's conditioning experience—is symbolized by adding a "hat" (ˆ) to the symbol for the objective variable. These subjective variables are assumed to be proportional to the corresponding objective variables. (Subjective duration is assumed to be proportional to objective duration and subjective number to objective number.)

$$\frac{\hat{\lambda}_{cs} + \hat{\lambda}_b}{\hat{\lambda}_b} > \beta$$

where β is the threshold or decision criterion. Assuming that the animal's estimates of numbers and durations are proportional to the true numbers and durations (i.e., that subjective number and subjective duration, represented by the symbols with hats, are proportional to objective number and objective duration, which are represented by the same symbols without hats), we have

$$\hat{\lambda}_{cs} + \hat{\lambda}_b = n_{cs} / t_{cs} \quad \text{and} \quad \hat{\lambda}_b = n_I / t_I,$$

so that (by substitution) conditioning requires that

$$\frac{n_{cs} / t_{cs}}{n_I / t_I} > \beta$$

Equivalently (by rearrangement), the ratio of CS reinforcers to background reinforcers, $n_{cs}{:}n_b$ must exceed the ratio of the cumulated trial time to the cumulated intertrial (background alone) time by some multiplicative factor,

$$\frac{n_{cs}}{n_I} > \beta \frac{t_{cs}}{t_I} \qquad (1)$$

It follows that, N, the number of CS reinforcements required for conditioning to occur in simple delay conditioning must be inversely proportional to the $I{:}T$ ratio. The left hand side of Equation 1 is equal to N, because: First, by the definition of N, the conditioned response is not observed until $n_{cs} = N$, so the numerator of the ratio on the left of Equation 1 is equal to N at the point of acquisition. Second, n_I, the denominator on the left of Equation 1 is implicitly taken to be 1 when the estimated rate of reinforcement is taken to be $1{:}t_I$. Thus, at the point of acquisition, the left hand side of Equation 1 is equal to

$$\frac{N}{1} = N$$

reinforcements to acquisition. The right hand side of Equation 1 is the threshold constant, β, times the ratio of cumulated amounts of exposure to the two kinds of intervals, the trial interval and the intertrial interval. The ratio of the cumulative exposures to each kind of interval is simply the ratio of the relative proportions of each kind of interval in the protocol, which is to say, the $T{:}I$ ratio. In other words, we can substitute $T{:}I$ for t_{CS} / t_I on the right hand side of Equation 1. And, of course, $T{:}I = (I{:}T)^{-1}$, so responding to the CS should begin when

$$n_{CS} > \beta(I{:}T)^{-1}. \qquad (2)$$

Equation 2 says that on average, the number of trials to acquisition should be the same in different protocols with different durations for I and T but the same $I{:}T$ ratio. It also says that reinforcements to acquisition should be inversely proportional to the $I{:}T$ ratio. These are two of the salient quantitative facts about simple conditioning that we wanted to understand.

The important conclusion to be drawn from Equation 2 and Figs. 2.2 and 2.3 is that the rate of conditioning is constant at constant $I{:}T$ ratios, as Rate Estimation Theory predicts. Conversely, when the $I{:}T$ ratio varies, the rate of acquisition (the inverse of reinforcements to acquisition) varies in proportion to it. This accounts for most of the quantitative findings in conditioning listed earlier:

1. *Effect of trial spacing.* Increasing I without increasing T results in a higher $I{:}T$ ratio, hence more rapid conditioning.

2. *Effect of delay of reinforcement.* Increasing T without increasing I results in a lower $I{:}T$ ratio, hence slower conditioning.

3. *Time-scale invariance.* Increasing I and T by the same factor does not change the rate of conditioning. The points in Fig. 2.2 with the same $I{:}T$ ratio show approximately equal rates of conditioning, even though the absolute values of I and T differ substantially among points at the same ratio (at the same point along the abscissa). The dashed line in Fig. 2.4 shows the time-scale invariance of acquisition in a different way, by plotting reinforcements to acquisition as a function of delay of reinforcement, with the $I{:}T$ ratio held constant. When this ratio is held constant, the delay of reinforcement has no effect on the rate of learning.

4. *No effect of partial reinforcement.* When reinforcers are omitted on some fraction of the trials, cumulative exposure to the CS per CS reinforcement increases by the inverse of that fraction, but so does cumulative exposure to the background per CS reinforcement. For example, reinforcing only $\frac{1}{2}$ the trials increases the amount of exposure to the CS per reinforcement by two. But each T seconds of exposure to the CS is accompanied by I seconds of exposure to the background. So, the partial reinforcement schedule increases

exposure to the background per (CS) reinforcement by two, as well. Thus, the ratio of these two cumulative exposures (t_{CS} and t_b) after any given number of reinforcers has been delivered remains unchanged. No decrement in rate of acquisition should be seen, and none is, indeed, found. In Rate Estimation Theory, this deeply important experimental result is another manifestation of the time-scale invariance of conditioning. Conditioning is time-scale invariant because it depends on the relative amounts of the two kinds of intervals, intervals when the CS is present and intervals when it is not present. Partial reinforcement does not change the relative amounts of these two kinds of intervals, and that is why it has no effect on the rate of learning.

5. *No effect of reinforcement magnitude.* When reinforcement magnitude is increased, it increases the *estimated* rate of reinforcement[1] for both the CS and the background by the same factor. These changes in reinforcement magnitudes cancel, leaving $I:T$ unchanged. Again, no improvement in rate of acquisition is expected, and none is found. If there were a contrast between the magnitude of reinforcements given during the intertrial intervals and the magnitude given during the CS, then Rate Estimation Theory predicts that the ratio of these contrasting reinforcement magnitudes would strongly affect rate of acquisition. However, when there are no reinforcements during the intertrial intervals (the usual case), Rate Estimation Theory predicts that varying magnitude of reinforcement will have no effect, because the "consistency check" stage in the computation of the decision variable implicitly assumes that the yet-to-occur first background reinforcement will have the same magnitude as the reinforcements so far experienced. (What other assumption could plausibly be made?)

6. *Acquisition variability.* The data points in Fig. 2.2 show an approximately constant range of vertical scatter about the regression line. In the model of acquisition just presented, this scalar variability in reinforcements to acquisition results from the increasing variability in the estimate of t_b, the total accumulated exposure to the background, in comparison to the relatively stable variability of the estimate of the average interval of CS exposure between reinforcements. Intuitively, the estimated interreinforcement interval in the presence of the CS $\{1 / (\hat{\lambda}_{CS} + \hat{\lambda}_b)\}$ becomes increasingly stable as n_{CS} increases, whereas the estimate of the background interreinforcement interval $(1 / \hat{\lambda}_b)$ gets more variable in proportion as that estimate gets larger—the

---

[1]Rate is now used to mean the *amount* of reinforcement per unit of time, which is the product of reinforcement magnitude and number of reinforcements per unit of time. Later, when it becomes important to distinguish between the *number* of reinforcements per unit of time and the magnitudes of those reinforcements, we will call this *income* rather than rate. It is the same quantity as expectancy of reinforcement, *H*, in Gibbon (1977).

scalar variability of remembered estimates of duration (see chap. 1). Because of the scalar property, the variability in the estimate of n_{CS} in Equation 1 is proportional to its size, hence constant on the log scale.

One of the originally listed facts about acquisition follows from additive partitioning and is treated at greater length in chap. 4. It is stated here for completeness:

7. *Dependence on contingency (effect of random control).* When the rate of reinforcement during the intertrial intervals and during the CS (the trial signal) are equal ($\lambda_b = n_i / t_i = n_{CS} / t_{CS}$). The rate of reinforcement credited to the CS itself must be equal to $n_i / t_i - n_{CS} / t_{CS}$, and this difference is zero. Thus, partitioning credits the background with all the reinforcements, both those that occurred during the intertrial intervals and those that occurred when the CS was also present. Hence, no conditioning to the signal (the CS) is expected, and none is found.

If, however, the background reinforcers are not in fact background reinforcers, but are delivered only during another CS (Durlach, 1983), they have no effect on the rate of conditioning, because the partitioning mechanism assigns them to the other CS rather than to the experimental chamber (the background). The partitioning process is described in detail in the chap. 4.

Summary of Simple Acquisition

Most of the presently known quantitative facts about the rate of acquisition in simple conditioning (no background reinforcements) follow directly from the assumption that the animal begins to respond to the CS when the ratio of two rate estimates exceeds a decision criterion: The numerator of the ratio is the subject's estimate of the rate of reinforcement in the presence of the CS; the denominator is the estimate of the background rate of reinforcement. In simple conditioning, when the background is never reinforced, the denominator is the reciprocal of the cumulative duration of the interval between trials, whereas the numerator is rate of reinforcement when the CS is present. If the decision ratio is taken to be a ratio of expected interreinforcement intervals rather than a ratio of expected rates of reinforcement, then the predictions follow from the assumption that conditioned responding begins when the expected interval between background reinforcements exceeds the expected interval between CS reinforcements by a threshold factor. These are equivalent formulations.

What is also obvious in the above description of the model is that it takes seriously the assumption that is at the heart of the information processing approach to the brain and behavior, namely, that behavior is the result of computations that the brain performs on signals carrying information about the animal's experience. In modeling learning, we model those computations.

GENERALIZING THE MODEL

Acquisition When There Are Background Reinforcers

When there is a nonzero rate of background reinforcement—that is, when USs occur with some frequency during the intertrial intervals—subjects nonetheless acquire a response to the CS, provided that the frequency of reinforcement in the presence of the CS is substantially higher than in its absence (Rescorla, 1968). Under these conditions, the ratio between the estimated rate of reinforcement when the CS is present and the estimated rate when it is absent does not grow as conditioning progresses. Thus, the model stated for the simple case cannot explain acquisition when there is a background rate of reinforcement.

Another way to frame the problem is as follows: The model for simple conditioning, when there are no background reinforcements, relies on the fact that a simple measure of the contingency between the CS and the US gets steadily stronger as conditioning progresses. This measure is the ratio of the rate estimates in the presence and the absence of the CS. When there is no contingency, this ratio is 1. Of course, the measure of contingency can depart from its null value (1) in either direction, depending on whether the rate of reinforcement goes up when the CS comes on—the case we have so far considered—or down. The latter case occurs for inhibitory CSs, stimuli that predict a decrease in the rate of reinforcement. One would like to have a measure of contingency that is symmetrical about 0. Such a measure should be 0 when there is no contingency. When there are equal but opposite contingencies, the resulting measures should be of equal magnitude but opposite in sign. A measure that is proportional to the logarithm of the ratio of the rates has this property, because $\log(1) = 0$ and $\log(1/R) = -\log(R)$. Thus, we can generalize the model of acquisition to explain the acquisition of a response to a CS that predicts a decrease in rate simply by assuming that the measure of contingency is the log of the ratio of the estimated rates of reinforcement in the presence and absence of the CS and that the subject begins to respond when the magnitude (absolute value) of this decision variable exceeds a decision threshold. The sign of the contingency measure and the nature of the reinforcement (appetitive or aversive) jointly determine the nature of the CR (approach or avoidance).

This generalization predicts that rates of acquisition in inhibitory and excitatory conditioning should be comparable. This can be tested by using Kaplan's (1984) two-key paradigm with either the standard excitatory protocol or its inhibitory complement, the explicitly unpaired protocol, in which reinforcements occur at some rate whenever the CS is absent but never when the CS is present. In Kaplan's paradigm, the CS is the illumination of either of two keys. If the CS predicts the absence of reinforcement (a CS–), the subject moves away from the illuminated key toward the other side. When the US is positive (food), this avoidance response is the CR to a CS–, a CS that predicts a decrease in the rate of reinforcement. If, in contrast, the CS predicts an increase in the rate of reinforcement (a CS+), then the subject moves toward the illuminated key (when the reinforcement is positive). If the just suggested generalization of the acquisition model is valid, then one should be able to predict the time to acquisition of the avoidance response from the time to acquisition of the approach response. If the approach response appears when

$$\frac{t_I}{t_{CS}/n_{CS}} = x,$$

then the avoidance response should appear when

$$\frac{t_I/n_I}{t_{CS}} = \frac{1}{x}.$$

The left hand side of the first equation is the ratio of the cumulative intertrial interval, t_I, to the average interval between CS reinforcements, $t_{CS}{:}n_{CS}$. The left hand side of the second equation is the ratio of the average interval between background reinforcements, $t_I{:}n_I$, to the cumulative CS interval, t_{CS}.

The proposed measure of contingency grows toward infinity as conditioning progresses, that is, as it becomes increasingly apparent that the contingency between CS and US is complete; the US never occurs in the absence of the CS. When there are background reinforcements, the contingency between the CS and US is weaker, because USs sometimes occur in the presence of the CS. Moreover, the measure of this contingency does not grow as conditioning progresses. Something, however, clearly does grow as conditioning progresses, because prolonged exposure to the protocol causes the subject to respond to the CS, provided there is a substantial contingency, that is, provided the rate of reinforcement changes substantially when the CS comes on (Rescorla, 1968). The question then is: What gets stronger with continued exposure to a protocol in which there are different nonzero rates of reinforcement in CS and non-CS intervals?

An obvious answer is that the odds that the contingency so far observed is reliable get stronger the longer the exposure to the protocol. In the initial formulation of Rate Estimation Theory (Gallistel, 1990), the odds ratio, rather than simply the ratio of the two rate estimates, determined the onset of conditioned responding in the course of training. The odds ratio is $(1 - p){:}p$, where p is the probability that the contingency so far observed is fortuitous. The odds are related to the measure of contingency—the ratio of the estimated rates of reinforcement—by way of the F distribution function. The odds that the contingency so far observed is not a fluke are jointly determined by the estimated strength of the contingency (the ratio of the expected interreinforcement intervals, which is the inverse of the ratio of the estimated rates) and by the numbers of reinforcements, n_{CS} and n_I, on which the estimate is based.

At first, the assumption that there is the neural equivalent of the F distribution function in the heads of pigeons and rats strikes most people as implausible, indeed, preposterous. It may perhaps lessen this implausibility somewhat to note that anyone who finds neural net modeling at least vaguely plausible should not find the suggestion that there is an F function in the head implausible, at least on neurobiological grounds. Multilayer neural nets are universal function approximators (Hornik, Stinchcombe, & White, 1989). This means that it is possible to adjust the connection weights in such a net so as to make the input–output mapping performed by the net approximate any computable function. The F distribution function is a very simple function relative to the much more complex functions that nets are commonly called on to compute. It is easy to create a neural net that performs the mapping required by the proposed extension of the model.

Why should there be such a network in the heads of pigeons and rats? Because it enables them to deal efficiently with the uncertainties about the true states of affairs that are inherent in their daily experience of those aspects of the world on which their foraging efficiency depends. Thus, neither neurobiological considerations nor evolutionary considerations give reason to reject the assumption that the requisite neural machinery is to be found in the brains of pigeons and rats.

There are, however, purely behavioral reasons to doubt whether the proposed generalization is valid, because this model does not correctly predict the quantitative properties of acquisition in the case where there are no background reinforcements. It predicts that subjects should begin to respond after many fewer reinforcements than are in fact required and it predicts that the dependence of rate of acquisition on the $I{:}T$ ratio should be nonlinear and much shallower than it is.

What is puzzling is that, as discussed in chap. 4, the assumption that the subject assesses the odds that rates are different does predict the rapidity of their adjustment to changes in the rates of reinforcement delivered by competing response options, both under circumstances where those changes are infrequent and when they are frequent. Adjusting to changes in rates of reinforcement would appear to be closely related to acquiring a response based on differential rates of reinforcement. It turns out that when a change in relative rates of reinforcement is infrequent, subjects show evidence of detecting the change soon after it occurs, but they are slow to adjust completely to it (see Fig. 4.4). They begin to adjust at a normatively appropriate time after the change, but they take a long time to complete their adjustment. In contrast, when they have experienced such changes several times within a few sessions, they adjust completely to the changes within a normatively appropriate interval. Indeed, they adjust about as rapidly as it is, in principle, possible for any device to adjust. This suggests that when they detect a change in the rate of reinforcement, how long they take to adjust to it depends on how long they expect it to last. The first time they detect a change, they do not know how long it can be expected to endure; hence, they do not adjust to it completely until they have observed it to last an appreciable interval relative to the duration of their initial experience of a rate of reinforcement. Thus, we suggest that subjects in simple acquisition experiments detect the CS–US contingency well before they begin to respond reliably to the CS. It would be interesting to seek behavioral evidence of this.

Trace Conditioning and the Acquisition of a *Timed* Response

There is no CR to the CS until the *whether* criterion has been met. The timing of the responses that are then observed is known to depend, at least eventually, on the distribution of reinforcement latencies that the animal observes. It is this dependence that is modeled by Scalar Expectancy Theory, which models the process leading to a timed CR under well-trained conditions, where the animal has decided (earlier in its training) that the CS merits a response (the *whether* decision), what the appropriate comparison interval for that particular response is, and what the appropriate threshold value(s) is (are). A model for the *acquisition* of an *appropriately timed* CR is needed to describe the process that makes these latter decisions during the course of training, because Scalar Expectancy Theory presupposes that these decisions have already been made. It models only mature responding, the responding observed once comparison intervals and thresholds have been decided on.

It is tempting to assume that no such decisions are necessary, that the animal, simply samples from the distribution of remembered intervals to obtain the particular remembered interval that constitutes the denominator of the decision ratios in Scalar Expectancy Theory on any one trial. This would predict exponentially distributed response latencies in experiments where the observed CS–US intervals were exponential, and normally distributed response latencies in cases where there was a single, fixed CS–US

interval. We are inclined to doubt that this assumption would survive detailed scrutiny of the distributions actually observed and their evolution
over the course of training, but we are not aware of published data of this
kind. Consider an experiment where the rat has come to fear a shock that
occurs at some random but low rate when a CS is present (as in, for example, Rescorla's 1968 experiments). The shock delays after CS onset are exponentially distributed, and this distribution is so shallow that it is common
for shocks not to occur for many minutes. It seems unlikely that the onset
of the rat's fear response is ever delayed by many minutes after the onset
of the CS under *these* conditions, where the shock is equally likely at any
moment. But this is what one has to predict if it is assumed that the rat simply samples from the distribution of remembered latencies. Also, casual
observation of training data from the peak procedure suggests that the termination of conditioned responding to the CS when the expected reinforcement latency has passed develops later in training than does the delay of
anticipatory responding (cf. Rescorla, 1967). This implies that it takes longer (more training experience) to decide on an appropriate stop threshold
than to decide on an appropriate start threshold.

The need to posit timing-acquisition processes by which the animal decides in the course of training on appropriate comparison intervals (and
perhaps also on appropriate decision thresholds) becomes even clearer
when one considers more complex paradigms like the time-left paradigm
with one very short and one very long standard interval. In this paradigm,
the subject compares the steadily diminishing time-left until reinforcement
on the time-left key to the expected delay of reinforcement on a standard
key. It begins a trial by pecking the standard key, because the expected delay there is shorter than the time left. The subject switches to the time-left
key, when it judges the time left has become less than the expected delay
on the standard key. Thus, the time left when the subject switches gives an
estimate of the expected delay on the standard key.

When there are two possible delays on the standard key and no way of
knowing which will occur, the subjective expectation turns out to be the
harmonic mean of those two delays. That is, the value for time left at which
pigeons judge the time-left key to be preferable to the standard key is the
harmonic mean of the two possible delays (Brunner, Gibbon, & Fairhurst,
1994). In this paradigm, there is a moment-of-commitment beyond which
the subject is stuck with its choice, that is, with either the standard key and
hence a standard delay or the time-left key and hence the time left, depending on which key it was pecking at the (unpredictable) moment of commitment. On trials where the subject ends up on the standard key, one observes the effects of three more timing decisions. After the moment when
the program has committed the subject to the Standard Side—hence, to one
of the two Standard Delays—the likelihood of responding rises to a peak at

the time of the first standard delay (first start decision); if food is not delivered then, it subsides (first stop decision), to rise to a second peak at the time of the second latency (second start decision). Thus, in this experiment, three different reference intervals (expectations) are derived from one and the same experienced distribution (the distribution of delays on the Standard side)—one expectation for the changeover decision, one for the decisions that cause the early peak in responding on the Standard Side and one for the decisions that cause the late peak.

Clearly, an account is needed of how in the course of training, the animal decides on these three different reference intervals and appropriate thresholds. There is no such account at present. Its development must await data on the emergence of timed responding (i.e., appropriate acquisition data).

A related issue concerns the acquisition of the CR in trace conditioning paradigms. In these paradigms, the US does not occur during the CS but rather some while after the termination of the CS. Thus, the onset of the CS does not predict an increase in the rate of US occurrence. Rather the offset of the CS predicts that a US will occur after a fixed latency. Experiments in rabbit eyeblink conditioning using probe trials on which the CS is unexpectedly lengthened give evidence that the subject has in fact learned to estimate the time of US occurrence using both CS onset and CS offset (Desmond & Moore, 1991). Two different populations of blink latencies are seen on the probe trials, one at the correct latency relative to the onset of the CS and one at the correct latency relative to the offset. On any given trial, one may see blinks belonging to either population or to both (that is, two blinks in response to one CS, one timed from CS onset and one from CS offset). The scalar variability of remembered latencies is evident in these data in that the second population, the population timed relative to CS offset, has a tighter distribution than the first population, the one that is timed relative to CS onset, even though these blinks occur later in the sequence that begins with the onset of the CS. This is, of course, because the remembered interval from CS offset to the US onset is shorter than the remembered interval from CS onset to US onset.

For acquisition of a response to the CS to occur under the conditions of trace conditioning, the animal must decide that the latency from CS onset to the US is appreciably much shorter than the US–US latency. As in the acquisition of a timed response, this would appear to require a decision process that examines the distribution of USs relative to a time marker.

We are not aware of published data on the rate of acquisition of a timed response to the CS, but Balsam (1984) has studied acquisition in trace conditioning parametrically. As in delay conditioning, it is the proportions among the temporal intervals in the trace conditioning protocol that determine the rate of acquisition, not their absolute durations, only now there are three relevant intervals, rather than two: the CS duration, T, the duration, G, of the gap between CS and US, and the duration, C, of a trial cycle (Balsam (1984) showed that both the rate of acquisition of a CR and the asymptotic strength of the response were approximately proportional to an expectancy ratio, r, defined as follows:

$$r = \frac{C}{T+G} - \frac{G}{T+G}\left(\frac{C}{T+G} - 1\right). \tag{3}$$

The interval $T + G$ is the delay of reinforcement, that is, the interval that elapses between the onset of the CS and the delivery of reward. Equation 3 says that if this delay is fixed, then the longer the trial cycle is, the faster acquisition is. Put another way, the shorter the delay relative to the inter-reinforcement interval, the faster acquisition is. This is the same relation that is observed in delay conditioning. (Note that when $G = 0$, that is, when there is no gap, Equation 3 asserts that acquisition is proportional to $C{:}T$.) However, the $C{:}T$ ratio is not the only proportion that matters. When the ratio between the interreinforcement interval and the delay of reinforcement is kept constant, both the rate of acquisition and the asymptotic strength of responding nonetheless depend strongly on the proportion

$$\frac{G}{T+G};$$

the greater the proportion of the delay occupied by the gap, the more slowly subjects acquire and the more poorly they respond to the CS. In other words, it is important not only that the CS signal a *relatively* short delay of reinforcement, but also that the CS occupy a *relatively* large proportion of that delay.

We do not have a model that can explain the direct proportionality between the expectancy ratio, r, defined by Equation 3 and the rate of acquisition, much less the direct dependence of this rate on the proportion of the delay occupied by the CS. However, it is clear that one aspect of the problem is a procedure for determining whether USs are or are not randomly distributed in time with respect to temporal markers like CS onsets and offsets. For this, we can suggest a normatively correct model.

We begin by noting that this is inherently a problem of distribution sensitivity. The subject must be sensitive not simply to the average values of the intervals but to the form of the distribution of the intervals. Brunner, Fairhurst, Stolovitzky, and Gibbon (1997) have shown that pigeons and rats are, indeed, sensitive to the spread of a distribution, rather than simply to its expectation (average). They manipulated the forms and spreads of distributions and showed that the onset and offset of conditioned responding could be controlled by the outer deciles of these distributions—the latencies after or before which 10% or 90%, respectively, of all reinforcements occurred.

Thus, we want to develop a distribution-based measure that would enable a subject to decide whether a time marker gave information about the timing of a US. Let US_n be the nth US following the last occurrence of a time marker. The cumulative distribution function for a US_n relative to the time marker is the cumulative number of US_n's that have been observed to occur, as a function of their occurrence latency. Whenever the time marker occurs for example, at each CS onset, the timer for this cumulative distribution is reset to zero. The reading on this timer, if and when a reinforcement then occurs, is the reinforcement latency relative to that marker for a US_1. The timer continues timing, and if there is a second US before the marker recurs, the timer reading at that moment is the latency for a US_2, and so on. When the marker recurs, the timer is reset. Over many recurrences of the marker, we accumulate a population of US_1 latencies, a population of US_2 latencies, and so on. When we plot the total number of US_1 reinforcements at or less than a given latency, as a function of that given latency, the asymptote of this plot is simply the total number of US_1 reinforcements. If we divide earlier points in the plot by this total, we get the normalized cumulative distribution function. This function gives for each possible latency, the fraction of total US_1's that occurred at or before that latency. We can, of course, do the same thing for any US_n, that is, we can plot the normalized cumulative distribution function of the latencies of the nth postmarker reinforcements.

The expected form of these distributions in the case where the time marker provides no information about the timing of the USs is known; they are Poisson distributions. Thus, a suitable measure is one from which we can estimate the likelihood that the distribution we have in fact observed differs from the appropriate Poisson distribution. Which Poisson distribution is the appropriate one is determined by n, that is, by whether we are considering the population of first postmarker USs or the population of second postmarker USs, or the population of nth postmarker USs. In what follows, we treat only the case where $n = 1$, but the same approach works for any value of n.

The cumulative distribution function for US_1's has two limiting cases. One comes from the random rate case, where the time marker gives no information about the timing of the next US. In that case, the cumulative distribution of latencies following the time marker is the cumulative exponential $1 - e^{-\lambda t}$, where λ is the rate of US occurrence. (The cumulative exponential is the first member of the family of cumulative Poisson distributions.) At the other limit, the time marker gives perfect information about the temporal location of the next reinforcement: Given the time of occurrence of the time marker, the time of occurrence of the next reinforcement is known exactly. If animal memory were capable of remembering reinforcement latencies with arbitrary precision, then the cumulative distribution function in this case would be a step from 0 to 1 at the reinforcement latency. However, as we know from chap. 1, scalar noise in memory limits the precision with which a fixed latency can be remembered. Because of the scalar variability in memory, the subjective distribution function will be the cumulative normal distribution rather than a step. The parameters (μ and σ, respectively) of the subjective cumulative normal distribution function in the fixed-latency case will be $\hat{l}_r$, which is the subjective estimate of the reinforcement latency, and the $\hat{l}_r(c.v.)$, where $c.v.$ is the coefficient of variation for that subject. The $c.v.$ is the trial-to-trial variability in the retrieved value when the exact same value in memory is read repeatedly, expressed as a fraction of the mean of the distribution of remembered values.

To decide whether the time marker gives useful information about the time of occurrence of the next US (that is, a US_1), the subject needs a measure of the extent to which the next US has been predictable. A normatively appropriate measure of the extent to which the time of reinforcement was predictable given a time marker is D_{max}, the maximum deviation between the obtained cumulative distribution function and the cumulative distribution function for the random rate case. This maximum deviation between the observed and expected cumulative distribution functions is the Kolmogorov-Smirnov statistic. It, together with the number of observations in the observed distribution, determines the probability that an observed distribution differs from an expected distribution. Figure 2.8 shows D_{max} for two cases, in both of which there is a fixed reinforcement latency. In one case, the reinforcement latency is equal to the overall expectation t/n. This is the case that we see in a traditional protocol, where the CS has a fixed duration and reinforcement in always delivered at the end of the CS. In that case, the reinforcement latency is equal to the expectation of reinforcement in the presence of the CS. In the other case, the reinforcement latency is $\frac{1}{5}$ of this expectation. One prediction of this model is evident from Fig. 2.8: The shorter the reinforcement latency in relation to the overall expectation of reinforcement in the presence of the CS, the faster a timed response should develop. This is because the shorter the latency in relation to the average interreinforcement interval, the greater D_{max}, which is the proposed measure of nonrandomness in the timing of reinforcement.

It may also be seen from Fig. 2.8 that the D_{max} measure would allow the subject to detect the temporal predictability of a reinforcement even when the latency of the reinforcement was equal to the expected interval between reinforcements, which is an interesting case. This case arises, for example, when a subject responds on a fixed Time schedule, where the time of the previous reinforcement predicts the time of the next reinforcement.

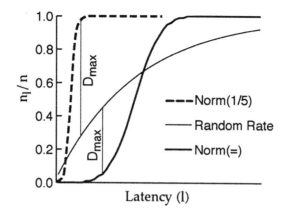

FIG. 2.8. Subjective normalized cumulative distribution functions for three different cases in which the overall expectation of reinforcement, t/n, is the same. These distributions give the fraction of all reinforcement latencies (ordinate) less than a given latency from a time marker (abscissa). The random rate distribution is the null hypothesis. If an observed distribution does not depart significantly from this distribution, then the time marker gives no information about the timing of the next reinforcement. Norm(=) is the observed distribution in the case that there is an unvarying reinforcement latency equal to the overall expectation of reinforcement. The less the coefficient of variation in memory noise is, the more step-like this distribution becomes. The assumed $c.v.$ in this figure is 0.25. Norm(1/5) is the observed distribution in the case where there is an unvarying reinforcement latency equal to $\frac{1}{5}$ the overall expectation of reinforcement. The measure of the extent to which a given distribution departs from the null distribution is D_{max}, the maximum deviation. The odds that this deviation is not fortuitous depend on D_{max}, and on n, the total number of reinforcements.

In this paradigm, there is no CS that predicts an increased rate of reinforcement, so Rate Estimation Theory clearly does not apply. However, the subject does develop a temporally patterned CR, with the probability of responding increasing in proportion to the fraction of the fixed interreinforcement interval that has elapsed (see Fig. 1.5).

This initial attempt at a theory for the acquisition of a CR that depends purely on the timing of reinforcement relative to a marker—rather than on the rate of reinforcement in the presence of a CS—captures one qualitative fact about acquisition in trace conditioning, namely, that it is faster when there is a relatively short gap between CS offset and US onset. Also, this model is time-scale invariant; its predictions depend only on the delay of reinforcement relative to the interreinforcement interval. Finally, this model makes it clear how a subject could distinguish a fixed interval schedule of reinforcement from a random interval schedule with the same expectation.

However, this model does not make quantitatively correct predictions about acquisition in trace conditioning. The number of reinforcements to acquisition should, according to this model, increase as the delay of reinforcement following CS onset is made longer relative to the interreinforcement interval, but it should not increase by as much as it in fact does. Also, this model does not explain why the rate of acquisition depends on how much of the delay is occupied by the CS, nor why filling the gap with another CS eliminates the effect of the gap (Balsam, 1984). It is clear that part of the story in trace conditioning is that the animal learns that the onset of the CS predicts a return to the background state prior to the eventual appearance of the US. When this return to the background condition is relatively long, both acquisition and asymptotic responding are greatly reduced, even if the delay of reinforcement is relatively short.

In summary, part of the problem in understanding the acquisition of a timed response and the acquisition of a CR in trace conditioning is to understand how the subject decides that a time marker—such as a CS onset or offset, or, with FI schedules, the occurrence of a US—gives information about the timing of the next US. We have suggested a normatively appropriate model for that decision. It is clear, however, that this model falls far short of a complete model.

3

Cue Competition and
Inhibitory Conditioning

Hull (1929) thought that "all elements of a stimulus complex playing upon the sensorium of an organism at or near the time that a response is evoked, tend themselves *independently and indiscriminately* [italics added] to acquire the capacity to evoke substantially the same response" (p. 498). He was wrong. The modern era in the study of conditioning began with the discovery that conditioning to one CS does not proceed independently of the other CSs present. The more or less simultaneous discovery of the effects of background conditioning (Rescorla, 1968), of blocking and overshadowing (Kamin, 1969a, 1969b), and of relative validity (Wagner, Logan, Haberlandt, & Price, 1968) made the point that what an animal learns about one CS strongly affects what it learns about other CSs. Or, possibly, what it has learned about other CSs strongly affects the behavioral expression of what it has learned about any one CS (cf. Miller's Comparator Hypothesis; Cole, Barnet, & Miller, 1995a; Miller, Barnet, & Grahame, 1992). The discovery of cue competition changed the character of associative models; it led to the model by Rescorla and Wagner (1972) and to other contemporary associative models that explain how experience with one stimulus affects the observed conditioning to another stimulus (e.g., Mackintosh, 1975; Miller & Matzel, 1989; Pearce, 1994; Pearce & Hall, 1980; Wagner, 1981). All such models attempt to explain how cues interact in conditioning. The general term for this interaction is cue competition. As we will see, an understanding of cue competition leads to an understanding of inhibitory conditioning, the conditioning that occurs when the CS predicts a reduction in the rate of reinforcement.

EXPERIMENTAL RESULTS

Some well-established facts concerning cue interactions are:

Blocking and the Effect of Background Conditioning. A CS that has already been conditioned blocks conditioning to a second CS that is presented together with it on so-called compound trials (see Fig. 3.1). Put another way, if the onset of a CS does not predict an otherwise unanticipated change in the interval between reinforcements (a change in the rate of reinforcement), a CR to that CS does not develop, no matter how often the US is paired with that CS. This is another demonstration that temporal pairing of a CS and a US is not sufficient for conditioning. If a CS is a *redundant* predictor of the US, conditioning does not occur even though the CS and US are temporally contiguous.

One manifestation of blocking is when the apparatus in which training is conducted functions as the blocking stimulus. In a famous experiment, described in the previous chapter, Rescorla (1968) showed that when reinforcers were delivered during the intertrial intervals at the same rate as during a CS, a CR did not develop to the CS despite many CS–US pairings. This procedure is called the truly random control, because it eliminates the contingency between the CS and the US without eliminating the US. It is now well understood that what happens in this case is that the US becomes conditioned to the experimental apparatus (the background or context) and this blocks conditioning to an intermittent CS (e.g., a tone) that does not alter the rate of US occurrence in that chamber.

Overshadowing. If two CSs are always presented and reinforced together, a CR generally develops to one but not the other as shown in Fig. 3.2 (Kamin, 1967, 1969b; Mackintosh, 1971, 1976; Reynolds, 1961; Wagner et al., 1968). Put another way, when it is inherently ambiguous which CS should be credited with the observed reinforcements, subjects tend to credit one of the CSs to the exclusion of the others. This CS is said to overshadow the other CSs.

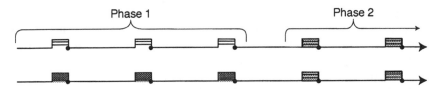

FIG. 3.1. Schematic protocol for a blocking experiment. There are two CSs, represented here by gray and by horizontal bars. Whichever CS is conditioned first (in Phase 1) blocks conditioning to the CS that is added in Phase 2. In the top protocol, the CS represented by the horizontal bars is conditioned first and it blocks the CS represented by the gray. In the bottom protocol, the roles of the CSs are reversed. No matter how many times USs (dots) are paired with the blocked CS, a CR to the blocked CS (the one introduced later on and in compound with the other CS) does not develop. Note that the addition of the second CS does not change the rate of reinforcement. Thus, the additional CS (the blocked CS) is not informative.

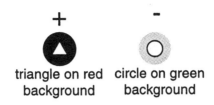

Training Stimuli

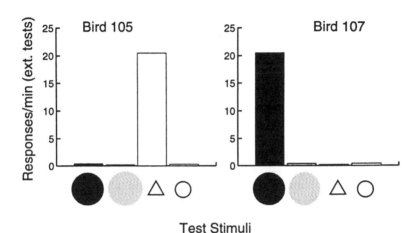

Test Stimuli

FIG. 3.2. Overshadowing. Two pigeons were trained to peck the key with a triangle on a red background and not the key with a circle on a green background. When tested with the four stimulus elements (red, green, triangle, circle) separately, one bird responded entirely to the red, whereas the other responded entirely to the triangle, although both of these elements had, of course, been paired with reinforcement throughout training. (Data from Reynolds, 1961.)

One Trial Overshadowing. The competitive exclusion of one CS by another CS under conditions where it is inherently ambiguous how much reinforcement should be credited to each is manifest after a single conditioning trial (Mackintosh & Reese, 1970).

Relative Validity. When one CS (called the common cue) occurs in combination with one CS on some trials and with another CS on other trials, the CS that gets conditioned is the one that can, by itself, predict the observed pattern of US occurrences. For some patterns, the common cue gets conditioned and its partners do not, even though one of those partners is paired with the US just as frequently as the common cue. For other patterns, one of the partner CSs gets conditioned and the common cue does not. In both kinds of conditions, the common cue is reinforced on half of all the trials on which it is presented. Thus, the relatively more valid cue gets conditioned as shown in Fig. 3.3 (Wagner et al., 1968).

Retroactive Reversal of Overshadowing and Blocking. Subjects do not respond to an overshadowed CS if tested before the overshadowing CS is extinguished, but they do respond to it if tested after the overshadowing CS is extinguished (see Baker & Mercier, 1989 for review; also Kaufman & Bolles, 1981; Matzel, Schachtman, & Miller, 1985). Thus, extinction of the overshadowing CS retroactively removes the overshadowing. Sometimes, the complementary effect, retroactive blocking, is also obtained. Subsequent reinforcement of an overshadowed CS retroactively blocks the over-shadowing CS (Cole et al., 1995a). Retroactive blocking is only reliably obtained in sensory preconditioning protocols, where the stimulus paired with a CS is another CS rather than a conventional US. It is not generally obtained when conventional CS–US overshadowing protocols are used (Grahame, Barnet, & Miller, 1992).

One way to look at these retroactive paradigms is that an initially ambiguous experience with reinforcement in the presence of two CSs is rendered unambiguous by subsequent experience with one CS alone. The only difference between a blocking paradigm and a retroactive reversal paradigm is in whether the disambiguating experience with a single CS precedes (blocking) or follows (retroactive paradigms) the ambiguous experience with the two CSs presented together.

Inhibitory Conditioning. When the onset of a CS predicts a decrease in the rate of reinforcement (see Fig. 3.4), a CR develops that is more or less

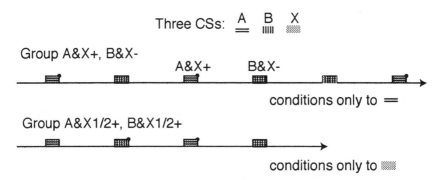

FIG. 3.3. The relative validity experiment (Wagner et al., 1968). In both protocols, the X stimulus is presented on every trial, and reinforced on half of those trials. But, in the upper protocol, the A stimulus is a more valid predictor of the US, and a CR develops only to it, not to X. In the lower protocol, the X stimulus is a more parsimonious predictor of the US. The CR develops only to it, despite the fact that the US is paired with both the A and the B stimulus on half of all the trials on which they are presented.

A

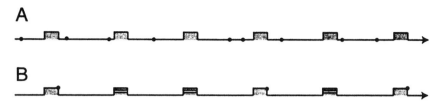

B

FIG. 3.4. Two protocols for producing conditioned inhibition. A. The *explicitly unpaired* procedure. The US (dot) occurs during intertrial intervals but never when the CS is present. Note that a CR to the CS emerges despite the fact that the CS and US never occur together, demonstrating that temporal pairing is not necessary for conditioning. B. The *feature negative* procedure. The US occurs whenever one CS (represented by gray) is present, but not when another CS (represented by horizontal bars) is also present. An inhibitory response to the second CS develops, although the CS is never paired with the US. There is yet another protocol, the *overprediction* procedure, which produces an inhibitory CR to a CS that is always paired with the US.

the antithesis of the excitatory response (e.g., avoidance of the CS rather than approach to it). Such a CS is called a CS−. When it is paired with an excitatory CS (a CS+), the CR elicited by the CS+ is reduced or abolished. This is called the summation test for inhibition, because it demonstrates that the inhibitory (negative) effect of the CS− cancels (partially or completely) the excitatory (positive) effect of the CS+.

Most contemporary associative models of conditioning offer explanations of these fundamentally important results. In a later chapter, we critique these models, noting especially their strong dependence on the assumption that experience is organized into trials. It has long been recognized that this assumption is highly artificial and probably, in the end, indefensible. This has led to the distinction between trial-based models and real-time models of conditioning. Only real-time models can claim to describe processes that happen in real time, neurobiological processes, for example. Trial-based models can be seen as describing neurobiologically realizable processes only if a way can be found to eliminate the model's dependence on the assumption that experience occurs in discrete trials. For most trial-based models, no way around this assumption has so far been found. The model of cue competition that follows is a real-time model; trials are not assumed.

TWO PRINCIPLES

In Rate Estimation Theory (Gallistel & Gibbon, 2000), the results from cue competition experiments are explained by two simple principles, which are implicit in the structure of the mechanism that estimates the rates of reinforcement to be credited to each of the experimental stimuli. Gallistel

(1990) laid down these determinative principles and developed their mathematical implications. The *rate additivity* principle requires that the estimated rates of reinforcement sum to the observed rates. The *predictor minimization* principle keeps the number of CSs that predict changes in the expected interval between reinforcements to the minimum consistent with additivity. This latter principle is a mechanized and quantified form of Occam's razor, the principle of explanatory parsimony.

The additivity of estimated rates leads directly to the prediction of blocking and the effects of background conditioning (Rescorla's truly random control). Because the target CS (the blocked CS) does not change the observed rate of reinforcement in those paradigms, the rate of reinforcement ascribed to it must be zero. Rate additivity also leads directly to an account of inhibitory conditioning. The onset of an inhibitory CS reduces the rate of reinforcement below that otherwise observed, hence, it must be credited with a negative rate of reinforcement (otherwise, additivity would fail).

Predictor minimization yields overshadowing, which occurs when it is inherently ambiguous which CS should be credited with how great a fraction of the observed reinforcements. Predictor minimization resolves the ambiguity by crediting the observed reinforcements entirely to one CS. Predictor minimization also yields the important result of Wagner et al. (1968), which is that the only CS to which a nonzero rate of reinforcement is credited is the relatively most valid CS, the one that by itself predicts as much of the variability in observed rates as can in principle be predicted.

The structure of the partitioning process in Rate Estimation Theory is entirely determined by the above two principles, in the sense that all of the explanations in Rate Estimation Theory that depend on partitioning are mathematically derivable consequences of these principles. The derivations are all exercises in solving systems of simple linear equations, which most of us learned to do in high school algebra. For someone with college-level training in linear algebra, the derivations can be entirely summarized in one paragraph, which is a testimony to the enormous compressive power of the notation. We give this summary first, because of its concision and precision. However, for many readers, the notation will be unfamiliar and the powerful concepts it refers to may never have been digested. Thus, we follow the mercifully short initial presentation of the rate estimation model with what are, we hope, intuitive explanations of why Rate Estimation Theory predicts what it predicts.

GENERAL SOLUTION TO THE RATE ESTIMATION PROBLEM

The problem the animal faces is to solve for the unknown rates of reinforcement predicted by each stimulus (CS) acting alone, given the rates observed when various combinations of them have acted together. The predicted rates are assumed to be additive. Rate additivity generates a system of simple linear equations. Solving this system of equations determines the solution to the rate estimation problem in every case in which there is independent evidence of the contribution of each CS, and hence, a unique solution.

Somewhat counterintuitively, it turns out that the general solution to the problem requires only the following quantities: (a) for each CS_i, the cumulative number of reinforcements, N_i, delivered when that CS was present; (b) the cumulative time, t_i, each CS has been present; and (c) the cumulative time, t_{ij}, that each pairwise combination of CSs has been present. The subscripts i and j range over the n CSs that have been observed. The background, that is, the experimental chamber, is always among these n CSs. It might seem that treating the experimental chamber as the background is somewhat arbitrary. One may reasonably argue that the laboratory environment is a still deeper background. Fortunately, the predictions of this model do not depend on any arbitary decisions about what stimuli should and should not be included among the potential predictors. The following is a perfectly general solution. Given any set of potential predictors of the observed rates, it finds a unique set of best predictors.

Let the sought-for rate estimates be represented by the column vector

$$\begin{pmatrix} \lambda_1 \\ \lambda_2 \\ \vdots \\ \lambda_n \end{pmatrix},$$

where λ_1 is the rate of reinforcement predicted by the first CS in the set of potential predictors, λ_2, the rate predicted by the second CS, and so on. Then

$$\begin{pmatrix} \lambda_1 \\ \lambda_2 \\ \vdots \\ \lambda_n \end{pmatrix} = \begin{vmatrix} 1 & \dfrac{t_{1\&2}}{t_1} & \cdots & \dfrac{t_{1\&n}}{t_1} \\ \dfrac{t_{1\&2}}{t_2} & 1 & \cdots & \dfrac{t_{2\&n}}{t_2} \\ \vdots & \vdots & \ddots & \vdots \\ \dfrac{t_{1\&n}}{t_n} & \dfrac{t_{2\&n}}{t_n} & \cdots & 1 \end{vmatrix}^{-1} \times \begin{pmatrix} \dfrac{N_1}{t_1} \\ \dfrac{N_2}{t_2} \\ \vdots \\ \dfrac{N_n}{t_n} \end{pmatrix}, \tag{4}$$

When there are redundant CSs, the determinant of the matrix in Equation 4 is zero, so a unique solution does not exist. In that case, unique solutions are obtained from reduced systems. Reduced systems are obtained by deleting one or more CSs from consideration. In the resulting systems of equations, the rank of the matrices is reduced by the number of CSs excluded from the predictive system and so is the dimensionality of the input and output vectors. Deleting different CSs produces different systems of equations and therefore different solutions. Among the different solutions thus obtained, the preferred solution is the one that minimizes the sum of the absolute values of the rate estimates (that is,

$$\sum_{i=1}^{i=n} |\lambda_i|).$$

When there is more than one such minimal solution, the choice among them must either be made at random or be based on extraneous considerations, such as the relative salience of the CSs. A spreadsheet implementation of this model is available on request from the first author of this book. Using it is one way for the skeptical but not mathematical to verify that the model predicts what we say it predicts in what follows.

Figure 3.5 shows the functional structure of the rate estimating process. The notation for Rate Estimation Theory is given in Box 2.1 on p. 41. There and in Fig. 3.5 and later figures, the variables that refer to hypothesized magnitudes in the brain of the subject have hats over them. The quantities in the exposition above were not hatted because the solution discussed there is the general solution to the additive rate estimation problem, whether or not it is an appropriate model of the psychological processes by

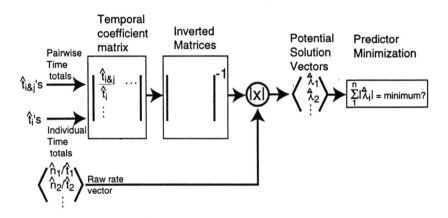

FIG. 3.5. The functional structure of the rate-estimating mechanism. See Gallistel (1992b) for an implementation that uses the matrix inversion and matrix multiplication functions in contemporary spreadsheet programs (e.g., Excel™). The hats on the variables indicate that they are quantities in the head.

which subjects solve the cue competition problem. By adding hats to the variables we convert this mathematics into a psychological theory, a theory about the processes that mediate conditioning.

INTUITIVE "DERIVATIONS"

Blocking

In a blocking protocol, an independently conditioned CS is combined on some trials with the target CS, without a change in the expected inter-reinforcement interval. Because the rate of reinforcement when the target CS is present does not differ from the rate when the other CS is presented alone, the additive combination of expected rates requires that the reinforcement rate attributed to the target stimulus be zero (see partitioning box in Fig. 3.6). Hence, the target stimulus does not acquire the power to elicit a CR no matter how often it is paired with the reinforcer.

Rate Estimation Theory predicts that if US magnitude is changed at the same time the second CS is introduced, then a rate—or rather an income—will be attributed to that CS (Dickinson, Hall, & Mackintosh, 1976). An income is the number of reinforcements per unit time multiplied by a reinforcement magnitude. If reinforcement magnitude goes up when the second CS is introduced, then income goes up and the newly introduced CS is credited with that increase. That is, it is credited with the amount of income not predicted by the first CS. If reinforcement magnitude goes down when the new CS is introduced, then it is credited with a negative effect on income.

We deal with incomes at much greater length in chap. 6. So far, we have ignored reinforcement magnitude, because in most conditioning experiments it does not vary. However, Rate Estimation Theory generalizes in a straightforward way to the case in which it is income that must be predicted rather than simply rate. No new assumptions are necessary. Income simply replaces simple rate in the calculations.

There is a close analogy between the explanation of blocking in terms of rate partitioning and its explanation in the Rescorla-Wagner model, which has been the most influential associative explanation of cue competition. In the Rescorla-Wagner model, associative strengths combine additively and, at asymptote, the sum of the associations to a given US cannot exceed the upper limit on possible net associative strength for that US. In the timing model, estimated rates of reinforcement (or estimated incomes) combine additively, and their sums must equal the observed rates of reinforcement (or incomes). However, in Rate Estimation Theory, unlike in the Rescorla-Wagner model, the constraint on the sum holds at every point in conditioning, not just at asymptote. Also, in Rate Estimation Theory the value to which

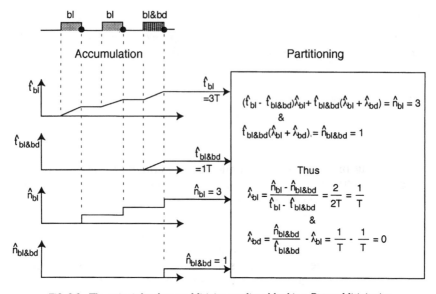

FIG. 3.6. The principle of rate additivity predicts blocking. Rate additivity implies the top two equations in the Partitioning Box. Solving them gives 1 / T for $\hat{\lambda}_{bl}$, which is the subjective rate of reinforcement for the blocking stimulus. Note that any value other than this would fail to account for the rate of reinforcement observed on trials when the blocking stimulus is presented alone. By additivity, the rate of reinforcement attributed to the blocked stimulus ($\hat{\lambda}_{bd}$) must be the raw rate for that stimulus, which is 1 / T, minus the rate estimate for the blocking stimulus, which is also 1 / T. Hence, the rate of reinforcement attributed to the blocked stimulus must be zero.

the estimated rates must sum is not an unobservable free parameter, as it is in the Rescorla-Wagner model. Indeed, there are no free parameters in the rate estimation process: The theoretically posited rate estimates in the subject's head are completely determined by the observed rates of reinforcement.

Background Conditioning and the Contingency Problem

In the truly random control protocol, the rate of reinforcement when the background alone is present is the same as the rate observed when a transient CS, such as a tone or a light, is also present (see Fig. 3.7). The principle of rate additivity requires that the background be credited with a rate that explains the rate observed when it alone is present. It also requires that the sum of this rate and the rate credited to the CS equal the rate observed when the CS is present. The unique solution to this double constraint ascribes a zero rate of reinforcement to the CS. This explains the profoundly

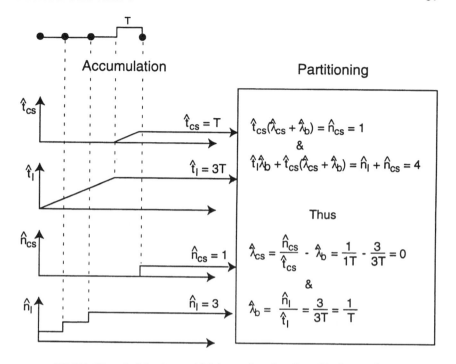

FIG. 3.7. The principle of rate additivity predicts the effect of background conditioning. When the rate of reinforcement during the intertrial interval equals the rate during a CS, the rate estimate for the background equals the raw rate estimate for the CS. When the rate estimate for the background is subtracted from that raw rate, the resulting estimate for the CS alone is 0. Thus, what matters is not whether the US is paired with the CS but whether the rate of US occurrence changes when the CS comes on (CS–US contingency).

important discovery that conditioning depends on a CS–US contingency rather than on the temporal pairing of CS and US (Rescorla, 1968). In Rate Estimation Theory, the ratio of the rate of reinforcement when the CS is present to the rate when it is absent (the background rate) is the measure of contingency. When this ratio equals 1, as it does in the truly random control, there is no contingency.

Response Elimination

Recall that responding to a conditioned CS may be abolished equally rapidly either by ordinary extinction, in which the CS is no longer reinforced, or by the so-called response-elimination procedure, in which the CS continues to be reinforced but the rate of reinforcement during the intertrial interval (background reinforcement), which has been zero, is now made equal to the rate of CS reinforcement. The partitioning process in Rate Estimation Theory has the property that the attribution of further reinforcements to the CS ceases as soon as the rate of background reinforcement is raised to equal the rate of CS reinforcement. This is because the rate estimates at every point in conditioning depend only on the totals accumulated up to that point. Thus, it does not matter whether the reinforcements in the background come before or after the CS reinforcements. In Fig. 3.7, the background reinforcements come before the CS reinforcement. In Fig. 3.8, they come afterwards, as they would when response elimination begins, but the result is the same: The three reinforcements during the intertrial interval have the effect of forcing the reinforcement that occurs during the CS to be credited to the background rather than to the CS.

Because the commencement of background reinforcement immediately robs all further CSs of credit for the reinforcements that occur in their pres-

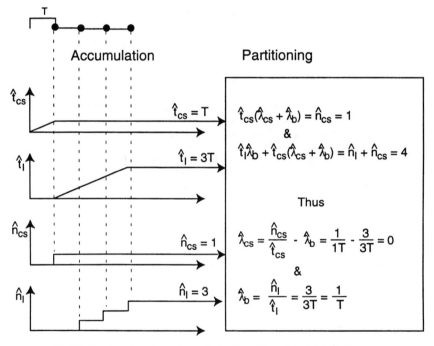

FIG. 3.8. Explanation of response elimination: When intertrial reinforcers appear, they force a corresponding proportion of *previous* CS reinforcements to be credited to the background rather than to the CS. Thus, the cumulative number of reinforcements credited to the CS stops growing as soon as the background begins to be reinforced at a rate equal to the rate of CS reinforcement. Note that the rate estimation process uses only the total cumulations, which are the same in this figure and the previous one. Thus, the equations for the two cases are identical. This is a form of path independence.

ence, the onset of background reinforcement marks the beginning of an interval in which no further reinforcements are attributed to the CS. Thus, ordinary extinction and response elimination are two different ways of reducing to zero the apparent rate of CS reinforcement. From the standpoint of the extinction-producing decision process—to be described in the next chapter—they are identical. Thus, the decision to stop responding to the CS occurs after the same number of omitted reinforcements in both cases, whether those omissions are real or apparent.

Signaling Background Reinforcements

Rate additivity also has the consequence that so-called signaled background reinforcers do not affect the estimate of the rate of reinforcement for the chamber alone; hence, signaling background reinforcers eliminates the blocking effect of such reinforcers. A signaled background reinforcer is simply a reinforcer that occurs in the presence of another CS (the signaling CS). Because there are never reinforcements when only the background is present, the background rate of reinforcement must be zero. The zero estimate for the background rate of reinforcement forces the reinforcers that occur during the signaling CS to be credited to it (proof in Gallistel, 1990), which is why signaled background reinforcements do not prevent the acquisition of a CR to the target CS (Durlach, 1983; Goddard & Jenkins, 1987). Note that this explanation requires a substantial amount of unreinforced exposure to the background in the absence of any other CSs, which has been shown to be necessary (Cooper, Aronson, Balsam, & Gibbon, 1990). The advantage that Rate Estimation Theory has over the alternative timing account of blocking and background conditioning offered by Gibbon and Balsam (1981) is that it explains why signaling background reinforcers eliminates the blocking effect of background conditioning.

Overshadowing

The principle of additivity does not always determine a unique solution to the rate estimation problem. In overshadowing protocols, two CSs are always presented together, but the CR develops to one CS and not the other (see Fig. 3.2), or, at least, more strongly to one than to the other. When two CSs have always occurred together, any pair of rate estimates that sums to the observed rate of reinforcement is consistent with the additivity constraint. Suppose, for example, that a tone and a light are always presented together for 5 s, at the end of which reinforcement is always given. Reinforcement is never given when these two CSs are not present, so the estimate of the background rate of reinforcement must be zero. One solution to the rate estimation problem credits a rate of one reinforcement every 5 s to the tone and zero rate of reinforcement to the light. This solution is consistent with the principle of rate additivity. But so is the solution that credits one reinforcement every 5 s to the light and zero to the tone. And so is the solution that credits one half of the reinforcements in 5 s to the light and one half of the reinforcements in 5 s to the tone, and so is every combination of rates that sums to one reinforcement in 5 s. Thus, the principle of rate additivity does not determine a unique solution to the rate estimation problem in cases where there are redundant CSs. There is an infinite number of solutions consistent with the principle of rate additivity.

The principle of predictor minimization eliminates redundant CSs in such a way as to minimize the number of predictors (CSs) credited with any predictive power, that is, credited with an effect on the rate of reinforcement. The requirement that a solution to the rate estimation problem minimize the number of predictors eliminates all those solutions that impute part of the observed rate of reinforcement to one of the two redundant CSs and part to the other. The principle pares the infinite population of possible additive solutions down to only the all-or-none solutions. There are never more of these solutions than there are CSs. In the case shown in Fig. 3.2, there would not appear to be in principle any nonarbitrary way of deciding which of the two all-or-none solutions should be preferred, so it is not surprising to find that one subject credited the triangle whereas the other credited the red background. The very arbitrariness of this outcome suggests that the principle underlying overshadowing is the elimination of redundant predictors. The situation is, we believe, analogous to the situation with ambiguous figures in perception. Ambiguous figures are stimuli that support two or more mutually exclusive percepts (e.g., the famous old-woman, young-woman illusion). The perceptual system resolves such conflicts in favor of one percept or the other, even if the resolution is arbitrary.

In some cases, there may be an auxiliary principle that favors one solution over another. There may be a priori biases about which kinds of CSs are likely to predict a given kind of US (Foree & LoLordo, 1973; LoLordo, Jacobs, & Foree, 1982). Or, a CS that has a greater observed range of variation (hence, higher contrast between its presence and its absence) might be preferred over a CS with a smaller range of variation. This would explain why manipulating the relative intensities of the two CSs can determine which CS is overshadowed (Kamin & Gaioni, 1974; Mackintosh, 1976).

The principle of predictor minimization requires that one of two redundant CSs be credited with no rate of reinforcement. Although this was the result in Fig. 3.2 (see also Fig. 3.9), it is not always the case that the subject fails completely to respond to the overshadowed CS. There are many cases in the literature where there was some response to both CSs (e.g., Kamin, 1969a; Mackintosh, 1971; Wagner et al., 1968), although in examining the literature on incomplete overshadowing, one must be wary of group averag-

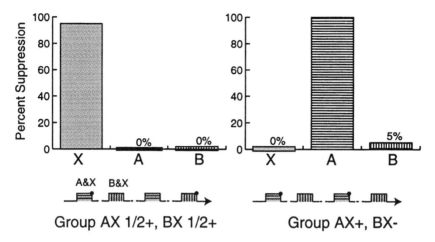

FIG. 3.9. The effect of relative validity on conditioned emotional response conditioning in the rat. Although foot shock (dots) is paired with both X and A on 50% of all presentations, X is the more valid predictor in Group AX 1/2+, BX 1/2+, whereas A is the more valid predictor in Group AX+, BX−. When responses to the individual stimuli are tested, only the more valid CS elicits a CR (fear-induced suppression of appetitive responding). These are the Stage I data from Table 3 on p. 175 of Wagner et al. (1968). Not all of the results in that paper show the all-or-nothing property that one sees in these data.

ing artifacts. If the data from the two pigeons in Fig. 3.2 were averaged, then one would conclude that there was no overshadowing in this experiment! Blocking is also sometimes incomplete (Ganesan & Pearce, 1988), although this is a rarer finding.

The explanation of overshadowing and blocking in many associative models depends on the assumed values of salience parameters, so these models can explain intermediate degrees of overshadowing (at least qualitatively) by an appropriate choice of values for these free parameters. The explanation of overshadowing and blocking in Rate Estimation Theory, in contrast, does not involve any free parameters: The principle of predictor minimization dictates that one or the other CS be given credit, but not both. The only way that intermediate degrees of overshadowing or blocking—in individual subjects—can be reconciled with Rate Estimation Theory is to assume that the subjects respond to the overshadowed CS not because that CS is itself credited with a rate of reinforcement, but because the overshadowed CS predicts the presence of the overshadowing CS and the overshadowing CS is credited with a rate of reinforcement. Many will recognize this as an appeal to something akin to what are called within-compound associations (Dickinson & Burke, 1996; Rescorla & Cunningham, 1978), which is a well-established phenomenon, often incorporated into associative models as well. This interpretation raises the question of how one can determine whether the response to a redundant CS is due to the primary conditioning of that CS (a rate of reinforcement credited to that CS) or to the second order conditioning of that CS to the other CS. Techniques for doing this have been developed by Holland (1990), so this explanation can be tested. Clearly, it would also be desirable to understand why one sees this phenomenon in some cases and not others.

One-Trial Overshadowing

The selective imputation of the observed rate of reinforcement to only one of two redundant CSs may occur after the first trial on which the two CSs are reinforced, because predictor minimization applies whenever ambiguity (multiple additive solutions) arises, and ambiguity arises the first time that there is a reinforcement of the jointly presented CSs. In the Rescorla-Wagner model, the overshadowing of one CS by another can develop only over repeated trials. Thus, experiments demonstrating overshadowing after a single trial have been thought to favor models in which an attentional process of some kind excludes one CS from access to the associative process (Mackintosh, 1975; Pearce & Hall, 1980). Rate Estimation Theory explains one-trial overshadowing without recourse to selective attention. Like ordinary overshadowing, it is an immediate consequence of the predictor minimization principle. That is, it is a consequence of the process for determining which stimuli get credited with which rates of reinforcement.

Relative Validity

The predictor minimization principle also predicts the relative validity effect first demonstrated by Wagner et al. (1968). Their two protocols had three CSs; A, B, and X. In both protocols, the X stimulus—the common cue—was reinforced on half the trials. In both protocols, it occurred together with the A stimulus on half the trials and together with the B stimulus on the other half. In one protocol, however, only the AX trials were reinforced, whereas in the other, half the AX trials and half the BX trials were reinforced. Subsequent, unreinforced test trials with each stimulus presented in isolation showed that subjects exposed to the first protocol (only AX trials reinforced) developed a CR to the A stimulus but not to the X or B stimuli. Subjects exposed to the second protocol (half of each kind of trial reinforced) developed a CR to the X stimulus but not to the A or B stimuli, despite the fact that both were reinforced just as frequently as the X stimulus (see Fig. 3.9).

Both protocols in this experiment give rise to two possible solutions, one involving only one CS and one involving two CSs. The predictor minimization principle dictates the one-CS solutions (the most valid CS). In the protocol where both AX and BX trials are reinforced half the time, the one-CS solution credits all of the reinforcements to X. An alternative solution credits to both A and B the rate of reinforcement credited to X alone by the one-CS solution. This two-CS solution credits nothing to X. The predictor minimizing machinery selects the one-CS solution (X) over the two-CS solution (A & B).

In the other protocol, where only AX trials are reinforced, the one-CS solution credits all reinforcements to A. Alternatively, reinforcements on AX trials could be credited to X, but this predicts an equal rate of reinforcement on BX trials. To explain the absence of reinforcements on BX trials, the alternative solution attributes an equal and opposite rate of reinforcement to B. The predictor minimizing machinery rejects this two-CS solution (X+, B−) in favor of the one-CS solution (A alone). Thus, predictor minimization explains both overshadowing and the effect of the relative validity of a cue. Predictor minimization is a mechanical or algorithmic implementation of Occam's razor, a principle sometimes formulated as, 'Explanatory entities should not be multiplied without good reason.' In other words, more parsimonious explanations, explanations that make use of fewer variables, are to be preferred over less parsimonious explanations. Predictor minimization selects the solutions that use the fewest predictive variables (CSs).

Retroactive Reversals

Rate Estimation Theory also predicts that the overshadowing of one CS by another will be reversed by subsequent extinction of the overshadowing CS. This result is a joint consequence of the additivity and predictor minimization principles. Predictor minimization credits the observed rate of reinforcement to only one CS, which leads to overshadowing in the first phase of conditioning. When the overshadowing CS is shown by subsequent experience not to predict the rate of US occurrence previously imputed to it, the additive partitioning of rates forces all the USs previously credited to the overshadowing CS to be credited retroactively to the overshadowed CS. That is, the additional experience radically alters the solution to the rate estimation problem. It disambiguates.

The retroactive effects of later reinforcements have already been seen in our explanation of response elimination. They are a consequence of the path independence of the partitioning process, its indifference to the order in which various CSs and CS combinations have been experienced. In Rate Estimation Theory, rate estimates depend only on the accumulated time and number totals. It does not matter how they accumulated.

In our analysis, the only alternative to the retroactive revision of previously computed rates of reinforcement is to conclude that the rate of reinforcement predicted by the overshadowing CS has changed. In the original formulation of Rate Estimation Theory (Gallistel, 1990), the conclusion that the rate had changed was prevented by a third constraining principle, the *rate-inertia* principle. The rate-inertia principle is that the rate attributed to a CS is not assumed to have changed unless the analysis for the nonstationarity of rate (the analysis that leads to the extinction decision) decides that it has. In the case of retroactive unblocking, there is no evidence of nonstationarity *if* the rates originally imputed to the overshadowing and overshadowed stimuli are reversed. After the reversal, which occurs in response to a subsequent disambiguating experience with one CS alone, there is no evidence that the rate of reinforcement imputed to either CS has changed since conditioning began.

Reversing rate estimates made under initially ambiguous conditions is not the same as deciding that there has been a change in the rates. The system concludes in effect that its earlier estimates of the rates were erroneous, as opposed to concluding that its earlier estimates were correct and that the rates themselves have now changed. The latter conclusion is prevented by the rate-inertia constraint. This constraint imposes an arbitrary resolution on another inherently ambiguous state of affairs. The second scenario—that the rates themselves have changed—is just as consistent with the animal's experience as is the conclusion that previous rate accreditations were erroneous.

It may be that under some circumstances, the rate-inertia constraint does not operate, in which case earlier estimates will not be revised in the light of later evidence. This would explain why retrograde blocking is sometimes observed and sometimes not (Grahame et al., 1992). In retrograde blocking, subsequent reinforced presentations of the overshadowed CS retroactively blocks conditioning to the overshadowing CS. Generally speaking, in perceptual theory, ambiguity-resolving constraints are context-specific. They apply in some circumstances, but not all. A principled analysis of which contexts will and will not support retroactive blocking is clearly necessary for this to be a satisfactory explanation.

The reversal of overshadowing by subsequent training with the overshadowing CS alone is difficult to explain for associative models that explain overshadowing in terms of the effect of cue competition on the strength of the association to the overshadowed CS (Baker & Mercier, 1989; Barnet, Grahame, & Miller, 1993a; Hallam, Matzel, Sloat, & Miller, 1990; Miller et al., 1992; Miller & Grahame, 1991; Miller & Matzel, 1989). It requires that the strength of the association to the overshadowed CS increase in the absence of any further experience with that CS. The strength of the association to the overshadowed CS must increase not simply as a consequence of the passage of time, but rather as a consequence of the animal's subsequent experience with the overshadowing CS. This violates a fundamental principle of most associative models, which is that the only CSs whose associations with the US are modified on a given trial are the CSs present on that trial (but see Dickinson & Burke, 1996; Van Hamme & Wasserman, 1994). These considerations have led to the suggestion that overshadowing is not due to an effect on associative strength but rather to a decision process that translates associative strengths into observed responses (Baker & Mercier, 1989; Cole et al., 1995a; Matzel et al., 1985). This suggestion moves associative theory in the direction of the kind of theory we are describing, particularly when it is coupled to the Temporal Coding Hypothesis (Barnet, Arnold, & Miller, 1991; Barnet et al., 1993a; Barnet, Grahame, & Miller, 1993b; Barnet & Miller, 1996; Cole, Barnet, & Miller, 1995b; Matzel, Held, & Miller, 1988; Miller & Barnet, 1993), which is that the animal learns the CS–US interval, in addition to the CS–US association.

In the relative validity protocol, also, the animal's initial conclusions about which CS predicts an increase in reinforcement can be reversed by subsequent, disambiguating experience with the CS to which it initially imputes the observed rates of reinforcement (Cole et al., 1995a). Here, too, the additivity and predictor minimization constraints together force this retroactive effect—for the same reasons that they force subsequent exposure to an unreinforced overshadowing CS to reverse the animal's original conclusions as to which CS predicted reinforcement in the first place. The kind of analysis we propose brings the study of learning close to the study of sensory psychophysics and perception, not only in that it has explicitly formulated decision processes, but also in that it has principles that constrain the interpretation of inherently ambiguous data, thereby resolving those ambiguities.

The timing-model explanations of the effects of background conditioning, overshadowing, and relative validity do not depend on assumptions about the values of free parameters. They are direct results of the two principles that determine the structure of the rate estimation machinery. In contrast, associative explanations of these phenomena depend critically on parametric assumptions. The explanation of the effects of background conditioning and relative validity were central features of the influential paper by Rescorla and Wagner (1972), which is the most widely cited contemporary theory of associative conditioning. It is, however, unclear that the Rescorla-Wagner model can explain both effects using a single set of parametric assumptions (Gallistel, 1990). Attention to whether and how explanations depend on parametric assumptions should be part of the evaluation of competing theories of conditioning.

Inhibitory Conditioning

The Explicitly Unpaired and Feature Negative Protocols. The additive partitioning of observed rates generates the phenomena of conditioned inhibition, without any further assumptions. Two protocols that produce what is called conditioned inhibition are the explicitly unpaired protocol and the feature negative protocol. In the first (see Fig. 3.10), reinforcements occur at some random rate except when a transient CS is present. Thus, when the CS comes on, the expected rate of reinforcement decreases to zero. If the reinforcers are positive reinforcers, the CR that develops is avoidance of the CS (Wasserman, Franklin, & Hearst, 1974). Note that this protocol is the inverse of the standard conditioning protocol: It reverses the contingency between CS and US. In the standard protocol, the US occurs only when the CS is present; in the explicitly unpaired protocol, it occurs only when it is absent. The fact that conditioning occurs equally readily in both cases is another reason for believing that it is CS–US contingency–not temporal pairing!–that drives the conditioning process.

In the feature negative paradigm, one CS (the CS+) is reinforced when presented alone, but not when presented together with the other CS (the CS–). Thus, on those trials where the CS– comes on along with the CS+, the rate of reinforcement decreases to zero from the rate predicted by the CS+. In time, the CR is seen to the CS+ but not to the combination of CS+ and CS–. When the CS– is then tested in combination with another separately conditioned CS+, the CR elicited by this other CS+ is reduced or eliminated (for reviews of the conditioned inhibition literature, see LoLordo & Fairless, 1985; Rescorla, 1969).

The additive partitioning of observed rates of reinforcement dictates that the subjective rate of reinforcement for the CS– in the above described inhibitory conditioning paradigms be negative, because the rate attributed to the sometimes co-occurring CS (the background or the CS+), which is positive, and the rate attributed to the CS– must sum to the rate observed when the CS– is also present. Objective rates cannot be negative, anymore than amounts of money can be negative, but subjective rates can be negative as easily as bank balances can. Subjective rates are quantities or sig-

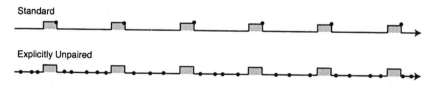

FIG. 3.10. The explicitly unpaired protocol has the same CS–US contingency as the standard protocol for simple excitatory conditioning, but inverted. The contingency is negative rather than positive.

nals in the brain, just as bank balances are numbers in a book or bit patterns in a computer.

Subjective rates are used in the process of arriving at estimates of expected interreinforcement intervals, just as debts (negative assets) are used in arriving at estimates of net worth. Adding a negative rate estimate to a positive rate estimate reduces the estimated rate of reinforcement, which lengthens the estimated interval between reinforcements, thereby weakening or eliminating the CR. The lengthening of the expected inter-reward interval when the CS− comes on is what elicits conditioned avoidance of the CS−.

In this analysis, the conditioned effects of the CS− have nothing to do with inhibition in the neurophysiological sense. From a timing perspective, these phenomena are misnamed in that it seems odd to call the reduction in an expected rate of reinforcement, or equivalently, the lengthening of an estimated interval between reinforcements an instance of inhibition. Moreover, when we come to consider recent results from backward second order conditioning experiments (in chap. 5), we will see that calling these CSs inhibitors leads to confusion and perplexity.

The Overprediction Protocol

Although conditioned inhibition is normally produced by omitting reinforcement when the target CS is present, it can also be produced by protocols in which the target CS is reinforced every time it is presented (Kremer, 1978; Lattal & Nakajima, 1998). In the first phase of the overprediction protocol (see Fig. 3.11), two CSs are separately presented and reinforced. In the second phase, they are presented together and accompanied by a third CS. Each presentation of the three-CS compound is reinforced. Because estimated rates add, the rate of reinforcement to be expected when two CSs are presented together is twice the rate expected when each is presented separately. But only one reinforcement is in fact given on these three-CS trials. There is a unique additive solution to the resulting discrepancy between the predicted and observed rate of reinforcement on these trials,

FIG. 3.11. The *overprediction* protocol (Kremer, 1978). Two CSs (represented here by gray and by horizontal bars) are independently conditioned, then presented together, with a third CS (here represented by vertical bars). Although the third CS is reinforced on every trial on which it is presented, this third CS becomes a conditioned inhibitor. The third CS will inhibit responses to other excitatory CSs. Notice that the rate of reinforcement experienced in the presence of this third CS is only one half the sum of the rates for the other two CSs, that is, one half of what the additive combination of rate estimates requires.

namely, that the rate of reinforcement ascribed to the third CS be equal in magnitude to the rates ascribed to each of the first two CSs but opposite in sign. Asymptotically, λ_1, $\lambda_2 = 1/T$, and $\lambda_3 = -1/T$. This protocol does indeed produce inhibitory conditioning of the third CS, despite the fact that this CS is paired with reinforcement on every occasion on which it is presented. Note that the predictor minimization principle does not come into play here, because there is a unique additive solution. Predictor minimization operates only when there is more than one additive solution.

A related protocol weakens the CR to two independently conditioned CSs by pairing them and giving only one reinforcement per paired presentation (Kamin & Gaioni, 1974). Here, there is no third CS to whose influence the missing reinforcements can be ascribed. Hence, the rates of reinforcement ascribed to each of the two CSs must be reduced when they are presented together without doubling the amount of reinforcement per presentation. It is readily shown that when the number of joint presentations has grown to equal the number of (initial) individual presentations, $\lambda_1 = \lambda_2 = \frac{2}{3}$ (N/T). At that point, the paired presentations have reduced the original (pre-pairing) rates (N/T) by a third.

CONCLUSIONS

The discovery of cue competition profoundly altered our understanding of what drives the conditioning process. It had generally been assumed that what drove conditioning was the temporal contiguity of CS and US (temporal pairing). Cue competition experiments have demonstrated over and over again that temporal pairing is neither necessary nor sufficient for conditioning. What drives conditioning is CS–US contingency, not the temporal contiguity of the CS and the US. The fundamental importance of this discovery needs to be emphasized, because the neurobiological community has not gotten the message. It continues to be taken as axiomatic by most researchers interested in the neurobiological basis of conditioning that the temporal pairing of the CS and the US is the essential event that drives the conditioning process. For example, Usherwood (1993) in an article entitled "Memories are Made of This," which appeared in *Trends in Neurosciences*, one of the more eminent review journals in the neurosciences, writes: "The temporal relationship between the conditioned and unconditioned stimuli is of critical importance for any type of conditioning; that is, the unconditioned stimulus must follow very briefly after the conditioned stimulus" (p. 427). This quote is representative of thinking about conditioning and learning among neurobiologists (see, for a more recent example, Tang et al., 1999). It is also wrong—utterly and completely wrong. Any understanding of the neurobiology of learning is going to have to rest on an understanding of the mechanisms by which the nervous system estimates contingency. Contingency and temporal pairing are not the same thing. When the US only occurs in the absence of the CS, there is no temporal pairing but a perfect CS–US contingency. When the US occurs at random, there is (fortuitous) temporal pairing but no contingency.

4

Extinction

Extinction is the process of eliminating (extinguishing) a conditioned response (CR) by repeatedly presenting the CS while withholding reinforcement. It presents interesting paradoxes. One, which both Pavlov (1928) and Hull (1943) discussed at length, is that the learning that takes place during extinction is caused by what Dickinson (1989) has called a "no-US," an event that ought to have occurred but did not. The problem is that a no-US has no physical attributes—no intensity, no qualia, no locus in space, and, perhaps most important from a theoretical standpoint, no locus in time. In a materialist and neurobiologically oriented endeavor, there is no room for nonphysical causes. Contemporary models of conditioning, such as the Rescorla–Wagner (1972) model deal with this problem, but only through the artifice of dividing the continuous flow of time into discrete trials. The notion of a trial is itself deeply problematic, for reasons we elaborate in a later chapter.

A second paradox of extinction is that partial reinforcement during training does not increase the number of reinforcements required for acquisition, whereas it does increase trials to extinction. This latter effect is called the partial reinforcement extinction effect. Both the effect of partial reinforcement on extinction and the lack of an effect on acquisition are paradoxical because inserting stretches of unreinforced CS presentations into the midst of reinforced presentations would seem to be equivalent to putting repeated extinction trials into the midst of the training trials. If reinforcement strengthens a connection and nonreinforcement weakens it—or if reinforcement strengthens excitatory connections and nonreinforcement strengthens competing inhibitory connections—then why does partial reinforcement have no effect on the number of reinforcements required for acquisition? And why does it not reduce the number of reinforcements that must be withheld to produce extinction (see Figs. 4.1A and 4.1B)?

One of the attractions of viewing conditioning from a timing perspective is that these paradoxes disappear. Extinction is explained without an appeal to nonphysical no-USs and without the artifice of carving continuous experience into discrete trials. Finally, the lack of an effect of partial reinforcement either on reinforcements to acquisition or on omitted reinforcements to extinction is seen to be another manifestation of time-scale invariance.

Some of the well established facts about extinction that we seek to explain are the following:

The Gradual Weakening of the CR.   It takes a number of unreinforced trials before the CR ceases. How abruptly it ceases in individual subjects has not been established.

The Partial Reinforcement Extinction Effect (PREE).   Partial reinforcement during the original conditioning increases trials to extinction, the number of unreinforced trials required before the animal stops responding

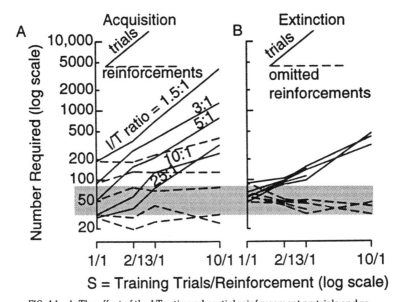

FIG. 4.1. A: The effect of the I:T ratio and partial reinforcement on trials and reinforcements to acquisition. B: The effect of the training schedule and of the I:T ratio on trials and *omitted* reinforcements to extinction. The gray band across the two data panels emphasizes the fact that omitted reinforcements to extinction are comparable to or even less than the number of reinforcements required for acquisition.

to the CS. This is the well known PREE. However, the increase is proportional to the thinning of the reinforcement schedule (see Fig. 4.1B, solid lines); hence, it does not affect the number of reinforcements that must be omitted (see Fig. 4.1B, dashed lines). Both delivered reinforcements to acquisition and omitted reinforcements to extinction are little affected by partial reinforcement. We defined the rate of acquisition to be the reciprocal of the number of reinforcements required before the subject began to respond to the CS. Similarly, we define the rate of extinction to be the reciprocal of the number of reinforcements that must be omitted before the subject stops responding to the CS. Figure 4.1 shows that partial reinforcement has little effect on either rate.

The Lack of Effect of the I:T Ratio on Rate of Extinction. The $I{:}T$ ratio has no effect on the number of reinforcements that must be omitted to reach a given level of extinction (see Fig. 4.1B, dashed lines), hence, also no effect on trials to extinction (see Fig. 4.1B, solid lines). This lack of effect on the rate of extinction contrasts strikingly with its strong effect on the rate of acquisition (see Fig. 4.1A).

Rates of Extinction May Be Similar to or Faster Than Rates of Acquisition. After extensive training in an autoshaping paradigm, the number of reinforcements that must be omitted to reach a modest extinction criterion (a decline to 50% of the pre-extinction rate of responding) is roughly the same as the number of reinforcements required to reach a modest acquisition criterion (one peck in three out of four CS presentations), provided that the $I{:}T$ ratio during acquisition is in the most commonly used range (see gray band across the two panels of Fig. 4.1). Thus, for some protocol parameters, the rate of extinction is similar to the rate of acquisition.

If a low $I{:}T$ ratio is used during acquisition, then the number of reinforcements that must be omitted in extinction can be much less than the number required for acquisition. In such cases, the rate of extinction is more rapid than the rate of acquisition, which makes it particularly puzzling that partial reinforcement has no effect on reinforcements to acquisition. If nonreinforcement antagonizes the effects of reinforcement, as has been almost universally assumed, and if the effect of a nonreinforcement can be made relatively much stronger than the effect of a reinforcement, how is it possible that mixing an average of nine nonreinforced trials with each reinforced trial does not reduce the overall effect of a given number of reinforced trials?

Rates of Extinction Are Comparable to Rates of Response Elimination. It is possible to extinguish a CR while continuing to reinforce every presentation of the CS. Instead of withholding reinforcements of the CS, the rate of background reinforcement—the rate at which USs are delivered during the

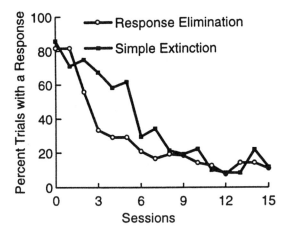

FIG. 4.2. Rate of response elimination under random reinforcement compared to rate of simple extinction. Two groups ($N = 6$) received 15 sessions of autoshaping training with one US per 30 s of CS exposure, a CS duration of 12 s, and a mean intertrial interval of 132 s ($I{:}T = 11$). Data shown are from subsequent sessions of extinction (no USs at all), or random control (ITI and CS both reinforced at the rate of one per 30 s). (From Aronson, Balsam, & Gibbon, 1991.)

intertrial intervals—is raised from zero to a rate that matches the rate of CS reinforcement. This procedure is called response elimination (Durlach, 1986), because there is a question whether the underlying process is the same as the process that mediates ordinary extinction.

One important quantitative fact relevant to the question of whether the mediating mechanism is the same in extinction and response elimination is that the rates at which the CRs disappear in the two paradigms appear to be about the same. After extensive training in the autoshaping paradigm, the decline of responding in ordinary extinction proceeds at about the same rate as the decline of responding when response elimination is produced by the response elimination procedure (see Fig. 4.2).

MODEL OF SIMPLE EXTINCTION

The fact that the $I{:}T$ ratio does not affect the rate of extinction implies that the decision to quit responding does not depend on a comparison between the rate of CS reinforcement and the rate of background reinforcement. Indeed, that is not the appropriate comparison. The question in extinction is whether the rate of CS reinforcement has changed. To detect a change in the rate of CS reinforcement, a recent estimate of it must be compared to an earlier estimate.

We propose that in simple extinction, the estimated interval of CS exposure since the last reinforcement, $\hat{t}_{CSnoR}$, is compared to the expected interval between reinforcements, which is $\hat{t}_{CS}/\hat{n}_{CS}$ (the cumulative exposure to the CS divided by the number of CS reinforcements. This decision variable can also be formulated as the ratio of two rate estimates, the estimate of the rate of CS reinforcement up to the last such reinforcement and the estimate of the rate since that last reinforcement, because

$$\frac{\hat{\lambda}_{CS}}{\hat{\lambda}_{CSnoR}} = \frac{\hat{n}_{CS}/\hat{t}_{CS}}{1/\hat{t}_{CSnoR}} = \frac{\hat{t}_{CSnoR}}{I\hat{R}I_{CS}}$$

where $I\hat{R}I_{CS}$ ($= 1/\hat{\lambda}_{CS}$) is the expected interreinforcement interval in the presence of the CS. The decision that reinforcement of the CS has ceased occurs when this ratio exceeds a criterion or threshold, β. The longer the cumulative interval of CS exposure without reinforcement the greater this ratio, because the estimate in the numerator (the duration of CS exposure without reinforcement) gets longer and longer, whereas the estimate in the denominator (the expected amount of CS exposure per reinforcement) remains almost constant. When this ratio exceeds the decision threshold, the animal quits responding (see Fig. 4.3). Intuitively, it quits responding when the cumulative duration of unreinforced CS exposure has become implausibly long. This decision is inherently based on a consideration of temporal proportions rather than absolute intervals, because it is the expected interval between reinforcements that determines how long an interval has to be in order to be considered implausibly long.

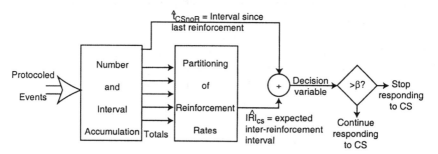

FIG. 4.3. Flow diagram for the extinction decision. At each CS reinforcement, the cumulative CS time to that point is stored in memory and the current rate of CS reinforcement ($\hat{\lambda}_{CS}$) is calculated using this total. The expected interval between reinforcements, $I\hat{R}I_{CS}$, is the reciprocal of this rate estimate. On each successive trial, a second clock cumulates time in the trial, $\hat{t}_{CSnoR}$, until reinforcement occurs, when it resets to zero. Subjects stop responding when the ratio between the currently elapsing interval without reinforcement and the expected interval between reinforcements becomes implausibly large.

The PREE. The quantitative effect of partial reinforcement on trials to extinction follows directly. Thinning the reinforcement schedule by a given factor multiplies the expected amount of CS exposure between reinforcements by that same factor. For example, reinforcing on average only every 10th presentation of the CS increases the amount of CS exposure per reinforcement ten-fold. The quantity thus increased is the denominator of the decision variable in extinction. For the decision ratio to reach a fixed threshold value during extinction, the numerator must increase by the same factor. Hence, the number of extinction trials—the number of segments of unreinforced CS exposure—required to reach the extinction criterion must increase in proportion to the thinning of the partial reinforcement schedule. Because the amount of unreinforced CS exposure must increase in proportion to the thinning factor, the number of reinforcements that must be omitted to reach a given level of extinction remains constant. In other words, there is a partial reinforcement extinction effect only if one looks at trials to extinction. From a timing perspective, this is not an appropriate unit. The appropriate unit is the number of omitted reinforcements, hence, the relative amount of CS exposure without reinforcement (Gibbon et al., 1980): If one takes the number of omitted reinforcements to extinction as the appropriate unit of analysis, there is no partial reinforcement extinction effect (see Fig. 4.1B, dashed lines).

The prediction that trials to extinction should increase in proportion to the thinning of the reinforcement schedule does not depend on parametric assumptions. The proportional increase is another manifestation of timescale invariance. It follows from the fundamental assumptions underlying our models of acquisition and extinction, namely: (a) It is estimated rates of reinforcement that matter (not probability of reinforcement); and (b) The decisions that underlie changes in conditioned responding depend on ratio comparisons between expected and observed intervals or rates.

The Absence of an Intertrial Interval Effect. The $I{:}T$ ratio has no effect on the rate of extinction, because the comparison that underlies the extinction decision does not involve the estimated background rate of reinforcement. It involves only estimates of reinforcements during the CS—the recent estimate versus the previous estimate. Thus, the striking difference between the effect of the $I{:}T$ ratio on acquisition and its lack of effect on extinction follows from another fundamental aspect of timing theory—different decisions rest on different comparisons, that is, on different decision ratios (cf. Miller's Comparator Hypothesis; Cole et al., 1995a; Miller et al., 1992). Different decisions rest on different comparisons because different comparisons are appropriate to detecting different properties of the animal's experience. The background rate of reinforcement is the appropriate comparison when the effect of a CS on the rate of reinforcement is in question; the previous rate of CS reinforcement is the appropriate comparison when the question is whether the rate of CS reinforcement has changed.

Rate of Response Elimination. From the perspective of Rate Estimation Theory, response elimination by shifting to a random control protocol is mediated by the same decision process as simple extinction. Hence, it should proceed at the same rate. At the beginning of response elimination, the rate of background reinforcement rises to the rate observed when the CS is present. The elevation of the background rate of reinforcement prevents further USs from being credited to the CS by the partitioning process, as explained in the previous chapter. Thus, from the standpoint of the whether-to-stop decision, it is as though the CS continues without USs, just as in standard extinction. Hence, the cessation of CS-specific reinforcements should be detected at about the same point after the change as in normal in extinction, and, in fact, it is (see Fig. 4.2).

The response elimination phenomenon is another example of the independence of the extinction decision from the rate of background reinforcement. The extinction decision rests on a comparison between the currently elapsing interval of CS exposure without a reinforcement credited to it and the expected interval between reinforcements credited to the CS. In normal extinction, there is no rate of background reinforcement. In response elimination, the rate of background reinforcement increases to equal the old rate of CS reinforcement. The cessation of responding to the CS proceeds at the same rate in both cases, because the background rate per se does not enter into the decision. Increasing the background rate leads to response cessation in the response elimination procedure only because USs are no longer credited to the CS by the partitioning process.

GENERALIZING THE MODEL

Just as we considered how to generalize the model of acquisition from the special case where there are no background reinforcements to the more general case where there is a background rate of reinforcement, so we now consider how to extend the model of extinction to the general case, in which the subject detects and responds to a change in the rate of reinforcement. In extinction, the rate of reinforcement abruptly goes to zero. But, of course, this is only the limiting case of a downward change. In the more general case, the rate of reinforcement may decrease by any amount, or it may increase. The rapid detection of changes in rates of reinforcement is presumably important to the efficiency with which an animal forages. It would presumably be advantageous to a foraging animal if it could rapidly perceive and respond to changes in rates of reinforcements in the various locations that it visits on its foraging expeditions.

There are experimental data on how rapidly foraging rats and pigeons can in fact respond to changes in the rates of reinforcement. The data come from the matching paradigm in operant conditioning, which we discuss at length in chap. 6. In the matching paradigm, there are two response options—two keys in the case of pigeons and two levers in the case of rats—which are simultaneously present. The options are commonly imagined to be equivalent to separate patches of territory in which the animal might forage. Responses on each option (key pecks or lever presses) are rewarded on *concurrent variable interval (VI) schedules.* A VI schedule makes a reinforcement available at a random interval following the harvesting of the previous reinforcement. Thus, the moment at which the next reward will become available on a given lever is unpredictable; what is predictable is the average interval between rewards, that is, the rate of reinforcement. Each response option has its own VI schedule. The animal is free to shuttle back and forth between the options harvesting rewards from them both. A scheduled reward waits to be harvested, it does not go away if the animal is not there to collect it. Thus, it pays to sample both options. If subjects sample them both efficiently—and they do—then they collect from both at close to the rate that they would collect if they could be in both places at the same time.

The animals sample the options efficiently by matching the relative amounts of time devoted to each option to the relative rates at which the options are reinforced (Davison & McCarthy, 1988; Godin & Keenleyside, 1984; Harper, 1982; Herrnstein, 1961). If the expected interval between reinforcements on one option is half the expected interval on the other option, the subjects distribute their time and responses two to one in favor of the first option, matching the ratio of their expected stay durations on the two sides to the ratio of the incomes derived from the two sides.

By looking at the transitions in matching behavior following sudden changes in the relative rates of reward, we can determine how rapidly subjects detect and respond to changes in the rates of reward. Dreyfus (1991) showed that when pigeons repeatedly encountered sudden, large, midsession changes in the relative rates of reward, they adjusted their time-allocation ratio to match the new relative rate of reward within a very short interval—within the span of one or two expected reinforcements on the leaner of the two postchange schedules. Mark and Gallistel (1994) showed the same thing in selfstimulating rats. In both of these experiments, the moment of change was (to some extent) anticipatable—in the Dreyfus experiment, because it always occurred at the same time in the session; in the Mark and Gallistel experiment, because it was signaled by the withdrawal and reappearance of the levers. Also, the subjects in these experiments experienced more than one change in the relative rates of reward in every session. In contrast, Mazur (1995) gave pigeons prolonged (multisession) experience with constant relative rates of reward, and then an unsignaled change. The transitions observed in Mazur's experiments took considerably longer than those observed by Mark and Gallistel (1994) and Dreyfus (1991).

Gallistel, Mark, King, and Latham (2001) have recently done a follow-up experiment to determine the effect of both a previous period of stable rates versus a previous period with frequently varying rates and the effect of a signaled versus an unsignaled change. In the phase of their experiment where changes in rates were frequent, a change of unpredictable magnitude and direction occurred at an unpredictable time once in each 2-hour long session. At the start of each session, there was another change of unpredictable magnitude and direction. This change—between the rates at the end of the previous session and the rate in force at the beginning of the new session—was signaled by the intersession, in contrast to the change that occurred somewhere during the session, which was unsignaled. Gallistel et al. found that—after a few experiences with these signaled and unsignaled changes in rates—the rats adjusted completely to a large change very rapidly, within the span of one or two expected interreinforcement intervals on the leaner of the two postchange schedules (see Fig. 4.4).

The data in Fig. 4.4 are representative in that rats that have repeatedly experienced these once-per-session changes in the relative rate of reward generally adjust to the new relative rate of reward within one or two expected interreward intervals on the leaner schedule, provided that there has been a large change in the relative rate of reward. When the change is small, it takes them longer to adjust to it, which is not surprising, because the smaller the change in the relative rate, the longer it takes to detect it. These data suggest that the brain of the rat may approximate an ideal detector of changes in the rate of reinforcement, a device that detects and responds to these changes as rapidly as they could in principle be detected. This suggestion is explored next.

When a rat has never experienced a change in the relative rate of reward, it takes much longer to adjust completely to the new relative rate. In the first phase of the experiment by Gallistel et al. (2001), the relative rate of reward remained constant for more than 30 two-hour sessions. Then, there was an abrupt, unsignaled change in the relative rate midway through a session, and this change remained in force for 20 more sessions. The rats detected this change soon after it occurred and began to adjust their time-allocation behavior accordingly. However, the adjustment extended over most of the remainder of the session (see Fig. 4.5A).

At the beginning of the next session, the ratio of the stay durations reverted strongly back toward the values it had before the change. The same thing happened, but to a lesser extent, at the beginning of the next session. In other words, from session to session, there was spontaneous recovery of the prechange pattern of time allocation. Mazur (1996) reports the same

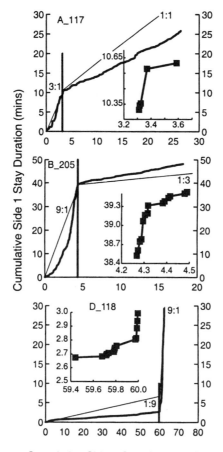

FIG. 4.4. Examples of abrupt adjustments in the relative amounts of time a rat allocates to each of two levers delivering brain stimulation reinforcement on concurrent VI schedules. The vertical lines indicate the time at which there was a step change in the relative rates of reinforcement. The curves plot the cumulative time the subject has spent on Side 1 against the cumulative time it has spent on Side 2. This plot is called a cum-cum function. The slope of this function is the ratio of the expected stay durations. Abrupt changes in slope indicate abrupt changes in this ratio. The thin sloped lines indicate the time-allocation ratios that would match the ratio of the programmed rates of reinforcement (given alongside each line, e.g., 3:1). When the slope of the cum-cum function matches the slope of the corresponding thin line, the animal is matching its time-allocation ratio to the ratio of the programmed rates of reinforcement. The insets show the interval immediately surrounding the abrupt change in behavior. Each data point in an inset marks the termination of a visit cycle (one visit to each side). Notice that the change in behavior in these examples is completed within the span or one or two visit cycles very soon after the change in the rates of reinforcement. Moreover, the abrupt and almost immediate adjustment to the change in relative rates of reward is sometimes an overadjustment (top panel). (Excerpted from a figure in Gallistel, Mark, King, and Latham, 2001. Copyright © 2001 by the American Psychological Association. Reprinted with permission.)

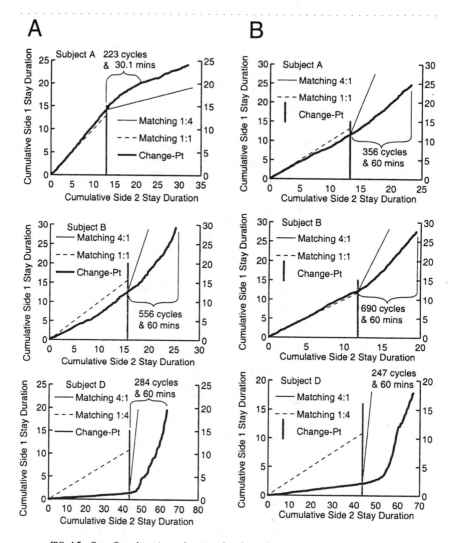

FIG. 4.5. Cum-Cum functions showing the slow adjustments to a change in the relative rates of reward that are observed after prolonged periods of stability. A. After more than 60 hours (more than 30 two-hour sessions) with no change, change-naive subjects experience an unsignaled change in the relative rates of reward. B. Slow transitions are again observed in these same subjects following a renewed period of prolonged stability (60 hours), even though, between the two phases of prolonged stability, there were phases during which these subjects experienced more than 80 changes and came to adjust very rapidly to them (as witness, Fig. 4.4). (Reproduced from Gallistel et al., 2001. Copyright © 2001 by the American Psychological Association. Reprinted with permission.)

phenomenon in pigeons that encountered a change in the relative rates of food reward after a long period of stability.

Gallistel et al. (2001) showed that the slow adjustment to a change in the relative rate of reward seen in subjects who have experienced a prolonged period of stability prior to the change, is a consequence of the prolonged period of stability rather than of inexperience with changes in rates of reward. After the phases in which subjects experienced frequent changes in the rates of reward, Gallistel et al. put them back into a phase of prolonged rate stability. This renewed phase of rate stability was followed by one more abrupt, unsignaled midsession change in rates. Although subjects had at this point experienced more than 80 changes in the rates of reward and had shown themselves capable of very rapid and complete adjustments to these changes, their behavior following this final change in rates of reward was indistinguishable from their behavior following the very first such change (see Fig. 4.5B). Thus, it is prolonged stability that induces slow adjustments not lack of experience. Put another way, subjects do not learn to make rapid adjustments to changes in rate; they make rapid adjustments when such changes have recently been frequent; they make slow adjustments when there have been no such changes for a long time.

Perceiving a Change in Rate:
How Good is the Rat?

The experiment by Gallistel et al. (2001) showed that when there is prolonged stability preceding a change, the adjustment to the change is slow, but when changes occur often, the adjustment is completed rapidly. In both cases, however, the adjustment begins soon after the change. Gallistel et al. (2001) showed that the beginning of a change more-or-less coincides with the emergence of objective evidence that there has in fact been a change in rates. In other words, they show that the rat approximates an ideal detector of rate changes.

An ideal detector applies the best possible analysis to the available evidence, an analysis that properly weighs all the information in the evidence. The available information is contained in the sequence of experienced interevent intervals. Because the intervals between events in a random rate process are highly variable, the distribution of interevent intervals after a change overlaps the distribution before the change. The smaller the change is, the greater this overlap is; hence, the harder it is to detect the change. The amount of information about the distribution of interevent intervals following an arbitrarily chosen point in time increases as more time elapses, for the obvious reason that the longer the observation interval is, the more interevent intervals are observed. Thus, the strength of the evidence for a change in rate increases as a function of the time elapsed since the change.

An ideal real-time detector makes an accurate moment-to-moment assessment of the strength of the evidence.

As was first discovered by Heyman (1979) and subsequently confirmed by Gibbon (1995) and Gallistel et al. (2001), the stay durations of pigeons and rats under these experimental conditions (concurrent VI schedules) are exponentially distributed. This means that subjects behave as if the decision to leave a side was itself the outcome of a random rate process. In effect, when they are on a given side, they keep flipping a leave/stay coin specific to that side until the coin comes up "leave," at which point they do. The expected duration of a stay is one over the probability of the coin coming up "leave" multiplied by the interval between flips. The relative "leave" bias on the coins for the two sides being visited in alternation is determined by the relative rates of reward on those two sides. When, for example, the rat is on a side where the expected interval between rewards is twice as long as on the opposite side, then the bias toward "leave" in the coin for that side is twice as strong as the bias in the coin flipped on the other side. Thus, the coin flipped on the leaner side comes up "leave" in, on average, half the time that it takes for the coin flipped on the other side to come up "leave." Thus, the ratio of the expected stay durations matches the ratio of the incomes.

Gallistel et al. (2001) analyzed mathematically how good the rats in their experiment were at detecting changes in the rates of reward. As is generally the case in matching experiments, their subjects responded for reinforcement on concurrent variable interval schedules of reward. Thus, they got two random rate time series as the behavior-determining inputs, one series from each lever. And, as we have just learned, their behavior generated two more random rate time series—the two sequences of visit durations. In asking whether the rat was an ideal detector, Gallistel et al. asked whether information that there had been a change in stay durations appeared in the behavioral output as soon as information that there had been a change in reward rates appeared in the input.

Formulating the question in terms of the information in the output up to time, t, versus the information in the input up to that same time, suggests that the appropriate analysis is Bayesian. Let r_0 be the first rate of reward on a given side, the rate in force during the portion of a session preceding a step change in rate. Let r_1 be the rate in force after the change and t_c be the time at which the change occurs. In responding to the change, the rat estimates all three of these quantities. Its estimate of the rates before the change determines its expected stay durations before the change, its estimate of the rates after the change, determines its expected stay durations after the change, and its estimate of t_c determines the moment at which its expected stay durations change. From a Bayesian perspective, how precisely it can estimate these parameters of its experience at any point in a session depends on two things: First, it depends on the information in the sequence of so-far experienced interreward intervals, which we designate by **t**. Second, it depends on the prior probabilities, the a priori relative likelihood of any given first rate, the a priori relative likelihood of any given second rate, and the a priori relative likelihood that any given session time will be the moment at which the rates of reward changed.

None of these quantities can be known exactly by an observer not privy to the computer program running the experiment. Their values must all be described by a probability density function, which gives for each possible combination of values for r_0, r_1, and t_c the likelihood of that combination relative to all other combinations. These parameters of the rat's experience define a three-dimensional space in which a probability cloud of varying density gathers during a session. When there is enough information to define these values narrowly, the cloud is small and dense; when there is not, it is large and diffuse. The requisite information emerges during the session as the sequence of intervals unfolds. From Bayes theorem,

$$P(r_0, r_1, t_c \mid \mathbf{t}) \propto P(\mathbf{t} \mid r_0, r_1, t_c) P(r_0, r_1, t_c). \qquad (5)$$

In words, the probability density function for the two rates of reward on a given side and for the time of change, *given the information in* **t**, is proportional to the product of two other probability density functions, $P(\mathbf{t} \mid r_0, r_1, t_c)$ and $P(r_0, r_1, t_c)$. The first of these gives for any triplet of assumed values for r_0, r_1, and t_c the relative likelihood of any given sequence of interevent intervals. The second function is the a priori probability density function for r_0, r_1, and t_c, the relative likelihoods of the various combinations of values for r_0, r_1, and t_c, absent the information in **t**. This function describes the distribution of the mist before the gathering of the session cloud.

The prior distribution, $P(r_0, r_1, t_c)$, is created when the experimenter specifies the range of possible rates in the experiment and the rules determining when a rate change can occur. However, using the actual experimental conditions to calculate $P(r_0, r_1, t_c)$ is mathematically cumbersome, and the form of $P(r_0, r_1, t_c \mid \mathbf{t})$, which is what we are really interested in, will not depend strongly on the details of the prior distribution. To simplify the calculation, we (Gallistel et al., 2001) assumed that the probability density functions for r_0 and r_1 were flat between 0 and 1/s and zero beyond 1/s. We also assumed that the probability density function for t_c was exponential with parameter 0.75 changes per hour. These assumptions determine $P(r_0, r_1, t_c)$, which may be calculated by discrete approximation: Consider a voxel with very small dimensions Δr_0, Δr_1, and Δt_c, surrounding the point $\langle \rho_0, \rho_1, \tau \rangle$ in the space defined by r_0, r_1, and t_c. By our just stated assumptions, the a priori probabilities that ρ_0 and ρ_1 are the correct values of r_0 and r_1 are Δr_0 and Δr_1, and the a priori probability that τ is the correct value for t_c is $\Delta t_c e^{-0.75\tau}$, The prior probability that $\langle \rho_0, \rho_1, \tau \rangle$ will be the two reward rates and the time of change is the product of these three prior probabilities.

To calculate the probability of a sequence **t** of observed interevent intervals, given an expected rate of occurrence r and an interval of observation of duration T, we again used discrete approximation, dividing the interval of observation into very small discrete intervals of length Δt. The number, N, of these intervals is $T / \Delta t$. When Δt is small relative to the expected interval between events, the probability of an event in any one such interval is$\approx r\Delta t$ and the probability of no event is $\approx 1 - r\Delta t$. Thus, the probability of any particular sequence containing l events and $N - l$ nonevents is $(r\Delta t)^l (1 - r\Delta t)^{N-l}$. Because Δt is very small relative to the interreward intervals, $N_0 \gg l_0$ and $N_1 \gg l_1$. Using this and the equality in the limit $(1 - \varepsilon)^{x/\varepsilon} \to e^{-x}$ as $\varepsilon \to 0$, gives $(1 - r\Delta t)^{N-l} \to e^{-Nr\Delta t} = e^{-rT}$. Thus $p(\mathbf{t}|r) = (r\Delta t)^l e^{-rT}$. This probability is proportional to $r^l e^{-rT}$, with Δt^l as the constant of proportionality. It is important to note that the probability of any particular sequence depends only on the number of events, l, because any specific realization of this number of events is just as improbable as any other.

When the interval of observation may contain a step change in rate at some unknown time t_c, we let N_0 be the number of discrete intervals before t_c and N_1 be the number after t_c—the number in the interval between the time of change and the current moment or end of observation, designated t_f. As $\Delta t \to 0$,

$$P(\mathbf{t}\,|\,r_0,r_1,t_c) = (r_0 \Delta t)^{l_0} (1 - r_0 \Delta t)^{N_0 - l_0} (r_1 \Delta t)^{l_1} (1 - r_1 \Delta t)^{N_1 - l_1} \qquad (6)$$

Using the equality $x^y = e^{y \ln x}$, one gets from Equation 6,

$$P(\mathbf{t}\,|\,r_0,r_1,t_c) \propto \exp[-t_c r_0 + l_0 \ln r_0 - (t_f - t_c) r_1 + l_1 \ln r_1], \qquad (7)$$

Given any particular set of assumed values for r_0, r_1, and t_c, Equation 7 tells us how to calculate the likelihood of an observed sequence, **t**, of interevent intervals. This, together with the prior probability of that particular combination of r_0, r_1, and t_c gives us the after-the-fact likelihood of that combination, the likelihood given the information in **t**. These likelihoods constitute the "session cloud," that is, the sought-for probability density function $P(r_0, r_1, t_c \mid \mathbf{t})$, which objectively describes the subject's experience during a session.

As a first approach to estimating how closely the shifts in behavior followed the shifts in rates of reward, Gallistel et al. (2001) calculated the $P(r_0, r_1, t_c \mid \mathbf{t})$ functions for the reward series on both sides and for the stay duration series on both sides. They then integrated these three-dimensional probability density functions with respect to the two rates to obtain the one-dimensional temporal probability density functions that define where in time the change in rates occurred (see Fig. 4.6A). One measure of how close the change in behavior was relative to the change in rates of reward is the statistical distance between the reward probability density

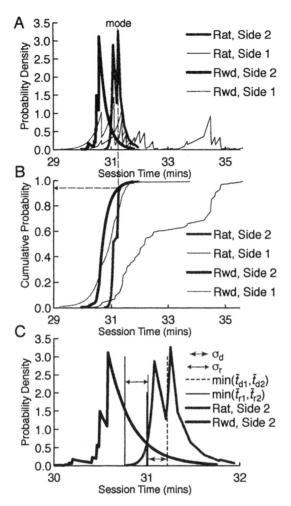

FIG. 4.6. A. Representative probability density functions for the location within the session of the changes in rates of reward (Rwd, Side 1 and Rwd, Side 2) and the answering changes in the rat's stay durations (Rat, Side 1 and Rat, Side 2). In this case, the probability density function for the earlier evident reward change is on Side 2 and so is the probability density function for the earlier evident response. In other cases, the sides for the two earlier probability density functions were different. B. Cumulative probability functions give the probability that a change has occurred as a function of the session time elapsed. Roughly speaking, the functions in A are the derivatives of these functions. (Not exactly, however, because when we computed the cumulative probability function for a change, we used at each time only the information available up to that time, whereas the probability density functions in A are based on the information from the entire session.) One of our measures of the quality of the rat as a detector of changes in rate is the probability that the reward rates had changed (horizontal dashed line terminating in arrowhead) at the mode of the probability density function for the earlier response (vertical dashed line descending from Panel A). C. The probability density functions from A with the earlier mean time for the reward change [$\min(\bar{t}_{r1}, \bar{t}_{r2})$] and the earlier mean time for an answering change in stay durations [$\min(\bar{t}_{d1}, \bar{t}_{d2})$]. The difference between these mean times divided by the square root of the sum of the variances of the two probability density functions is a measure of how closely the first change in expected stay duration followed the first change in reward rate. (From Gallistel et al., 2001. Copyright © 2001 by the American Psychological Association. Reprinted with permission.)

function with the earlier mean [min($\bar{t}_{r1}$,$\bar{t}_{r2}$)] and the stay duration probability density function with the earlier mean [min($\bar{t}_{d1}$,$\bar{t}_{d2}$)] as seen in Fig. 4.6C.

Figure 4.7 is a histogram of the statistical lags between the stimulus changes and the answering behavioral changes. As one would expect, the lags were mostly positive (80%), meaning that the evidence for the first change in stay durations developed later than the first evidence for a change in rates for reward. They were also mostly small, meaning that there was little lag between the first evidence of a change in reward and the first evidence of a change in stay durations. Negative lags came from cases in which the mean of the stay duration probability density function was earlier than the mean of the reward probability density function. These arose in one of two ways: (1) Small negative lags occurred when the rat made a large change in its stay duration when there was still only weak evidence for a change in a rate of reward. The large change in response to weak evidence makes the probability density function for the change in stay duration peak before the probability density function for a change in reward rate. (2) Large negative lags occurred when there was a spontaneous change in the rats stay durations prior to the change in rates of reward. These "anticipatory" changes were presumably fortuitous; they occurred less than 10% of the time.

The comparison whose results are plotted in Fig. 4.7 is not entirely fair to the rat because the probability density functions underlying it were computed from the data over the entire session. Thus, they reflect the information in interreward intervals that had not yet occurred when the rat changed its behavior. To estimate both the quality of the rat's real-time as-

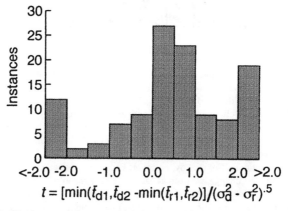

FIG. 4.7. Histogram of the statistical distances (t) by which the probability density function for the first change in stay durations lagged the probability density function for the first change in reward rates. The first change is defined in both cases to be the probability density function with the earlier mean (see Fig. 4.6C). (From Gallistel et al., 2001. Copyright © 2001 by the American Psychological Association. Reprinted with permission.)

sessment of the incoming information about reward rates and its decision criterion, Gallistel et al. (2001) took the mode (peak) of the probability density function for the first change in the rat's stay durations as the best estimate of when exactly the change in the rat's behavior occurred. They then calculated the cumulative probability of a change in reward rates at this point in the session. This second measure asks, How much evidence was there that the reward rate had changed at the moment when the change in the rat's behavior is most likely to have occurred? As in the first calculation, the probability that the change in reward rates had occurred was calculated from the reward series with the earlier probability density function.

The histogram in Fig. 4.8 gives the results of this calculation. In 80% of the 118 transitions plotted, the moment of maximum likelihood for the first change in stay durations occurred before the objective probability that there had been a change in the rates of reward exceeded .99. This implies both that the rat was making an accurate assessment of the evidence for a change in rates of reward and that it was using a low decision criterion. Any insensitivity in the rat's assessment of the information that there had been a change in reward would shift the data in Fig. 4.8 to the right, that is, it would lead to a delayed reaction on the part of the rat, hence greater evidence of a change in reward rate at the time of that reaction. A high decision criterion would have the same effect. The data in Figs. 4.7 and 4.8 show that the rat approximates an ideal detector of changes in the rates of reward.

One way to appreciate the sophistication of what the rat is doing is to compute for successive small increments in time the probability density functions for the expected reward rates and for the expected stay durations, and observe their evolution over time. Figure 4.9 gives representative

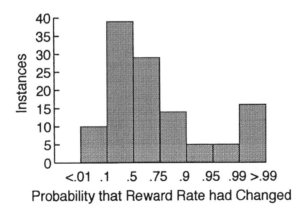

FIG. 4.8. Histogram of the objective probabilities that the reward rates had changed at the moment at which the first change in the rat's stay durations is most likely to have occurred. (From Gallistel et al., 2001. Copyright © 2001 by the American Psychological Association. Reprinted with permission.)

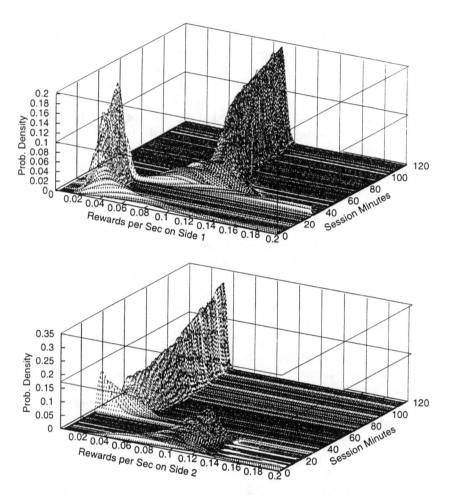

FIG. 4.9. Above panels: Probability density (y axis) for reward rate (x axis) as
a function of session time (z axis). Each successive probability density function (curve in an x-y plane) specifies probabilistically the reward rate based
on the information contained in the sequence of interreward intervals up to
that point in the session. Note that early in the session after only a few rewards, the reward rates are both poorly defined (a shallow broad curve) and
misleading (the curves peak in the wrong place). As more rewards are obtained, however, the curves soon become narrow, sharply peaked, and consistently located in the same region of the rate axis. At about Minute 30 of the session, the programmed reward rate changed. At this point, the probability
density functions for the reward rate become transiently shallower and
broader, but they soon rise and resharpen as the new, higher rate of reward
becomes well defined. Note, however, that the functions for the new rate over-

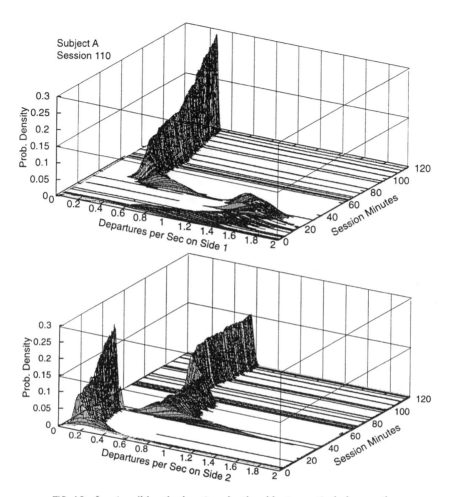

FIG. 4.9. *(continued)* lap the functions for the old rate, particularly near the transition point. This reflects the fact that there is a measurable amount of objective uncertainty regarding whether the rate has changed or not (for any observer not privy to the program). Above panels: Probability density for the rat's leaving rate (the reciprocal of its expected stay duration) as a function of session time. Notice that in the period before the change in the relative rates of reward, there were nonetheless several spontaneous changes in the rat's expected stay durations. Despite this instability in its prechange behavior, there is a clear reaction to the change in the programmed rates of reward; in response to this increase in the relative rate of reward on Side 1, the rat's expected stay duration abruptly shifted to a longer duration (a lower leaving rate). In response to the decreased rate of reward on Side 2, the rat's leaving rate on that side increased. (From Gallistel et al., 2001. Copyright © 2001 by the American Psychological Association. Reprinted with permission.)

examples. Note that at the beginning of the session, the initial reward rates (the r_0's) are poorly defined (low broad probability density functions), but that as the session went on, they become sharply defined until the moment when the rates of reward change. Around that moment, the probability density function for the reward rate "collapses" and then rises again at a new location on the plane (at the r_1 location). The expected stay durations do the same thing: They become sharply defined during the prechange period; collapse abruptly when the reward probability density functions collapse, then rise again at a new leaving rate. The plots of the probability density functions' evolution through time render visible the dramatically sudden and complete change in the rat's behavior provoked by the change in the rates of reward it experiences. Under these circumstances, rats "acquire" new expected stay durations and "extinguish" their old expected stay durations about as fast as they could in principle do so.

The Rat Is Not Tracking the Noise in the Inputs

If the rat reset the bias on its stay/leave coins after every reward it got, then it would, of course show an adjustment to a change in the interreward intervals as soon as such a change was manifest. Indeed, Mark and Gallistel (1994) suggested that this was the explanation for the extremely rapid adjustments they observed. They plotted the ratio of the stay durations within very small windows of time against the ratio of the reward rates within those same windows and showed a strong correlation. However, Gallistel et al. (2001) later showed that the correlation they observed was an aliasing artifact, produced by totaling stay durations and interreward intervals within windows that were only about twice as wide as the expected interreward intervals on the leaner side. Gallistel et al. (2001) recorded actual event times. When they analyzed their event time data to see whether stay durations depended on the durations of the immediately preceding interreward intervals, they found no such dependence. Provided that the most recent interreward intervals fall within the expected range of intervals, they have no effect on expected stay durations. Thus, the ideal detector behavior of the rat is not seen because the rat bases its expected stay durations on maximally local estimates of the expected rates of reward; it is the result of a sophisticated mechanism for detecting genuine changes in rate.

Modeling the Rat's Change-Detecting Mechanism

Knowing that the rat approximates an ideal detector of changes in random rates is an important guide in creating models for the computational process that mediates its adjustment to such changes. It means that viable models must approximate normative solutions to this problem. What follows is one such model. It is not a Bayesian model, it takes a frequentist approach to the statistical problem of detecting changes in the parameter of a random rate process.

Detecting a change in a random rate is equivalent to detecting a change in the slope of a cumulative event record, which is the plot of the number of events as a function of elapsed time (Fig. 4.10). Assume that observation begins at time t_0, which is the time of occurrence of the event number, n_0. Let $t > t_0$ be a subsequent point in time, $T = t - t_0$ be the interval of observation, and $N > 0$ be the number of events observed, including the event, if any, at t, but not including the event at t_0. If the rate has been constant, then the cumulative record approximates a straight line, with slope N/T.

If the rate has changed somewhere within the interval of observation, then the cumulative record will have an inflection point (change in slope) where it changed. Let t_c be the time at the inflection point and n_c the event count. If there is an inflection point in the record, then its location may be estimated to be the point at which the record deviates maximally from a straight line (d_{max} in Fig. 4.10). Because the cumulative record is incremented in discrete steps, this point always coincides with an event. Let $T_a =$

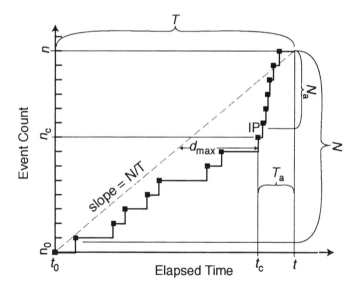

FIG. 4.10. A cumulative record of events (cumulative number of events versus time on the clock). So long as the average rate of event occurrence remains constant, this function will approximate the dashed straight line. When the rate changes, there will be an inflection point (IP), with coordinates $\langle t_c, n_c \rangle$. The location of a putative inflection point may be estimated by finding the point of maximum deviation (d_{max}) of the observed function from the expected straight line. (From Gallistel et al., 2001. Copyright © 2001 by the American Psychological Association. Reprinted with permission.)

$t - t_c$ be the interval since the putative inflection point and N_a be the number of events observed after that point.

On the null hypothesis that the events are randomly distributed in time, the probability, p_e, that any one of the events (ignoring event order) falls in the interval T_a is T_a/T. The probability P_f of observing N_a or fewer events in that interval is given by the cumulative binomial probability function, as is the probability P_m of observing N_a or more events. When the number of events in T_a is approximately the expected number, then the ratio P_f/P_m is approximately unity and the log of this ratio is approximately 0. As the observed number of events since the putative time of change becomes improbably low, the ratio becomes very small and its log approaches minus infinity. As the observed number becomes improbably high, the ratio becomes very large and its log approaches infinity. The absolute value of the log of this ratio (the logit[1]) is proposed by Gallistel et al. (2001) as the subjective measure of the strength of the evidence that there has been a change in rate.

This model for the process that detects changes in rate is closely related to our generalizerd model of acquisition. In that model, we assumed that the decision variable was the odds against the hypothesis that the CS had no effect on the rate of reinforcement. These odds are $(1 - p){:}p$, where p is the probability of the observed difference in rates on the null hypothesis. This odds ratio—or the logarithm thereof—is a measure of the strength of the evidence for a CS–US contingency. Our measure of the contingency itself was the ratio between the expected interreward interval when only the background was present and the expected interreward interval when the CS was also present. The odds that a contingency is reliable are related to this measure of contingency by way of the F distribution function, which is computed by something called the incomplete beta function.

Similarly, in the model for detecting changes in rate, the decision variable is the log of the odds against the hypothesis that there has been no change. The measure of the size of the putative change is the ratio of the estimated interevent intervals before and after the estimated time of change. The odds that a change of this size is genuine, when there were n_b events before the change and n_a events after it, is related to the size of the change via the cumulative binomial probability distribution, which, it turns out, is likewise computed by the incomplete beta function. Thus, the generalized model of extinction is very similar to the generalized model of acquisition. Both models assume a mechanism whose input-output characteristics ap-

---

[1]The logit is usually defined to be the ratio of two complementary probabilities. Our ratio is between two overlapping probabilities, which therefore do not sum to 1. We use overlapping probabilities because the resulting measure is better behaved when the expected and observed numbers of events are the same and near or equal to zero. Away from unity or when the expected number of events is >> 0, our ratio approximates the usual ratio.

proximate those of the incomplete beta function. It takes as inputs one quantity representing the strength of a contingency or the size of a change, and two quantities representing event counts, and it generates for an output a quantity proportional to the likelihood that the input measure—the measure of contingency or change—did not arise by chance.

The effect of perceiving a substantial contingency between a CS and reinforcement is that, at least after some while, the subject begins to respond to the CS. The effect of perceiving a change in the rate of CS reinforcement is that the subject resamples the interreward intervals in the period after the perceived time of the change and sets the bias on its stay/leave coins by the outcome of this postchange sample. It also resets the change-detecting mechanism, making t_c, the perceived moment of change, the new time 0.

The Rapidity of the Adjustment to a Perceived Change in the Rate of Reward

The generalized model of extinction has the same problem as the generalized model of acquisition. In an unmodified form, both predict that the latencies of behavioral change should be normatively correct. Subjects should begin to respond to a CS when there has been a number of differential reinforcements sufficient to indicate a CS–US contingency beyond any reasonable doubt and they should extinguish when the interval since the last reinforcement indicates beyond any reasonable doubt a reduction in the rate of reinforcement. Neither prediction is correct; the numbers of reinforcements required for acquisition and the numbers of omitted reinforcements required for extinction are not predictable by normative statistical considerations; they are much too great. This implies that in simple acquisition and simple extinction, there is something else going on in addition to (or instead of) the assessment of the strength of the evidence.

Our generalized models are probably best regarded as models of the process by which an animal perceives a contingency or change in rate. One reason to cast the models in perceptual terms is that it makes it clear that a change in rate is itself an experienced event. Other events may be predicted based on their latency from the moment at which this change was perceived to occur.[2] We believe this is the key to understanding why subjects adjust their behavior more slowly when they encounter a change after a prolonged period of stability. Although, their adjustments in such cases begin about as soon as they could in principle begin, they proceed much

---

[2]Not the moment at which the perception occurs, which is the moment at which the change is detected (the termination points of the thin lines in Fig. 4.5A), but rather the moment at which the change is perceived to occur. This moment, which corresponds to the inflection point in the cumulative reinforcement function, will always be earlier than the moment at which the perception occurs.

more slowly to completion (see Fig. 4.5) than when the rat frequently experiences such changes (see Fig. 4.4). Moreover, as noted already, the rat or pigeon reverts to its previous choice pattern at the beginning of each of the next two or three sessions after the change (Gallistel et al., 2001; Mazur, 1995).

Both of these phenomena have long been known in simple extinction, under the headings of *learning to learn* and *spontaneous recovery* or *reinstatement*. If a subject is given repeated acquisition training followed each time by extinction, it comes to acquire and extinguish very much faster, often in a trial or two. This phenomenon is called learning to learn (cf. Ricker & Bouton, 1996). Secondly, when a CR is extinguished in the course of one session, it spontaneously recovers at the beginning of the next few extinction sessions. Even when a CR has been entirely eliminated by multiple extinction sessions in one context (one experimental chamber), so that spontaneous recovery is no longer observed, it may be reinstated by changing the context (Bouton & Ricker, 1994; Brooks, Hale, Nelson, & Bouton, 1995).

Pavlov realized that this spontaneous recovery was theoretically important. It showed that extinction did not involve the return to the status quo ante. In associative terms, it meant that extinction did not reduce the strength of the associations built up during acquisition. Rather, it created new, competing inhibitory associations. In more theoretically neutral terms, it means that extinction does not wipe out previously acquired knowledge (e.g., knowledge of what the rate of reinforcement used to be), rather, it adds new knowledge (e.g., the knowledge of what the rate has most recently been). Reinstatement, of course, makes the same point. What has been learned in previous conditioning is not wiped out by subsequent contradictory training. On the contrary, what the subject learns is, to speak informally, "That was then, and this is now."

When a subject experiences an abrupt cessation of CS reinforcement after a long period of stability (or an abrupt change in the relative rates at which two levers deliver reward), the subject cannot know how long the change will last. We suggest that the slow adjustment seen the first time that a subject is extinguished or the first time it encounters a change in the relative rate of reward after a long period of stability is because it is a strategy based on the implicit assumption that when a change follows a long period of stability, it may prove transient.

We think that the temporal weighting rule (Devenport & Devenport, 1994; Devenport, Hill, Wilson, & Ogden, 1997) points the way to the treatment of reinstatement phenomena from a timing perspective. The general principle, indicated by a variety of findings, is that animals track their experience on several different time scales, and they know how long ago they had a given experience (Clayton & Dickinson, 1998, 1999). When previous experiences offer conflicting testimony as to what to expect now, both the relative duration and the relative recency of those experiences become important decision variables. When recent experience indicates one state of affairs, but more remote, albeit more extensive experience indicates a different state of affairs, the animal favors the more recent experience, so long as it is relatively very recent. As that experience becomes relatively less recent, the animal begins to base its behavior more on the more remote, but more extensive, past.

When a subject frequently experiences abrupt decreases and increases in the rate of reinforcement, it learns how long such changes may be expected to endure. This, we believe explains the much greater rapidity with which the experienced subject makes a complete adjustment to a step change in the relative rate of reward (Dreyfus, 1991; Mark & Gallistel, 1994). It has learned that the changes in rate last about half a session or more, so it adjusts completely to the new relative rate as soon as it detects the change in the rates. Similarly, the subject that has repeatedly been conditioned and extinguished to the same CS has learned that a single failure of reinforcement predicts a long sequence of failures. And, it has learned that a single renewed reinforcement predicts a long sequence of reinforcements (Ricker & Bouton, 1996).

We arrive at a conception of acquisition and extinction that looks something like this. Subjects compute estimates of the strength of the evidence for CS–US contingencies and the strength of the evidence for changes in rates of reinforcement by processes that are normatively correct. That is, they make an approximately correct assessment of the strengths of the evidence, and their perceptions of contingency and rate change are determined by these assessments. In almost any story one would want to tell about acquisition and extinction, the adjustments to changes in the rates of reward in the concurrent variable interval paradigm ought to be treated as examples of acquisition and extinction. In behaviorist terms, the subjects are acquiring stronger responses to the newly richer alternative and partially extinguishing on the newly poorer alternative. We have just seen that when subjects have to make such adjustments frequently in the concurrent variable interval (matching) paradigm, they make them about as fast as they could in principle do so. The same is known to be true for simple acquisition and extinction—the learning to learn literature. Therefore, the processes underlying acquisition and extinction must make assessments of the relevant evidence that are approximately normatively correct; otherwise, subjects could not adjust as rapidly as they demonstrably do adjust under conditions where they acquire and extinguish frequently.

When, however, there is uncertainty about how long a perceived contingency or a perceived change in rate may be expected to persist, then subjects do not adjust as rapidly as they could. Their rate of adjustment in such cases appears to be determined by other variables. In the case of simple acquisition, the determining variable is the ratio between the estimated interreinforcement intervals in the presence and absence of the CS. In the case of simple extinction, the determining variable is the ratio between the interval without reinforcement and the expected interreinforcement interval. In the more general cases—when there is a nonzero rate of background reinforcement or when there is a reduction to a lower but nonzero rate of CS reinforcement, we do not yet have a quantitative rule. It would be highly desirable to find a quantitative formulation that handled both the special cases, involving transitions from or to zero rates of reinforcement, and the more general cases, in which all rates of reinforcement are nonzero.

One implication of the conclusion that subjects have normatively appropriate processes for assessing evidence for both contingency and changes in rates of reward is that during simple acquisition, subjects must know that the CS predicts the US well before they begin to respond regularly to the CS. This suggests that we attempt to develop behavioral measures that demonstrate this early knowledge. The claim is that in simple acquisition and simple extinction, subjects know that there is a CS–US contingency or that the CS is no longer being reinforced, well before this knowledge is clearly manifest in the usual measure of conditioned behavior (response frequency).

5

Backward, Secondary, and Trace Conditioning

The timing theory framework offers a fundamentally different interpretation of the results from three dichotomies commonly recognized in the structure of conditioning protocols: trace conditioning versus delay conditioning, backward conditioning versus forward conditioning, and secondary conditioning versus primary conditioning. A long series of brilliantly conceived and executed experiments in the laboratory of Ralph Miller have recently shown that the traditional associative interpretations of these dichotomies are untenable. The experiments bring a new unity to our understanding of the different results obtained from these contrasting protocols, by showing that in each case the differences depend not on differences in the associative strengths produced but rather on the remembered information about the temporal relationship between the stimuli. This has led Miller and his colleagues (Miller & Barnet, 1993) to the *Temporal Coding Hypothesis*.

The Temporal Coding Hypothesis is a fundamental revision or extension of the traditional concept of the role of temporal relationships in conditioning. The traditional conception is that temporal relationships determine whether or not associations form, how rapidly they may be strengthened, and their asymptotic strength. The associations do not, however, encode the temporal relationships between the associated stimuli. They do not even specify the sequence in which two stimuli have occurred, much less do they specify the durations of the intervals involved. Thus, they do not endow the subject with knowledge of the temporal relations between the stimuli. The Temporal Coding Hypothesis is that, in addition to creating associations, conditioning protocols induce a coding of the temporal relations among the stimuli. In this chapter, we argue that the assumption that there are associations between the stimuli in the protocol, over and beyond knowledge of the temporal relations between the CSs, is gratuitous. The assumption that the subject knows that stimulus such-and-such follows stimulus such-and-such at such-and-such a latency is doing all the work. The assumption that the subject has become rewired so that stimulus such-and-such activates stimulus such-and-such is not contributing to the explanation of the observed behavior.

The experiments from the Miller laboratory repeatedly demonstrate that the concept of associations of differing strength cannot explain the results obtained. In most of their experiments, the relative strengths of the associations apparently reverse when the conditions under which those relative strengths are measured are changed. These seemingly paradoxical reversals are readily understood, however, if one assumes that the animal has in fact encoded the temporal relations between the stimuli. This places the interpretation of these experiments within the realm of Scalar Expectancy Theory, the theory of how knowledge of the temporal intervals between stimuli controls conditioned behavior.

DELAY CONDITIONING VERSUS TRACE CONDITIONING

The conditioning treated at great length in the chapter on acquisition was delay conditioning, in which the US occurs during the CS—usually coincident with its offset. In trace conditioning, in contrast, there is a gap between the end of the CS and the onset of the US. The conditioned responding that develops in trace conditioning is generally noticeably weaker (less certain) than responding that develops during delay conditioning, even when the latencies between CS onset and US onset are equated (Bolles, Collier, Bouton, & Marlin, 1978). In associative theory, this has traditionally been explained by the assumption that the trace of the CS in memory begins to get in some sense weaker as soon as the CS is no longer present. In its weakened or decaying state, the trace of the CS is not as readily associated with the US. (See Wagner, 1981 and Sutton & Barto, 1981 for associative models in which a version of this idea plays a pivotal role.)

The distinction between delay conditioning and trace conditioning appears in a different light when viewed from the perspective of our timing models, which assume that the animal reacts to the onset of the CS either because it predicts an increase in the rate of US occurrence (Rate Estimation Theory) or because it predicts imminent reinforcement (Scalar Expectancy Theory). Rate Estimation Theory does not apply to the analysis of a trace conditioning protocol, because, in such a protocol, the rate of US occurrence in the presence of the CS is zero. The rate of US occurrence is elevated only during a period after the CS has gone off. From a timing perspective, the only reason that an animal would respond to the CS in a trace conditioning protocol is because its onset predicts its offset (after a remembered duration). The offset in turn predicts a period of elevation in the rate of US occurrence. In other words, the response to CS onset in trace conditioning is an instance of secondary conditioning.

An experiment by Desmond and Moore (1991) demonstrates that subjects in a trace conditioning experiment learn the intervals to the US from both the onset and the offset of the CS. They conditioned rabbits to blink in response to a short tone that predicted a mild shock to the area around the eye. During training, the shock came a short while after the tone went off (trace conditioning). When they then tested the rabbits with longer tones, they observed two populations of blinks, one timed from the onset of the CS and one from the offset. The population timed from tone offset occurred later than the population timed from tone onset, but it had a tighter distribution. This is to be expected given the scalar variability of remembered intervals: the remembered interval from tone onset to the US is longer than the remembered interval from tone offset, and so blinks based on the former interval should have a more variable latency.

A recent experiment by Cole, Barnet, and Miller (1995b) gives evidence that the learning that occurs during trace conditioning is no weaker than the learning that occurs during delay conditioning. They show how to arrange circumstances so that a CR based on trace conditioning is stronger than a CR based on delay conditioning. Their results imply that the differences between delay conditioning and trace conditioning are best understood from a timing perspective. We postpone a fuller presentation of this important experiment until we have discussed two other commonly recognized dichotomies—the dichotomy between forward and backward conditioning, and the dichotomy between primary and secondary conditioning. The experiments by Cole, Barnet, and Miller cast new light on all three dichotomies.

FORWARD VERSUS BACKWARD CONDITIONING

It is commonly assumed that associations form readily if the reinforcement follows the CS (and/or the response)—*forward conditioning*—but weakly or not at all when the temporal order is reversed—*backward conditioning*—or when the two occur simultaneously—*simultaneous conditioning*. In neurobiologically oriented associative modeling, selective sensitivity to forward temporal pairing is usually taken to be a basic property of the associative mechanism (e.g., Gluck & Thompson, 1987; Grossberg & Schmajuk, 1991; Hawkins, Abrams, Carew, & Kandel, 1983; Montague & Sejnowski, 1994; Tang et al., 1999; Usherwood, 1993). However, it has recently been shown by the ingenious use of secondary conditioning protocols that two stimuli (whether two CSs or a CS and a US) get "associated" equally readily regardless of the order in which they are presented (Barnet et al., 1991; Matzel et al., 1988; Miller & Barnet, 1993; Miller & Grahame, 1991). The failure of backwardly or simultaneously conditioned animals to develop a CR is a performance failure, not a learning failure. The animal fails to respond to the CS not because it has failed to note a relation (i.e., "form an association") between the two stimuli but because of what it has learned about their relation, namely, the signs and durations of the temporal intervals between their onsets and offsets.

From the perspective of Scalar Expectancy Theory, the source of the performance failure in simultaneous and backward conditioning is apparent: At CS onset, the estimated interval to reinforcement is 0 in the case of simultaneous conditioning and negative in the case of backward conditioning. The relevant decision mechanism is the one that determines *when* to initiate the CR–the most basic decision mechanism in Scalar Expectancy Theory. The *when* decision mechanism compares the interval elapsed since the onset of the CS with the expected interval between CS onset and US occurrence. In making the comparison, it uses the ratio of the two intervals– the elapsed interval divided by the expected interval. When this ratio is more than $1 - b$, conditioned responding appropriate to the anticipated reinforcement begins. When this ratio is greater than $1 + b$, conditioned responding appropriate to the reinforcer's imminent arrival stops. The constant b is usually small (on the order of 0.2). It specifies how far the decision threshold is from 1, which is the value of the decision ratio when the elapsing interval equals the remembered interval.

In simultaneous conditioning, the denominator of the decision ratio is close or equal to 0, so the ratio becomes greater than $1 + b$ very soon after the onset of the CS. Hence, there is little or no CR to the CS. In the case of backward conditioning, the denominator is less than 0 (i.e., it is negative), because the animal expects the onset of the US to precede the onset of the CS. A negative ratio betokens an event that has already occurred, so the decision not to respond to the CS occurs as soon as the CS comes on. This is the formal realization of the intuition that the animal does not respond to the CS in backward conditioning because, when the CS comes on, it expects that the US will already have occurred (cf. the Temporal Coding Hypothesis of Miller & Barnet, 1993).

Recent experiments by Cole, Barnet, and Miller (1995b) and Barnet and Miller (1996) support this interpretation of the data on backward conditioning. Before we elaborate on them, we consider the timing interpretation of secondary conditioning, because the experiments make ingenious use of secondary conditioning.

SECONDARY VERSUS PRIMARY CONDITIONING

The principal forms of secondary conditioning are second-order conditioning and sensory preconditioning. The protocols for secondary conditioning are identical with the protocols for first-order (or primary) conditioning; the only difference being that neither of the stimuli is conventionally regarded as a US (a reinforcer). They are both CSs. This is awkward for associative models, because the associative mechanism is commonly assumed to require a reinforcer to set it in motion. The awkwardness is reflected in the names given to the conditioning produced by pairing two neutral CSs. When this occurs *after* a phase in which one of them has been paired with a US, it is called second-order conditioning. Traditionally, associative theories assume that the CS previously paired with a so-called primary reinforcer has acquired secondary reinforcing properties. Thus, pairing an already conditioned CS with a neutral CS conditions the neutral CS by secondary reinforcement.

Secondary reinforcement cannot be invoked to explain the conditioning that occurs when two neutral CSs are paired *before* one of them is paired with a primary reinforcer. That is why when secondary conditioning precedes primary conditioning, it is given a different name—*sensory preconditioning*. The name suggests that in some sense this is not really conditioning; it's preconditioning, whatever that may be. There are reasons to think, however, that second-order conditioning and sensory preconditioning are one and the same at the level of the conditioning process (cf. Barnet, Grahame, & Miller, 1991), and, indeed, that, at the process or mechanism level, they differ neither from one another nor from primary conditioning. At the process level, these distinctions are artifacts of the associative conceptual framework, more specifically of the assumption that the learning process is set in motion by a reinforcer that strengthens a connection, causing the animal to do something it would not have done before the connection was strengthened.

Timing models do not require a reinforcer. They assume that the animal times intervals between salient stimulus and response events (and cumulates the intervals during which a salient stimulus has been present) whether or not the stimulus is biologically or emotionally important to the animal. Timing (and counting) are assumed to be basic brain processes, which, like all other basic biological processes, go on continually, whenever there is anything to time or count.

In timing models, reinforcement is necessary for performance, not learning. Reinforcement engages the operation of the behavior systems that employ decision mechanisms to determine CRs (cf. Fanselow, 1989; Timberlake & Lucas, 1989). The intervals the animal has learned become manifest in its observable behavior only when decision mechanisms are engaged, that is, only when predicted events are important to the animal.

The explanation of secondary conditioning from a timing perspective requires only the assumption that animals can sum two estimated intervals. This is not a new assumption in the theory. We have taken for granted throughout the development of our argument the assumption that animals can sum intervals. For example, this assumption was central to our explanation of why partial reinforcement does not increase the number of reinforcements required to reach some acquisition criterion. Our treatment of partial reinforcement assumed that the animal cumulates (sums) successive unreinforced intervals of CS exposure. (For direct experimental evidence of this, see Gibbon & Balsam, 1981; Roberts & Church, 1978.)

To apply the timing analysis to the understanding of secondary conditioning, we assume simply that the beginnings of the intervals being summed may be indicated by different stimulus events. That is, the intervals being summed need not be marked by the onsets and offsets of the same stimulus. A CS_1–CS_2 interval—learned during a secondary conditioning phase—may be added to a CS_2–US interval to obtain the expected CS_1–US interval. This explanation of secondary conditioning is—in its intuitive essentials—the same as the explanation offered by the Temporal Coding Hypothesis (Miller & Barnet, 1993) and by Honig's (1981) Temporal Map Hypothesis.

This brings us at last to an account of recent experiments on conditioned lick suppression, which shed an interesting light on all four of the dichotomies we have just described—delay versus trace conditioning, forward versus backward conditioning, secondary versus primary conditioning, and second-order conditioning versus sensory preconditioning.

In the lick-suppression paradigm, the thirsty animal first learns to lick a spout for water. This establishes the appetitive responding that will subsequently be suppressed by the conditioned emotional reaction (fear) to various CSs. At some point in the experiment, the fear of the CS is established by pairing it a few times with a brief shock to the feet. If the shock coincides with CS offset, this is called delay conditioning. If the shock occurs some while after the offset of the CS, it is called trace conditioning. Delay and trace conditioning are the two basic forms of primary conditioning. The conditioned fear aroused by the CS is manifest in the suppression of licking. On test trials, when the shock is omitted in order to allow the experimenter to observe the CR uncontaminated by the unconditioned response, the latency to resume licking after the CS comes on is the measure of the strength of the CR. The longer the latency, the greater the strength of the CR.

One experiment (Cole et al., 1995b) looked at trace versus delay conditioning, backward conditioning, and secondary conditioning. In the second-order conditioning version of this experiment, the subjects were first given primary conditioning, using either a delay protocol or a trace protocol. In the delay protocol, the CS lasted 5 s, and the shock coincided with its offset (see top protocol in Fig. 5.1A). In the trace protocol, the CS also lasted 5 s, but the shock did not occur until 5 s after its offset (see second-to-top protocol in Fig. 5.1A).

Some subjects were immediately tested for their degree of suppression to the conditioned CS, and they showed the expected difference between the results of delay versus trace conditioning: The trace-conditioned subjects showed less fear of the CS than the delay-conditioned subjects. This outcome is doubly predicted in associative theory, because: (a) Trace conditioning is weaker than delay conditioning, even when the CS–US latency is the same. As already explained, this is traditionally taken to indicate that the associations formed to stimulus traces are weaker than the associations formed when the stimulus is present at the moment of reinforcement; and (b) In the present case, the trace group had a greater delay of reinforcement (10 s versus 5 s). Prolonging the interval from CS onset to reinforcement is traditionally thought to weaken the strength of the association by reducing the degree to which the stimulus onsets are temporally paired.

The subjects that were not immediately tested for the strength of primary conditioning next experienced a brief phase of *backward* second-order conditioning (see final protocol in Fig. 5.1A). During this training, the CS they had already learned to fear was followed by another CS, also lasting 5 s. As usual, the phase of second-order conditioning was kept brief, because the primarily conditioned CS is not reinforced during second-order conditioning. From the standpoint of the primary conditioning, the second-order conditioning phase is a brief extinction phase; it must be kept brief to prevent extinction of the primary conditioning.

From the standpoint of associative theories, the group that received primary trace conditioning followed by backward second-order conditioning ought to show no conditioned responding to the second-order CS, for two reasons: First, the primary conditioning itself was weaker in this group, because it was trace conditioning rather than delay conditioning. Second, the secondary conditioning was backward conditioning. Backward pairing is commonly assumed to produce no (or very little) conditioning.

From a timing perspective, however, this group should show a strong CR to the secondary CS, as may be seen by looking at the diagram of the three protocols in Fig. 5.1A. In fact, their response to the secondary CS should be stronger than the response of the group that received primary delay conditioning followed by backward secondary conditioning. In the latter group, the expected interval to shock when the secondary CS comes on is 0. (This

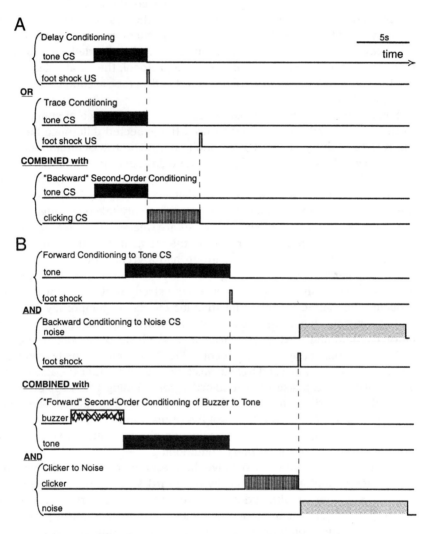

FIG. 5.1. Diagram of experiments by Cole et al. (1995b; A) and Barnet et al. (1997; B). The intervals during which primary CSs were presented are filled with dark gray; those during which secondary CSs were presented, with light gray. The dashed vertical lines are aids to perceiving the expected temporal relation between the secondary CS and the reinforcer when the remembered CS–US intervals from the different phases of conditioning are summed to yield the expected interval between the onset of the second-order CS and the US.

may be seen in Fig. 5.1A by following the dashed vertical line from the shock in the primary conditioning phase down to the onset of the secondary CS.) They should show little CR for the same reason that animals given simultaneous primary conditioning fail to respond to the CS. By the time they realize that the CS has come on, they have nothing to fear. In fact, this group showed very little fear (very little lick suppression). But for the group that got trace conditioning, the expected interval to shock is 5 s when the secondary CS comes on. They should be afraid and they were.

The reaction to the secondary CS in the group that got primary trace conditioning followed by backward second-order conditioning was not significantly weaker than the reaction to the primary CS in the control subjects that got simple delay conditioning. This comparison is not entirely valid, because the stimulus used in the secondary conditioning is generally found to be more potent in this kind of conditioning than the stimulus used for primary conditioning. Nonetheless, the comparison emphasizes that the fear elicited by combining what the animal has learned about the temporal relations between the four stimuli (three CSs and the shock US) during different phases of conditioning can be a strong fear. These are not marginal effects.

Cole et al. (1995b) also did a sensory preconditioning version of the experiment. The design was exactly the same except that the phase of secondary conditioning preceded rather than followed primary conditioning, which is why this phase is called sensory preconditioning rather than second-order conditioning. As already explained, this variation in procedure is important from an associative perspective. When the secondary conditioning occurs before the primary conditioning, it cannot be explained in terms of secondary reinforcement. How one explains sensory preconditioning is an unresolved question for associative theories in which the concept of a reinforcer is important. From a timing perspective, in contrast, this variation in procedure is of little theoretical importance. It means only that the primary conditioning phase is an extinction phase for the secondary conditioning, rather than vice versa. This becomes a serious consideration only if the second phase of conditioning (whether primary or secondary) is prolonged. But it is not, precisely in order to avoid this problem. From a timing perspective, one should get basically the same result in the sensory preconditioning version of this experiment as in the second-order conditioning version. That was in fact the case.

Again, the strength of the fear reaction to the secondary CS, the CS never directly paired with shock, was as strong as the reaction to the primary CS in the group that received simple delay conditioning, although again, this comparison is somewhat vitiated by the fact that the CSs used in different roles were deliberately not counterbalanced. The strong fear reaction to the secondary CS was observed only in the group that received the supposedly weaker form of primary conditioning—trace conditioning. In the group that received the supposedly stronger form of primary conditioning, the fear reaction to the secondary CS was much weaker.

In the light of these results, it is difficult to know how to obtain from conditioned behavior even an ordinal indication of the strengths of the associations that are supposed to mediate it. In the associative analysis, the secondary CS arouses fear by way of two associative bonds conducting in series—the association between the secondary and primary CS, followed by the association between the primary CS and the reinforcement. Because, these associations are in series, their combined conductance must be less than their individual conductances. The reactions to the primary CS imply that the association conditioned by the delay protocol is stronger than the association conditioned by the trace protocol. The secondary conditioning protocol was the same for both groups. Thus, the strength of the primary conditioning should control the strength of the reactions to the secondary CSs. But, the relative strengths of the reactions to the secondary CSs are the reverse of the relative strengths of the reactions to the primary CSs. From an associative perspective, these reversals in the apparent strengths of the primary associations are paradoxical.

A second experiment (Barnet, Cole, & Miller, 1997) makes the same point. Again there were second-order conditioning and sensory preconditioning versions of this experiment. That is, the secondary conditioning phase followed the primary conditioning phase in one version, but preceded it in the other. There were two 10-s-long CSs in the primary phase, one forwardly conditioned, one backwardly conditioned (top two protocols in Fig. 5.1B). There was no fixed temporal relation between these two CSs, but there was a fixed temporal relation between each CS and shock. Shock always occurred at the offset of the one CS but immediately preceding the onset of the other CS. In the secondary conditioning phase, two different secondary CSs, each 5 s in duration, were forwardly paired with the two primary CSs (bottom two protocols in Fig. 5.1B). Thus, the onset of one secondary CS preceded by 5 s the onset of the forwardly conditioned primary CS, whereas the onset of the other secondary CS preceded by 5 s the onset of the backwardly conditioned primary CS.

The strengths of the fear reactions to the primary CSs showed the usual difference between forward and backward conditioning; that is, reactions to the backwardly conditioned, primary CS were weaker. However, the strengths of the reactions to the secondary CSs were reversed. The secondary CS that predicted the backwardly conditioned primary CS elicited more fear than did the secondary CS that predicted the forwardly conditioned primary CS.

Within the context of an associative theory, it is unclear how one is to account for the apparent reversals in the strengths of primary associations when one shifts from testing the primary CSs to testing the secondary CSs. In contrast, a look at a diagram of the temporal relations (see Fig. 5.1B) makes the timing account more or less self-evident. What one needs to consider is the expected interval to shock at the onset of a CS—the comparison quantity in Scalar Expectancy Theory. In the tests of the primary CSs, when the forwardly conditioned CS comes on, the expected interval to shock is 10 s. When the backwardly conditioned CS comes on, however, it is 0 s, which, as previously explained, should result in little fear, given the decision rule specified by Scalar Expectancy Theory. On the other hand, when the secondary CS that predicts the forwardly conditioned primary CS comes on, the expected interval to shock is 15 s. Moreover, and probably more importantly, the onset of a still better warning stimulus—one that more precisely predicts the shock—is expected in 5 s. When the secondary CS that predicts the backwardly conditioned primary CS comes on, however, the expected interval to shock is only 5 s—and no further warning stimulus is expected. The shock is coming very soon and there will be no further warning.

The diagrams in Fig. 5.1 make it clear why one might wish to speak of subjects' forming a temporal map during conditioning (Honig, 1981). The ability to remember temporal intervals and to add, subtract, and divide them—the central capabilities in our timing models—gives the animal precisely that.

A third experiment (Barnet & Miller, 1996) shows the utility of the timing perspective in understanding both backward conditioning and conditioned inhibition. This intricately designed experiment requires for its interpretation both Rate Estimation Theory and Scalar Expectancy Theory. No other experiment that we know of brings into play so much of the theoretical analysis we have so far developed.

Recall that in Rate Estimation Theory, a CS is a conditioned inhibitor if its estimated rate of reinforcement is negative. When a CS to which a negative subjective rate of US occurrence is attributed is presented together with a previously conditioned excitor, the negative rate of reinforcement sums with the positive rate attributed to the excitor. The expected rate of reinforcement is thereby reduced. This test—presenting the putative conditioned inhibitor together with a conditioned excitor—is called the summation test for conditioned inhibition. Recall also that in Scalar Expectancy Theory, when there is a fixed interval between CS onset and reinforcement, the remembered reinforcement latency is used to time a CR that anticipates the reinforcement. All of these principles come into play in what follows.

The experiment, which is diagrammed in Fig. 5.2, involved three training phases. The first phase forwardly conditioned an excitor to be used in the summation test. The second phase backwardly conditioned an inhibitor to be used in the summation test. The third phase paired a third CS with the so-called inhibitor (secondary conditioning of an inhibitor).

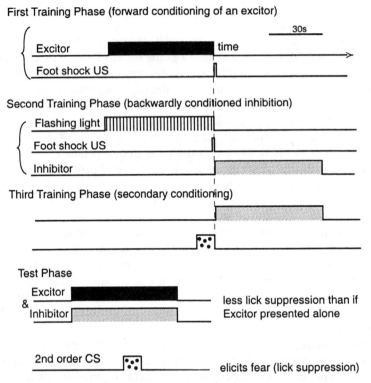

FIG. 5.2. Schematic of experiment by Barnet and Miller (1996) in which the inhibitor CS reduces (inhibits) fear, but a second-order CS, whose only connection to shock is that it predicts the inhibitor CS, nonetheless elicits (excites) fear. A consideration of the temporal relations diagrammed here makes this seeming paradox intelligible.

In the first phase, each presentation of the excitatory CS lasted 30 s and there was a 1-s foot shock coincident with its offset. Thus, the expected rate of reinforcement in the presence of this excitor was 2 shocks per minute.

A prolonged phase of backward inhibitory conditioning followed, carried out in the same chamber as the excitatory conditioning, but with a different CS. Each of the 12 twenty-minute sessions in this phase contained eight 30-s presentations of the inhibitory CS, with each presentation of this CS immediately preceded by a 1-s shock. The background against which the shock was presented was a flashing house light that came on 30 s before the shock. In the analysis of this experiment from the perspective of Rate Estimation Theory, it is assumed that this flashing house light constituted the background, and that the backwardly conditioned CS, which came on when the shock and the background terminated, can be treated as having suppressed the background and hence, the rate of reinforcement predicted by it, which was 2 shocks per minute.

Finally, there was a phase of secondary conditioning in which the subjects learned that yet another CS predicted the onset of the "inhibitory" CS. The reason that scare quotes now appear around inhibitory will soon become evident (the about-to-be demonstrated excitatory conditioned reaction to the secondarily conditioned CS makes it confusing to call the primary CS a conditioned inhibitor). The secondary CS lasted only 5 s, and the 30-s "inhibitory" CS came on at its offset.

As always, the phase of secondary conditioning was kept brief to avoid extinction of the primary conditioning. We note in passing, that the account of extinction offered by Rate Estimation Theory in chapter 4 makes it clear why this works. According to Rate Estimation Theory, extinction does not occur until the ratio between the interval without CS reinforcement and the expected interval between CS reinforcements gets quite large. Thus, a largish number of expected reinforcements must be omitted for a subject to decide that the rate of reinforcement has changed—on the order of 50. Until the subject decides that the rate of reinforcement has changed, there is no extinction. In contrast, in associative theories of extinction, the biggest decrements in net associative strength should occur in the early extinction trials. This is a consequence of the first-order kinetics universally posited in quantitative models of associative strengthening (and weakening). Therefore, a moderately numerous sequence of unreinforced trials ought to have a big impact on the strength of the association, but in fact such strings have no detectable impact (Prokasy & Gormezano, 1979).

The secondary conditioning was conducted in a different chamber from the primary conditioning, as was the summation test and the test for the subjects' CR to the secondary CS. This was done in order that all the conditions in which shock never occurred were run in a background that gave the animal no reason to expect shock.

The summation test showed that despite the backward pairing of shock and the "inhibitory" CS, the CS nonetheless became a conditioned inhibitor. Presenting this backwardly conditioned CS together with the excitor CS diminished the subject's fear of the excitor—the standard test for conditioned inhibition. From an associative standpoint, this is puzzling, because backward conditioning is not supposed to produce associations of any kind, excitatory or inhibitory. But in Rate Estimation Theory, this is the expected result. In Rate Estimation Theory, it does not matter where background USs occur relative to the CS. All rates are treated as Poisson rates, which means that a reinforcement is equally likely at every moment that the rate in question is in force. The backward conditioning experience taught the animal that the CS suppressed an excitor. When the backwardly conditioned CS was combined with another independently conditioned excitor, it did not eliminate the fear caused by the excitor, but it did reduce it. This is to be expected if the inhibitory power of the backwardly conditioned CS arose from its suppression of an excitatory background (the flashing light) rather than from its direct suppression of shocks themselves. When the backwardly conditioned suppresser is pitted against the other excitor in the summation tests, it proves inefficacious, that is, the other excitor is not suppressed, so it is not surprising that the subjects are uncertain what to expect.

That backward conditioning should establish an effective inhibitor is itself interesting. Together with the results of the first two experiments in this series (the experiments diagrammed in Fig. 5.1), this result would appear to pose a challenge to the widely held view that forward temporal pairing is important in the establishment of an association. However, the theoretically most interesting part of this experiment comes from the results of the test for the effect of the secondary CS—the CS whose onset predicted that the "inhibitor" would come on in 5 s. The secondary CS excited fear (manifest in a strong suppression of licking) even though its only connection to the shock was via a primary CS that inhibited fear.

From an associative perspective, the animal's fear in the presence of the secondary CS is perplexing. This CS was not only never presented together with shock, it was never even presented in an environment in which shock occurred. The connection between this CS and shock was mediated by the "inhibitory" CS, the CS that was backwardly paired with shock. This CS passed the summation test, the standard test for inhibition of a CR (in this case, inhibition of fear). How can a CS that predicts a stimulus that itself inhibits fear, nonetheless elicit fear? And strong fear at that. The degree of suppression to the secondary CS was slightly (though not significantly) greater than the degree of suppression produced by the primary excitor. It is this result that has led us to place scare quotes around "inhibitor" and its cognates. If a stimulus has an inhibitory effect, then another stimulus, whose only connection to the reinforcer is that it predicts the inhibitory stimulus, ought itself to inhibit the CR. But it does not inhibit the CR; on the contrary, it strongly excites it.

Rate Estimation Theory does not provide any illumination here, but Scalar Expectancy Theory does. It predicts this result, for reasons that have already been explained and diagrammed in Fig. 5.1. In the backward conditioning phase, the animal learned that the interval from the onset of the "inhibitory" CS to the onset of shock was −1 s. In the secondary conditioning phase, it learned that the interval from the onset of the secondary CS to the onset of the "inhibitory" CS was 5 s. The expected interval to shock when the secondary CS comes on is the sum of these two intervals, which is 4 s. The subjects should have feared an impending shock, and they did.

Rate Estimation Theory and Scalar Expectancy Theory are not in conflict here. Rate Estimation Theory deals only with the rate of reinforcement the animal expects when the inhibitory CS is present. That expectation is 0 shocks, because the backwardly conditioned CS suppresses the excitor. The rate estimation mechanism takes account of the analytic impossibility of directly observing a negative rate. Scalar Expectancy Theory deals with the timing of a CR controlled by the expected interval to the reinforcement (the *when* decision, in contrast to the *whether* decision). Scalar Expectancy Theory gives (in part) a quantitative formalization of Honig's (1981) Temporal Map and Miller and Barnet's (1993) Temporal Coding Hypothesis. Intuitively, any animal with a temporal map—any animal that has learned the temporal relations between the various stimuli—will show what Barnet and Miller (1996) found. Their findings are not intuitively surprising, once the various training conditions are understood; they are only surprising from the standpoint of traditional associative accounts of conditioning, in which the animal does not acquire knowledge of the temporal intervals.

In a second version of this experiment, Barnet and Miller (1996) added an extinction phase following the backward conditioning phase. In this version, the animal was first taught that a shock immediately preceded the onset of the "inhibitory" CS (the backward conditioning phase) and then that this was no longer true (the extinction phase). In the extinction phase, the "inhibitory" CS was repeatedly presented in the absence of shock—and (importantly) also in the absence of the flashing light that presaged shock (the effective background stimulus for the shock experience during the backward conditioning). From a timing perspective, the extinction phase should persuade the animal that, although it once was true that the inhibitory CS was preceded by a shock, that is no longer true. However, it should not affect the animal's estimate of the power of the backwardly conditioned CS to suppress an excitatory background stimulus (the flashing light), because this stimulus was absent during extinction. The extinction experience, if anything, confirmed that when the "inhibitory" CS was present, the flashing light was not present.

This second version of the experiment (the version with an interpolated extinction phase) emphasizes the importance of the distinction between the *whether* decision and the *when* decision. The extinction phase removes the expectation that is used in the excitatory *when* decision. This decision leads to a fear response to the secondary CS (and the consequent suppression of licking). But the extinction does not remove the expectation that makes the primary CS an effective conditioned inhibitor, the expectation that the primary CS can suppress CSs that predict shock, thereby lowering the expected rate of shock reinforcement.

The results from this second version (with interpolated extinction) were as expected from the joint application of Scalar Expectancy Theory and Rate Estimation Theory. The extinction phase did not affect the results of the summation test. Despite the intervening extinction phase, presenting the "inhibitory" CS together with the excitor diminished the subjects' fear of the excitor, thereby moderately reducing the amount of lick suppression, just as in the version without an extinction phase. The extinction phase, however, greatly reduced the animals' fear of the secondary CS. Thus, the extinction phase removed the basis for the anticipatory reaction to the secondary CS (the reaction that occurs before the primary CS comes on), without removing the basis for the reduction in fear caused by the actual presence of the "inhibitory" CS.

Further versions of this basic experiment replaced the backward conditioning of the inhibition with a phase of conventional, feature-negative inhibitory conditioning. In this more conventional protocol, the "inhibitory" effect of one CS was created by pairing that CS from time to time with an otherwise reinforced CS (hence, an excitor) and omitting the reinforcement on those trials. This is the procedure, first employed by Pavlov himself, which gave rise to the concept of a conditioned inhibitor. The CS that predicts the omission of reinforcement becomes a conditioned "inhibitor."

The use of the more conventional procedure for establishing conditioned "inhibition" eliminates the expectation that figured in the previously described prediction of Scalar Expectancy Theory, because there no longer is a fixed temporal interval between the onset of the "inhibitory" CS and the onset of the reinforcer. However, the additive partitioning of observed rates forces the attribution of a negative rate of reinforcement to the influence of the "inhibitory" CS. Moreover, according to Scalar Expectancy Theory, the animal learns the duration of the secondary CS during the phase of secondary conditioning. Thus, when a stimulus that has been secondarily conditioned to the "inhibitory" CS comes on, the animal expects that after an interval equal to the duration of the secondary CS (Scalar Expectancy Theory), the rate of shock will go down (Rate Estimation Theory). The two models together predict that, in this version of the experiment, the secondary CS will alleviate fear, just as does the conditioned inhibitor itself. And this was the result that was in fact obtained. In other words, timing theory explains why and how the conditioned "inhibition" created by the standard protocol (the one Pavlov himself used) differs from the conditioned inhibition created by the backward conditioning protocol. In the process, it shows why these phenomena are better thought of not in terms of inhibition and excitation, but rather in terms of the content of conditioning, what it is the animals really learn, which is the intervals and the rates.

Summary

Scalar Expectancy Theory may be applied to the interpretation of the differences found when one uses trace rather than delay conditioning, secondary rather than primary conditioning, and backward rather than forward conditioning. These phenomena follow directly from central assumptions of Scalar Expectancy Theory: First, that the *when* response is based on a ratio comparison of a currently elapsing interval to an expected reinforcement latency. Second, that the expected reinforcement latency may be based the sum of several intervals in memory. This interpretation deals felicitously with contemporary experimental results that pose strong challenges to associative interpretations of these phenomena. The problem for an associative analysis is that both the strength and the sign of a primary association seem to reverse when the strength is tested with secondarily conditioned CSs rather than with the primarily conditioned CSs. These reversals are readily understood when account is taken of the symbolic content of conditioning, namely, the animals knowledge of the temporal intervals in the protocols to which it has been exposed.

CHAPTER

6

Operant Choice

Skinner operant (handwritten annotation)

Operant or instrumental conditioning and classical or Pavlovian conditioning were once thought to depend on fundamentally different learning mechanisms. In the Pavlovian paradigm, reinforcement (the US) is given whether the subject makes a conditioned response (CR) or not, whereas in the operant paradigm reinforcement is contingent on the CR. However, as we noted earlier, the discovery of autoshaping raised serious doubts in many quarters about the claim that there are in fact two distinct learning processes in conditioning. Autoshaping is now the method of choice for teaching pigeons to peck keys and rats to press levers. An autoshaping protocol is identical to the protocol that Pavlov used to teach dogs to salivate in response to tones and other conditioned stimuli (CS). The only difference is that the dog subject is replaced with a pigeon or a rat, the tone CS is replaced with key illumination or lever extension, and the CR that emerges as a consequence of the subject's exposure to the contingency between the CS and reinforcement is key pecking or lever pressing. Just as dogs salivate to stimuli that predict food, so pigeons peck at a bright round stimulus that predicts grain and rats attempt to manipulate a lever whose extension predicts food. These are unconditioned responses to acquired knowledge. The pigeon and the rat have not learned *to* peck the key or press the lever, they have learned *that* the illuminated key or moving lever predicts food. The behavior that we observe is elicited by the knowledge the subjects have acquired.

Because the behaviors that are now routinely trained using the autoshaping protocol were long thought to be paradigmatic examples of operant behavior, the discovery that they could be so readily conditioned by the Pavlovian protocol led many to doubt that the underlying learning processes were really different in any fundamental sense. It is now common to assume that Pavlovian and instrumental (operant) conditioning do not differ in the laws of associations formation that mediate them. They are assumed to differ only in the associative structures that support them. Instrumentally conditioned behavior is assumed to depend to varying degrees on stimulus–response and response–outcome associations (e.g. Colwill & Rescorla, 1990; Rescorla, 1990, 1991, 1992), whereas classically conditioned behavior depends only on stimulus–outcome associations.

From the perspective of timing theory, there is even less reason to think that operant and classical conditioning protocols tap different learning mechanisms. The basic learning mechanism, namely the learning of temporal intervals and their reciprocals (rates), is assumed to be the same in all examples of what is usually considered conditioning. To be sure, an operant and a classical paradigm may involve somewhat different decision mechanisms, but that is no reason to group all classical paradigms in one category and all operant paradigms in another, because, as we have stressed repeatedly, within each group different protocols involve different decision mechanisms, that is, different decision variables. We begin our analysis of operant choice behavior by distinguishing two different decision mechanisms that may govern the process of choosing one response rather than another.

OPTING VERSUS ALLOCATING

Most of the theoretical literature on operant choice attempts to specify the effect of a given pattern of reinforcement on the subjective value (attractiveness) of an option (a key or lever that the subject may peck or press). Implicit in most such analyses is the assumption that there is an invariant mapping between the relative subjective values of two options and observed preference, that is, the relative frequency with which they are chosen or the relative amounts of time or numbers of responses devoted to them. This will not, however, be the case if different decision mechanisms operate in different contexts. Suppose, for example, that in one context, choosing serves to select the best option, whereas in another, choosing serves to allocate time or effort among the options so as to optimize net gain. In the first case, the choice mechanism is optimal to the extent that it always selects the best option. In the second case, the choice mechanism is optimal to the extent that it allocates time and effort in the best way. These are different goals. We assume that they cannot be and are not mediated by one and the same choice mechanism. Rather, the animal invokes different choice mechanisms, depending on its construal of the situation it faces. We call choice behavior mediated by the first mechanism *opting* and choice behavior mediated by the second mechanism *allocating*.

The Opting Decision

The desirability of distinguishing between opting and allocating became apparent in the course of a "failed" experiment in the laboratory of one of us (JG). The experiment was intended to be a variant of the well known matching paradigm in which subjects choose between two manipulanda reinforced by concurrent variable interval (VI) schedules. These schedules make reinforcement available at a variable interval following the collection of a reinforcement. Usually, the distribution of intervals is approximately exponential. Schedules are said to run concurrently when two response options are presented continuously and simultaneously, each reinforced on its own schedule. As we mentioned in an earlier chapter, Herrnstein (1961) discovered that, under these circumstances, the ratio of the responses allocated to the response options during a session tended to match the ratio of the reinforcements obtained from them. The study and analysis of this matching phenomenon has formed a substantial part of the experimental and theoretical literature on operant choice in the last four decades (Commons, Herrnstein, & Rachlin, 1982; Davison & McCarthy, 1988; Herrnstein & Prelec, 1991; Nevin, 1982).

In the failed version of this experiment, pigeons were first trained with the keys presented one by one rather than together. Six pigeons received 25 sessions of initial training in which each of two differently illuminated keys (red, green) was presented 15 times per session. Each time a key was presented, it remained on until the pigeon had collected a reinforcement from it. The amount of time that elapsed on any one trial between the illumination of the key, which signaled its availability as an option, and the arming of the reinforcement mechanism, varied from trial to trial in accord with the intervals programmed into a standard VI scheduling tape. The average scheduled interval differed depending on which key was illuminated; it was 20 s for the red, 60 s for the green key. When these subjects were then shifted to concurrent training (both keys illuminated at the same time), they did not show a degree of preference for the richer key that matched its relative richness (i.e., a 3:1 preference). All six birds preferred the richer key exclusively; they almost never chose the leaner key. This is called overmatching. Overmatching is seldom observed when concurrent VI schedules constitute the options, and this degree of overmatching—98% to 100% choice of the richer schedule in six out of six subjects—is without published precedent. The effect of the initial training, with each key presented separately, on subsequent preference under concurrent conditions was robust and enduring. Three of the six subjects showed exclusive preference for the richer key throughout 25 sessions of concurrent training.

It was found in the course of related experiments in this series that breaking the usual concurrent-schedules paradigm up into discrete trials, each trial terminating in a reinforcement on one or the other of the two simultaneously operative keys, does not produce overmatching. On the contrary, it reliably produced some degree of undermatching, provided that the schedule on the key not being pecked elapsed in the discrete trial procedure exactly as in the continuous procedure; that is, provided that the concurrent intervals did not begin anew with each trial. Thus, it was presumably the presentation of the options individually during initial training, not the breaking up of the experience with each key into discrete one-reinforcement trials that resulted in an exclusive preference for the richer key.

We suggest that in the course of the initial training, the subjects learned to construe the situation as one in which either one option was available or the other, not one in which the goal was to allocate behavior among concurrent options in such a way as to maximize overall gain. What construal means in practice is that the subjects' choice behavior when confronted with a choice between two alternatives was mediated by the opting mechanism. We assume this to be the mechanism commonly posited in the analysis of forced-choice psychophysical paradigms: The expected delays of reinforcement for the two options are represented internally by (memory) signals with scalar sampling variability (see Fig. 6.1). The remembered interval for a given option—the signal generated for that option when memory is consulted—varies from one consultation of memory to the next. The decision mechanism reads (samples) memory to get the value associated with each option and it always chooses the option with the lower sampled value. The choice of the option with the longer interreinforcement interval occurs only as a result of sampling error, that is, only on trials in which the sampled signal for the leaner option happens to be shorter than the sampled signal for the richer option. Thus, when the distributions from which the choice mechanism is sampling are well separated, the leaner option is almost never chosen. That is why pigeons trained with only one VI option available at any one time almost invariably chose the richer of the two options when they are subsequently offered as concurrently exploitable options. The subjects' choice behavior is no longer mediated by the decision process used to allocate behavior among concurrently exploitable options, because it has learned that these options are not concurrently exploitable.

Matching and the Allocating Decision Mechanism

Many discussions of matching behavior and in particular, the controversy over matching versus maximizing rest, we believe, in part on the implicit assumption that rational choice should always take the form of an opting deci-

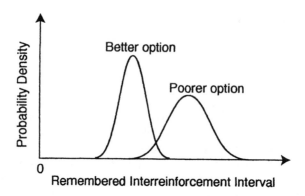

FIG. 6.1. The signals representing the parameters of the outcome (in this
case, the interval between reinforcements) have scalar variability (noise). To
the extent that the probability density functions for the distributions of these
signals overlap, there is some likelihood that, on a given occasion, the signal
for the poorer option will be better than the signal for the better option. In this
example, the better option is the one with the shorter interval, hence the
smaller variability. If the outcomes differed in magnitude but not rate of reinforcement, then the better option would be the one with the greater variability. How the variances due to magnitude and interreinforcement interval combine when the product of these two subjective variables is computed remains
to be determined.

sion, that is, the mechanism should always choose what it believes to be the
subjectively better alternative at the moment of choice. Part of the fascina-
tion of matching behavior for students of choice and rational decision making is that it appears to violate this principle; the animal frequently leaves the
better alternative for the poorer alternative. It does so even when the alternatives differ greatly in richness, so that it is unlikely that the animal is mo-
mentarily confused or in error about which is on average richer.

It is not obvious, however, that either the subject or the theorist should
attend to the average rates of reinforcement. In a concurrent VI schedule,
when the scheduling mechanism times out, the scheduled reinforcement is
held for the subject to collect when it next responds on the manipulandum.
The longer the subject has been away from a manipulandum, the more certain it is that a reinforcer has been scheduled on it. Thus, the longer a subject has stuck with one choice, the more certain it is that, at that moment,
the other choice is more likely to pay off. This consideration is the foundation of the *local maximizing* account of matching behavior (Shimp, 1969). In
this account, the subject learns the relation between time away from a
manipulandum and probability of immediate payoff. It leaves the richer option for the leaner only when it estimates the momentary probability of a
payoff from the leaner option to be higher than the momentary probability
of a payoff from the richer option. This account adheres to the principle

that the decision mechanism always chooses what appears to be the better option at that moment.

Local maximizing accounts of matching must be distinguished from *global maximizing* accounts (Baum, 1981; Rachlin, 1978; Staddon & Motheral, 1979). The latter emphasize the important point that matching (on concurrent VI schedules and in many other situations) is the rational way to behave in that it maximizes overall return. Because immediate reward is reliably available at the leaner alternative if it has long gone unvisited, subjects should leave the richer alternative for the leaner from time to time. Thus, adaptive advantage is very likely the *ultimate* (evolutionary) cause of matching behavior. The question is, What is the *proximate* cause of the decisions to leave richer alternatives to the sample leaner ones? Global maximization is a theory about ultimate causation, whereas local maximization is a theory of proximate (or molecular) causation.

Leaving Is Markovian. The local maximizing account predicts that the likelihood of the subject's switching from one option to the other at any moment increases with the duration of its stay (the interval during which it remains with one option, also called the dwell time). However, Heyman (1979) showed that the momentary probability of a changeover from one option to the other was constant; it did not vary as a function of the number of responses that the pigeon had made on the key it was currently pecking (see Fig. 6.2). If, as has often been suggested (Myerson & Miezin, 1980; Pliskoff, 1971), the rate of switching is the fundamental dependent variable in matching situations, this means that the rate of switching (the momentary likelihood of stay termination) does not change as stay duration increases. That in turn implies that the frequency of visits terminating at a given duration declines by a fixed percentage for each increment in duration. In other words, the frequency of observed departures is an exponential function of dwell time, which it is (see Fig. 6.3).

The discovery that the likelihood of leaving an option at any one moment depends only on the average rates of reinforcement, and not on the momentary likelihood that the switch will be reinforced, led Heyman (1979, 1982) to suggest that the decision process in matching was an elicited (unconditioned) Markov process, in which the rates of reinforcement directly determine the likelihoods of the subject's leaving one option for the other. These likelihoods are hereafter called the *leaving* rates.

Heyman argued that leaving behavior (the decision to terminate a stay) is not conditioned in the Skinnerian or operant sense of conditioned, that is, it is not shaped by the prior consequences of such behavior; it is simply what the animal is built to do given certain information about its situation. Once again, we have here to do with the distinction between learning *to* and learning *that*. The traditional understanding of operant behavior—and the one

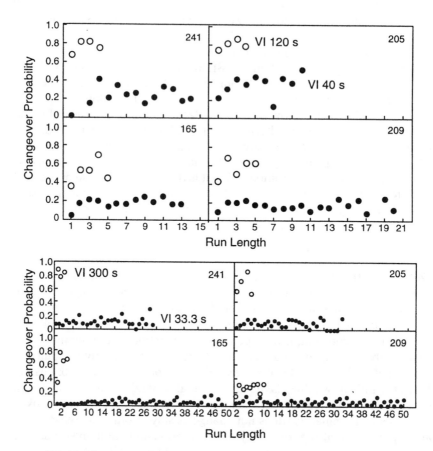

FIG. 6.2. The probability of a changeover key response (a switch to the other option) as a function of the number of responses since the last changeover. Note that probability increases little if at all with the length of the run, despite the fact that the longer run, the more certain it is that there is a reinforcement waiting to be collected from the other option. Note also that the lower the probability of switching, the longer runs last. Expected run length is the reciprocal of the switching probability (leaving rate); Figs. 3 & 4 on pp. 45 & 46 of Heyman, 1979. Copyright © 1979 by the Society for the Experimental Analysis of Behavior, Inc. Reproduced with permission.)

that Skinner insisted was the only scientifically valid understanding—was that the animal learned to distribute its responses in such-and-such a way. Despite Skinner's behaviorist strictures, it is now clear that there is an alternative to this conception. The behavior we see—in this case matching behavior—can be a manifestation of the knowledge that the animal has acquired, knowledge *that* something is the case. In this case, knowledge that the two rates of reward are r_0 and r_1 *elicits* inversely proportional leaving rates.

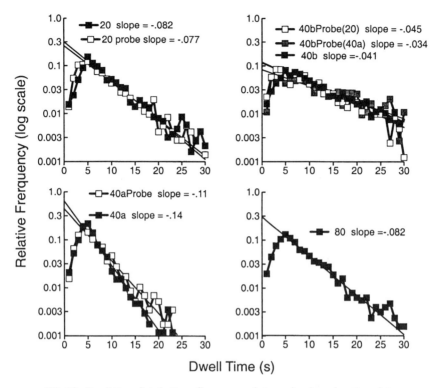

FIG. 6.3. Dwell time distributions (frequency of stays of a given duration plot-ted against duration) averaged over 6 subjects. The ordinate is logarithmic, so the linear decline seen after the changeover duration implies an exponential distribution of stay durations. The slope of the line is the leaving rate. The leav-ing rate depends on the rate of reinforcement available in the alternative schedule; hence, it is approximately four times greater when a VI 40 s schedule has been paired with a VI 20 s schedule (lower left panel) than when the same schedule has been paired with a VI 80 s schedule (upper right). Notice, also, that the leaving rate is unchanged on the probe trials, when a different alterna-tive is offered. What matters is the remembered alternative rate of reinforce-ment, not the alternative offered on the probe trial. (Fig. 4 on p. 213 of Gibbon, 1995. Reproduced by permission of the author & publisher.)

Effects of Relative and Overall Rates of Reward on Leaving Rate. Hey-man (1979) also noted an important property of the leaving rates, namely, that they summed to a constant. Myerson and Miezin (1980) showed that the same was true in the data of Baum and Rachlin (1969). They further con-jectured that the value of the constant to which the leaving rates summed would be an increasing function of the overall reinforcement rate (the sum of the two reinforcement rates). As they noted, this assumption is incorpo-rated into Killeen's (1975) model of choice in the form of an arousal factor that depends on the overall rate of reinforcement. This makes intuitive sense because the greater the sum of the leaving rates, the more rapidly the subject cycles through the options. To collect reinforcements from both options at close to the rate at which they become available, the duration of a visit cycle (the time to sample both options once) must be no longer than the average overall interval between reinforcements. This interval—the expected interval between reinforcements without regard to source—is the reciprocal of the sum of the rates of reinforcement at the different sources. On the other hand, it is a waste of effort to cycle between the options many times during one expected interreinforcement interval. Thus the time taken to cycle through the options should increase as the expected interval between reinforcements increases, and it does (see Fig. 6.4).

Effect of Relative Reward Magnitude on Leaving Rate. Although reinforcement magnitude has no effect on rate of acquisition, it has a dramatic effect on preference (see Fig. 6.5). Indeed, it has a scalar effect, that is, relative stay durations are strictly proportional to relative reward magnitudes. Catania (1963) reported matching when the relative magnitude of the reinforcements was varied rather than their relative rate. When the obtained

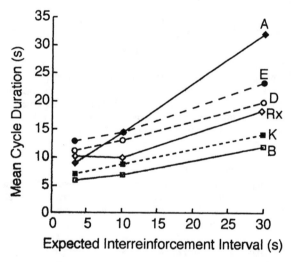

FIG. 6.4. Cycle duration as a function of the expected interval between programmed reinforcement in 6 self-stimulating rats, with concurrent and equal VI schedules of brain stimulation reinforcement. The overall rate of reinforcement changed, both between sessions and once in each 2-hour session. The expected interreinforcement interval is the reciprocal of the expected overall rate of reinforcement, which is the sum of the reciprocals of the two VIs. The cycle duration includes the changeover (travel time), which averaged several seconds and varied somewhat as a function of overall reinforcement density. (Unpublished data from Mark, 1997, doctoral thesis.)

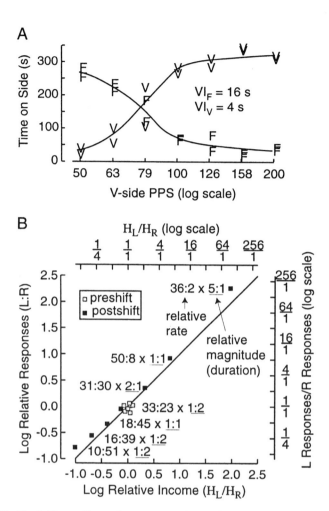

FIG. 6.5. A. Times allocated to competing levers delivering brain-stimulation rewards on concurrent VI schedules to a rat moving back and forth between them. The magnitude of the rewards delivered on the F side was fixed. The magnitude of the rewards on the V side was varied from one 10-minute trial to the next by varying the pulse frequency in the 0.5 s trains of rewarding pulses. Preference varies from a strong preference for the F side to a strong preference for the V side, depending on the magnitude of the V reward. The strength of the preference is the ratio of the two time allocations. (Reproduced with slight modifications from Leon & Gallistel, 1998.) B. Preference for the L(eft) key over the R(ight) key in a pigeon responding on concurrent VI schedules, as a function of the relative incomes. Relative income is the product of the ratio of the reward magnitudes (underlined) and the ratio of the experienced rates of reward: $H_L / H_R = (\lambda_L / \lambda_R)(M_L / M_R)$. The preshift data are from initial control sessions in which the scheduled rates of reinforcement and the reward magnitudes were both equal. (Data from Keller & Gollub, 1977.)

rates of reinforcement were approximately equal but the duration of food access per reinforcement was, for example, twice as great on one side, the subjects (pigeons) spent approximately twice as much time on the side that produced double the income. The *income* from an option is the amount of reward obtained from that option per unit of session time (time in the apparatus), not per unit of time invested in that option. This latter, amount of reinforcement per unit time invested in an option, is the *return* on the investment. The average income is the product of the average rate at which rewards are obtained and the average magnitude of a reward. Put another way, the income from an option is proportional to the rate of reinforcement of that option (reinforcements per unit of session time), with the reinforcement magnitude as the constant of proportionality (scaling factor). Expected income is the quantity that Gibbon (1977) called expectancy of reinforcement and symbolized H, which symbol we use here.

Catania's result implies that it is really relative income that matters in matching behavior, not rate or probability of reinforcement. If the same result—time-allocation ratios that match income ratios—is obtained over a wide range of relative magnitudes of reinforcement; that is, if the effect of the relative magnitude is independent of the effect of relative rate, then strong conclusions follow: (a) Subjective rate and subjective magnitude are simply proportional to objective rate and magnitude; (b) Subjective rates and subjective magnitudes combine multiplicatively to determine subjective incomes, which are the decision variables that determines how time is allocated among alternatives; and (c) The observed time-allocation ratio is equal to the ratio of the subjective incomes; that is, the ratio of the expected stay durations equals the ratio of the underlying expectancies.

Keller and Gollub (1977) varied both relative reinforcement magnitude (duration of the bird's access to the grain hopper) and relative rate of reinforcement. They found that, for some training conditions at least, the time-allocation ratio was approximately equal to the income ratio (see Fig. 6.5B; also Harper, 1982, for a similar result under group conditions). This has not been consistently replicated (e.g., Logue & Chavarro, 1987; see Davison & McCarthy, 1988, for review), although none of the failures to replicate have varied both relative reinforcement magnitude and relative reinforcement rate over a large range, so it is difficult to know how seriously to take the observed departures from matching.

Leon and Gallistel (1998) tested the extent to which the effect of varying the relative rate of reinforcement was independent of the relative magnitude of the reinforcers, varying both parameters by an order of magnitude or more. They used brain stimulation reward and varied reinforcement magnitude, M, by varying the pulse frequency in the 0.5 s trains of pulses that constituted individual reinforcements. Thus, the relative magnitude of the reinforcement was varied without varying relative duration. On one side (the F side), the reward magnitude was fixed; on the other (the V side), the reward magnitude varied from trial to trial, from a level near the threshold for performance to the saturation level (the largest possible reward producable in that subject by stimulating through that electrode).

The programmed relative rate of reward varied from 4:1 in favor of the F side to 1:4 in favor of the V side. The actually obtained rate ratio, $\lambda_v{:}\lambda_f$, varied by about 2 orders of magnitude, from about 10:1 in favor of the F side to about 1:10 in favor of the V side. Thus, the experiment tested the extent to which the ratio of times allocated to the F and V sides remained proportional to the relative obtained rate of reward in the face of large differences in the relative magnitude of reward, hence, large differences in the extent to which the animal preferred one side or the other at a given relative rate of reward.

Leon and Gallistel (1998) found that, except when one of the reward magnitudes was close to the threshold for performance, changing the relative rate of obtained reward by a given factor changed the time-allocation ratio by about the same factor. Thus, over about three orders of magnitude (from time-allocation ratios of 30:1 to 1:30), the time-allocation ratio equaled the ratio of subjective incomes (the product of the subjective magnitude of the brain stimulation reward and its subjective rate; see Fig. 6.6).

The When-to-Leave Decision. The findings just reviewed imply that allocating behavior is mediated by a stochastic decision mechanism in which the leaving rate for one option is determined by the subjective incomes from the other options. Mark and Gallistel (1994) suggested a model for the when-to-leave decision that directly incorporates these principles. The decision to leave is triggered by a Poisson process, a process formally equivalent to the process of emitting a particle in the course of radioactive decay. The leaving rate (emission rate) is assumed to be determined by the incomes from the two options in accord with two constraints. One constraint is that the ratio of the leaving rates equals the inverse ratio of the incomes. The expected stay duration, $E(d)$, is the reciprocal of the leaving rate. We formulate this constraint in terms of expected stay durations rather than leaving rates, because the symbol for the leaving rate on side i would normally be λ_i, but we have already used that symbol to represent the reinforcement rate on that side. Also, it is the stay durations that are actually measured. Formulated in terms of expected stay durations, the first constraint is

$$E(d_1)/E(d_2)=H_1/H_2 \qquad (8)$$

The other is that the sum of the leaving rates (that is, the sum of the reciprocals of the expected stay durations) be proportional to the sum of the subjective incomes:

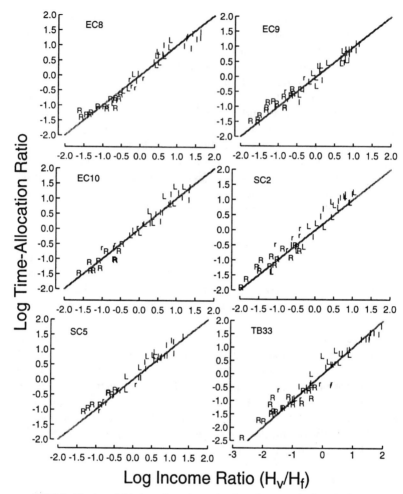

FIG. 6.6. The log of the time-allocation ratio plotted against the log of relative income for 6 rats responding for brain stimulation reward on concurrent VI schedules, with relative rate of reward, λ_v/λ_f, and relative subjective reward magnitude, M_v/M_f, varying over about two orders of magnitude (1:10 to 10:1). The different symbols identify different subconditions. The gray lines represent the identity function (slope of 1 and an intercept at the origin). Modified slightly from Leon and Gallistel (1998).

$$\left(\frac{1}{E(d_1)} + \frac{1}{E(d_2)}\right) = c(H_1 + H_2) \qquad (9)^1$$

---

[1]The formulation of this assumption in Mark and Gallistel (1994) contains a mathematical error, which is here corrected.

Whereas Mark and Gallistel (1994) built the empirically derived constraints directly into the structure of the mechanism that makes the when-to-leave decision, Gibbon (1995) suggested a psychological mechanism from which these principles may be derived. He proposed that the decision to leave is based on repetitive sampling from the population of remembered incomes or expectancies. (Each individual reward may be thought of as giving rise to a remembered income or reinforcement expectancy equal to the subjective magnitude of the reward divided by the subjective duration of the interval required to obtain it.) The subject leaves the option it is currently exploiting whenever the income sample for the other option is greater than the sample from the population for the currently exploited option. Gibbon showed that the likelihood that a sample from one exponentially distributed population of remembered incomes would be greater than a sample from another such population was equal to the ratio of the (scaled) rate parameters for the two distributions. This explains why the ratio of the leaving rates equals the inverse of the income ratio.

Gibbon further assumed that the rate at which the subject samples from the populations of remembered incomes (called its level of arousal) is proportional to the overall income (the sum of the average incomes from the two options). The higher the rate of sampling from the two populations, the sooner a sample will satisfy the leaving condition. This explains why the duration of a visit cycle (the sum of the expected stay durations, plus the travel or switching time) goes down as the overall rate of reinforcement goes up.

These models of the decision process that leads to matching explain the surprising results from a series of experiments designed initially by Williams and Royalty (1989) to test a key assumption underlying most previous models of matching, namely, that matching behavior depends on either the probability that a response will be reinforced, or on the return from an option, or both, that is, the amount of reward obtained per unit of time (or responding) invested in that option (Davis, Staddon, Machado, & Palmer, 1993; Herrnstein & Vaughan, 1980). The assumption that the relative strength of a CR depends on the relative frequency with which it is reinforced was arguably the most basic assumption in Skinner's analysis of operant behavior, and it has been taken for granted in most behaviorist theorizing about behavior. Thus, these experiments address foundational assumptions in traditional theorizing, assumptions that have often been taken to be so plausible as to be self-evidently true.

In these experiments, the subject is trained with two different pairs of concurrent variable interval (VI) options. One pair might be a red key reinforced on a VI 20 s schedule and a green key reinforced on a VI 40 s schedule. During training, the presentation of this pair alternates with the presentation of another pair consisting of a white key reinforced on a VI 40 s schedule and a blue key reinforced on a VI 80 s schedule. Once matching behavior is observed on both pairs, brief unreinforced probe trials are intermingled with the training trials. On a probe trial, the pigeon confronts one key from each pair. Its preference between these two keys is measured by its time or response-allocation ratio. In a conventional analysis of operant behavior, these probe trials test the relative strengths of the responses to the two keys presented on the probe trials.

The results from these experiments are difficult to reconcile with the assumption that operant choice depends on the probability of response reinforcement. When the key reinforced on a VI 40 s schedule is the leaner of two options, the subject makes many fewer responses on it than when it is the richer of the two options, because it spends much more of its time on the alternative in the first case than in the second. Because subjects cycle between the options so rapidly, the amount of time (hence, the number of responses) they invest in each option has little effect on the incomes realized. The return a subject realizes from an option is the income divided by the subject's investment (time and responses allocated to the option). Because the income remains almost constant while the investments varies (Heyman, 1982), the return realized from an option (and the probability that a response on that option will be reinforced) increases as the investment in it decreases.

Theories that assume that relative probability of reinforcement (relative return) is what determines choice rely on this very fact. They assume that the animal adjusts its investments until the probabilities of reinforcement (or returns) are equal, that is, they assume that the subject learns *to* equate its returns. Thus, when the leaner key from the richer pair is paired with the richer key from the leaner pair, the subject should prefer the leaner key from the richer pair, because the probability of reinforcement (the return) it has experienced on that key is much higher than the probability of reinforcement it has experienced on the richer key from the leaner pair, despite the fact that both keys have produced about the same income. In fact, however, the subject prefers the richer key from the leaner pair by a substantial margin (Belke, 1992; Gibbon, 1995). The empirical results are strongly in the opposite direction from the result predicted by the conventional assumption that the relative strength of operants depends on the relative probability of their having been reinforced in the past. These important results directly challenge the hypothesis that operant behavior depends on the probability of response reinforcement.

It might be thought that the preference for the richer key from the leaner pair is a consequence of a contrast effect, that is, the value of that key had been enhanced over and above what one would expect from its rate of reinforcement by the contrast with a poorer alternative during training. But this would not explain the surprising strength of the preference. On the probe trials, the VI 40 s key from the leaner pair is preferred 4:1 over the VI 40 s key from the richer pair (Belke, 1992; Gibbon, 1995). In contrast, it is only preferred 2:1 to the VI 80 s key with which it is paired during training. Moreover, when the richer key from the richer pair is pitted against the richer key from the leaner pair, the richer key from the leaner pair is preferred 2:1 (Gibbon, 1995), a result that is exceedingly counterintuitive. This last result seems to rule out explanations in terms of contrast.

These surprising results are a consequence of the principles embodied in the Mark and Gallistel (1994) and Gibbon (1995) models of the when-to-leave decision. Solving simultaneous Equations 8 and 9 for the leaving rates (the reciprocals of the expected stay durations), yields: $1/E(d_1) = cH_2$ and $1/E(d_2) = cH_1$. Thus, the leaving rate for a key should be proportional to the income from the other key. Or, in terms of expected stay durations, the richer the alternative, the shorter the expected stay duration. It follows that the expected stay duration for the VI 40 s key for which a VI 80 s key has been the alternative is four times longer than the expected stay duration for a VI 40 s key for which a VI 20 s alternative has been the alternative, and twice as long as the expected stay duration for a VI 20 s key for which a VI 40 s key has been the alternative (cf. slopes in Fig. 6.3, which are the empirically determined leaving rates).

Note that this explanation assumes that the decision to leave a key during a probe trial depends not on the income attributed to the key actually presented as an alternative on that trial. Rather, the decision appears to depend on the income that has generally been available elsewhere when the key the bird is now pecking was one of the options. In deciding whether to leave a key, the subject considers the income it remembers having obtained elsewhere in the past, not the income promised by the alternative presented on the probe trial.

Recall that if a subject is initially trained with concurrent VI keys presented separately, that is, not as options that can be concurrently exploited, then it shows an exclusive preference for the richer key when the keys are later presented simultaneously. That result and the results of these probe experiments imply that the decision mechanism that mediates matching is invoked only when past experience indicates that two or more options may be exploited concurrently. Moreover, only the options that have been exploited concurrently affect the leaving rate for a given option. Options that have not been exploited at the same time as the option currently chosen, but which are now present, do not enter into the decision to leave the currently chosen option in order to sample another option.

How the Allocating Mechanism Produces Exclusive Preference

An option that is never tried produces no income. Thus, the subjective income from an option must depend on the extent to which the subject tries that option, at least in the limit. As we have already noted, the empirically observed sampling rates for concurrent VI options are such that large variations in the pattern and amount of sampling have little effect on the incomes realized from the options (Heyman, 1982). This is not true, however, with many other scheduling algorithms. For example, when reinforcements are scheduled by concurrent ratio schedules, which deliver reinforcement after numbers of responses that are approximately exponentially distributed about some mean value, then any response-allocation ratio less than an exclusive preference for the richer schedule results in an income ratio greater than the response-allocation ratio. The response-allocation ratio equals the income ratio only in the limit when all of the responses are allotted to the richer option and, hence, all of the income is obtained from that option (Herrnstein & Loveland, 1975). Thus, the exclusive preference for the richer schedule, which is observed with concurrent variable ratio schedules of reinforcement, does not imply that this behavior is controlled by the opting mechanism rather than the allocating mechanism.

In the model that we propose for the understanding of matching behavior, the animal's tendency to allocate its investments in proportion to the incomes realized from its options is not conditioned in the usual operant sense by the previous consequences of such behavior, but that does not mean that the observed allocation ratio is independent of the consequences of past allocations, because past allocations may determine the experienced incomes from those options. The allocation ratio observed at asymptote is a consequence of the dynamics of the experimental system consisting of the reward-scheduling algorithm, the animal's reaction to the initial sequence of interreward intervals generated by that algorithm and the effect that reaction has on the subsequently experienced sequence. The dynamics depend on both the function that relates experienced incomes to allocation behavior, which is determined by the structure of the when-to-leave decision mechanism, and the feedback function, which relates allocation behavior to experienced incomes (Baum, 1981, 1992; Myerson & Miezin, 1980). The feedback function is determined by the scheduling algorithm. Our model predicts that whenever the income ratio is greater than the response-allocation ratio, the response-allocation ratio will shift in favor of the richer alternative. Under conditions where the income ratio remains greater than the response-allocation ratio except in the limit, where all responses are allotted to the richer alternative, our model of the allocating mechanism predicts that concurrent variable ratio schedules must eventuate in exclusive preference for the richer schedule.

The subtle role of the feedback effect in determining the asymptotic behavior produced by the allocating mechanism is evident, we suggest, in the different results obtained from correction and noncorrection methods in discrete trials probability learning paradigms. In these paradigms, a choice of one option (usually one arm in a T maze) is reinforced with one probability, while the choice of the other is reinforced with the complementary probability. When a correction procedure is used, which allows the animal to visit the other side if the side first visited does not pay off, the animal observes the true (undistorted) relation between the interreinforcement intervals on the two sides of the T maze. There is no feedback from its sampling behavior onto the experienced interreinforcement intervals. This results in a preference for the higher probability side that is equal to the percentage of trials on which the reinforcement is located there (Bitterman, 1965; Brunswik, 1939; Estes, 1964). (The measure of preference is the relative percentage of trials on which a side is visited first.) But when a noncorrection procedure is used, which terminates a trial after the animal has chosen one side, an unusually long sequence of visits to the richer side results in a proportional lengthening of the experienced interreinforcement interval on the leaner side. This destabilizing positive feedback leads eventually to exclusive preference for the side that is reinforced with higher probability (Fischer, 1972; Mackintosh, 1974).

HYPERBOLIC DISCOUNTING AND SELF-CONTROL

The principle that the decision variables on which choices are based are subjective incomes—reward magnitudes divided by interreward intervals— is equivalent to the hyperbolic discounting principle, which has often been used to describe the effect of delaying reinforcement on the subjective value of the reinforcement (Fantino, 1969; Killeen, 1982; Mazur, 1984, 1986; McDiarmid & Rilling, 1965). In Mazur's (1984) formulation

$$V = \frac{A}{1 + kD},$$ (10)

where V is the value, A is amount (magnitude), and D is the delay. Equation 10 is a necessary modification of the income formula when it is applied to very short delays. Without the 1 in the denominator the income produced by a given amount of food would go to infinity as the delay went to zero. Clearly, as the delay becomes negligible, the income ought to become asymptotically equal to the subjective magnitude of the food. This is accomplished by adding the one to the denominator. Psychologically, this may be thought of as taking into account that below some value, differences in the objective delay are psychologically negligible. Put another way, delays are scaled relative to the delay that is perceived as immediate, that is, as lasting no longer than a single unit of subjective time. The irreducible unit of time may be thought of as the latency to begin timing a delay (see Gibbon et al., 1984). If the reinforcement is delivered in less than this latency, then there is no effect of delay.

The income or expectancy principle predicts subjects' irrational preference for immediate, but small reinforcement over delayed, but larger reinforcement. When repeatedly offered such a choice, subjects repeatedly choose the immediate small reinforcement, even though doing so reduces their net return from the experimental session. This seemingly irrational preference has been termed a lack of self-control brought on by the prospect of immediate reinforcement (Rachlin, 1974, 1995). If a common delay is inserted between the choice and the outcomes while retaining the initial small difference in delays, then, as the common delay is made longer, there comes a point at which subjects prefer the bigger outcome, despite the fact that it is delayed (slightly) longer. Because this result—the choice of the outcome that increases net return (from the session)—is what economists believe that animals (including humans) ought to do if they were rational, this result could be characterized as showing that delaying outcomes increases self-control (Rachlin, 1974). However, both results—the irrational (nonnormative) preference for an immediate, smaller outcome, over a delayed but bigger outcome and the move toward rational (normative) preference when a common delay is inserted in front of both outcomes—are a consequence of the fact that animal's choose on the basis of the expected incomes from the alternatives, *calculated only for periods when the alternatives are actually available.* Time outs, intertrial intervals, et cetera—the periods when no alternative is available—are sunk time so far as the decision mechanism is concerned (Bateson & Kacelnik, 1996) as are periods when the discriminative stimulus specifically associated with reinforcement is absent (Mazur, 1991).

The economist uses session time in calculating the return to be realized from choosing one or the other option, but animal subjects appear to use only the time when the options are available to them. We call this important principle the *principle of subjectively sunk time.* Subjectively sunk time is treated like a sunk cost in rational decision making, a cost that should not be taken into account in deciding the relative value of two options because it has already been incurred or is otherwise inescapable no matter what the choice. Subjectively sunk time is composed of all the intervals when reinforcements are not actually pending (for example, intertrial intervals). Generally, the subject has no control over these intervals: They will be experienced no matter what it chooses to do, which is why it treats them as sunk time.

Thus, the basic results in the self-control literature follow from two principles: (a) The decision variables in choice situations, are incomes (Gibbon's, 1977, expectancies), reward magnitudes divided by the intervals between rewards (Mazur, 1997), and (b) Intervals when no option is present do not figure in the computation of subjective income (cf. Mazur, 1991). If the delay to obtain a smaller reward is shorter by some fixed amount than the delay to obtain a larger reward, then the subjective income from the smaller-but-shorter option must exceed the subjective income from the bigger-but-longer option as the two delays are decreased by the same additive factor, because the delay for the shorter option approaches zero first, and, at zero delay, subjective income becomes asymptotically large. As both delays are increased by the same additive amount, the subjective income from the bigger-but-longer option must become the greater of the two subjective incomes, because, in the limit, the fixed difference in the delays becomes negligible.

HARMONIC AVERAGING AND THE PREFERENCE FOR VARIABILITY

What if a given option sometimes produces one income and sometimes another, how does the animal average these income data to obtain an expected income? Does it compute the expected income in the normative way by summing the amounts of reinforcement to get the total amount of reinforcement and summing the delays to get the total time it has had to wait, then dividing total reinforcement by the total time waiting time? Or, does it divide each amount of reinforcement by the delay to obtain it, thereby obtaining an income datum for each reinforcement, then average these income data? If subjects do the latter, then a subjective expectation computed from a series of variable reward delays will be the harmonic mean of those delays, which is what you get if you convert delays to rates, average the rates, and then convert the average rate back into an expected delay.

The harmonic mean is always less than the arithmetic mean, except in the limiting case where the values being averaged are all the same, because in taking the reciprocals before averaging, more weight is given to short intervals than to long intervals. Thus, harmonic averaging inflates expected income. The objective expected income is the ratio of the expectations, that is, average amount divided by average delay. But subjects base their choice behavior on the expectation of the ratio, that is, on the average income.

The most often replicated result supporting this conclusion is the robust preference that subjects show for a reward given at variable delays over a reward delivered always at a delay equal to the arithmetic mean of the variable delays (Autor, 1969; Davison, 1969; Fantino, 1969; Herrnstein, 1964; Mazur, 1984; Pubols, 1962). Harmonic averaging predicts that in order for a reward given at a fixed delay to have the same value as rewards given after variable delay, the fixed delay must be made equal to the harmonic mean of the variable delays. This appears to be at least approximately true (Bateson

& Kacelnik, 1995; Gibbon, Church, Fairhurst, & Kacelnik, 1988; Killeen, 1968; Mazur, 1984).

Recently, harmonic averaging has been demonstrated in experiments that pit (as one option) two equally probable incomes, one from a short and one from a long delay, against a single income (the other option). In the titration version of this experiment the single income is adjusted to find the point at which it equals the average of the two other incomes (Bateson & Kacelnik, 1996). Whether the single income is adjusted by manipulating its delay or the amount of the reward, the results are the same: The single income at the point of subjective equality is equal to the average of the two incomes (the expected ratio), *not* to the expected income from the two-income option (the ratio of the expectancies). These experiments also show once again that only the interval between choice and reinforcement is used in computing the income from an option; the intertrial interval, the latency to choose, and the feeding time are irrelevant (the principle of subjectively sunk time).

In the time-left version of the two-against-one experiment, two equally probable fixed delays are pitted against a delay whose value gets smaller as a trial progresses. This latter option is called the time-left option. At the start of a trial, both options are presented to the subject. It is free to switch back and forth between them up to the unpredictable moment of commitment. Scheduled commitment times (effective choice points) vary unpredictably from trial to trial. When the commitment time scheduled for a given trial arrives, the option (key) that the subject is not currently exploiting (pecking) goes blank and is no longer operative. The subject must stick with the key it was on at that moment until it collects the reinforcement. Thus, during the period before the moment of commitment, when both options are still available, a rational subject should be on the key that has the greater expected income at that moment.

The delay to reinforcement on the time-left key is some initially long value minus the time that has elapsed since the trial began, so the expected income from that key grows as the trial goes on. In contrast, the delay (or delays) on the standard key are fixed; although initially shorter than the time-left key, they do not get shorter as the trial progresses. What pigeons do in this paradigm is to begin pecking on the standard key, then switch to the time-left key when they judge that the time left is less than the standard delay—or less than the expectation of the standard delays in cases where there is more than one standard delay.

When there is only one possible delay on the standard key, pigeons judge reasonably accurately when the time left has become shorter than the standard delay. That is, the midpoint in their cumulative changeover distribution occurs approximately at the interval at which the time left is in fact shorter than the standard (Gibbon & Church, 1981; Gibbon et al., 1988).

Put another way, the likelihood of the subject's having switched to the time-left option grows with the elapsed trial duration such that it crosses the 50% level at about the standard delay. Moreover, the scalar variability assumption in Scalar Expectancy Theory accurately predicts the form of the cumulative changeover function. Because of the scalar increase in the standard deviation of the memory sampling distribution assumed in Scalar Expectancy Theory, the slope of the sigmoidal cumulative changeover function should get shallower as the standard interval gets longer, as, in fact, it does (Gibbon & Church, 1981; Gibbon et al., 1988).

Subjects switch to the time-left option when they judge the time left to be shorter than the expected delay on the standard key. Thus, when the standard option yields one of two equally probable delays, the changeover point gives the subjective expectation of those two delays. The experimentally observed changeover point is the harmonic mean of the two standard delays. Moreover, the form of the function is the same as the function for a single delay at the harmonic mean of the two delays (see Fig. 6.7).

If the relative amounts of food associated with each delay are varied, then the cumulative changeover function varies more or less as predicted from the assumption that the subject averages the two incomes (i.e., weights the reciprocal of each delay by the amount of reward received at that delay) and switches to the time-left key when the expected income on

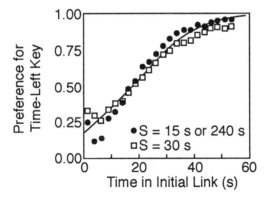

FIG. 6.7. Cumulative switch over functions—probability of having switched to the time-left key as a function of the time since the options were presented—obtained with double standard (equally probable delays of 15 or 240 s—square symbols) and with a single standard equal to the harmonic mean of the two delays in the double standard condition (30 s—circle symbols). If the subject correctly computed the expectation of the two equiprobable delays of 15 and 240 s (= 127.5 s), it would prefer the time-left side even at the outset of the trial, when the delay of reward for that choice is 60 seconds. The curve through the data is the prediction of the SET model for the case in which the standard delay is 30 s. (Redrawn from data originally published by Brunner, Gibbon, & Fairhurst, 1994, Figure 2 on p. 333.)

that key (the amount of reward on that key divided by the time left) is greater than the average of the standard incomes (Brunner, Gibbon, & Fairhurst, 1994).

An important aspect of these results is that the subjects demonstrably remember the two different reward latencies on the standard side. That they remember the two intervals is shown by their response rates to the standard key *after* the moment of commitment, on those trials in which they end up committed to that key. Their rate of responding on the standard key after the moment of commitment rises to a peak at the latency of the shorter of the two possible delays. If reinforcement is not delivered at that delay, responding subsides, then rises again in anticipation of the longer delay. The latencies at which responding peaks are not affected by the amount of reinforcement, whereas the computation of central tendency is.

Together, these results imply that the subjects remember separately each latency, each reinforcement magnitude, and which magnitude goes with which latency, and that they compute a central tendency from the combination of these separately remembered attributes of their past experience.

Perhaps the most surprising use of harmonic averaging occurs when there is more than one food delivery per choice of a given option, each delivery at a different delay. One might expect that the subjective income from that one choice would be the total amount of food obtained divided by the time to collect it. In fact, however, the income from a multiple-reward outcome appears to be computed by treating each reward (each food delivery) as if it were a separate outcome, dividing the amount of that reward by the delay to receive it, and averaging the different incomes thus computed. This is called parallel discounting, because the rewards are treated as if they were delivered by reinforcement schedules operating in parallel with different delays, with the income from each schedule computed separately. Using rats as subjects, Brunner and Gibbon (1995) titrated a single income—five pellets delivered one immediately after the other, beginning an adjustable delay after the choice—against an alternative in which there were appreciable intervals between the delivery of successive pellets. To do this, they varied the delay between the choice and the delivery of the first of the five spaced pellets. The delay at the point of subjective equality varied with the interval between successive pellets in the alternative in a manner best predicted by the parallel hyperbolic discounting model, thus confirming the conclusion reached in previous experiments with multiple rewards per choice (McDiarmid & Rilling, 1965; Schull, Mellon, & Sharp, 1990).

The use of harmonic averaging (the expected ratio) in the computation of the values of options raises two sorts of questions. First, what triggers this kind of averaging? Is it employed only by the opting decision mechanism? Or is it employed by both the allocating and the opting mechanisms? Second, what is the ultimate cause of this way of computing the central tendency? From an evolutionary perspective, what selection pressures have selected for a computation of subjective value that, on the face of it, is not optimal (cf. Bateson & Kacelnik, 1996)? It may well be the case that this way of computing the expected value of an option is a secondary consequence of some other adaptation. But, in that case, what other adaptation?

One answer does not seem likely, namely, that animals are incapable of arithmetic averaging. In acquisition, they appear to use arithmetic averaging, not harmonic averaging. That is, in comparing the rate of CS reinforcement to the rate of background reinforcement, rats and pigeons appear to compute rate by dividing the expected amount of reward by the expected interval between rewards (see chap. 2 on acquisition). If subjects used harmonic averaging in computing the rate of CS reinforcement during acquisition, the rate of acquisition (number of reinforcements to acquisition) at a given $I{:}T$ ratio would be faster with partial reinforcement than with continuous reinforcement, because, from a timing perspective, partial reinforcement produces a variable delay of reinforcement. However, the rate of acquisition is unaffected by partial reinforcement (for review of relevant literature, see Gibbon & Balsam, 1981).

If variable CS durations were harmonically averaged in acquisition, then a variable delay of reinforcement should produce faster acquisition than the usual fixed delay, when the expected delay of reinforcement is the same in the two conditions. In an unpublished experiment, we compared the rates of acquisition for two groups of pigeons, each presented with a single CS, with a fixed 96 second intertrial interval between presentations. Each presentation of the CS was reinforced by 4 seconds access to grain. For one group, the duration of the CS was fixed at 21 s. For the other, the duration was geometric approximation to an exponential distribution with an expectation of 21 seconds. The harmonic average of these variable durations was only 5.9 seconds. If these durations were harmonically averaged by the acquisition process, then the ratio between the expected duration of an intertrial interval and the expected duration of a CS would be much greater for the variable duration group than for the fixed duration group, which should lead to faster acquisition in the former. In fact, however, the group given the variable duration CS acquired if anything more slowly than the group given the fixed duration CS (see Fig. 6.8).

In a further test of the hypothesis that CS durations are harmonically averaged by the acquisition process, we ran two groups of birds, each of which saw two different CSs (a red key and a key with an X pattern), in a randomly intermixed sequence, with a 48 second intertrial interval between successive CS presentations. In one group, one of these CSs had a fixed duration of 21 s, while the other had a distribution that was a geometric approximation to the exponential distribution with an expectation of 21 s. In a comparison group, the durations of both CSs were fixed at 21 s. Again, the

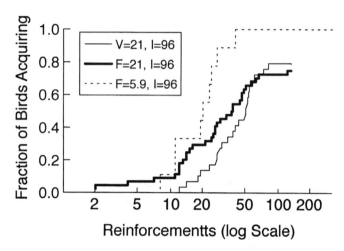

FIG. 6.8. Cumulative fraction of subjects acquiring a conditioned response to the CS as a function of the cumulative number of reinforcements of that CS. For the function labeled $V = 21$, $I = 96$, the durations of the CS varied geometrically with an expectation of 21 s and there was on average 96 seconds of exposure to the background alone between presentations of that CS. For the function labeled $F = 21$, $I = 96$, the duration of CS presentation was fixed at 21 seconds. For the function labeled $F = 5.9$, $I = 96$, CS duration was 5.9 seconds. (Data from an unpublished experiment by Aronson, Fairhurst, Gallistel, and Gibbon.)

acquisition of responding to the variable duration CS was if anything slower than the acquisition of responding to the fixed duration CSs. Rates of acquisition to a CS of fixed duration were comparable whether it was the only CS or one of two CSs, and likewise for a variable duration CS. Therefore, the data from the two different tests of the hypothesis are combined in Fig. 6.8. Note that the cumulative distribution for variable duration CSs lies to the right of the cumulative distribution for the fixed duration CSs. For comparison, we include the distribution for a group that had a fixed duration CS of 5.9, with 96 seconds of exposure to the background alone between each CS presentation (the same amount as in all other groups). As expected, the distribution for this group, with a more favorable I/T ratio, lies to the left.

In sum, it appears that animal subjects can and do compute the ratio of the expectancies. However, in many choice situations, the decision variable is the expectancy of the ratio.

THE EQUIVALENCE OF DELAYED REWARDS
AND PROBABILISTIC REWARDS

From a timing perspective, it does not matter whether one is pitting a variable delay against a fixed delay of reinforcement or a probabilistic reinforcement against a certain reinforcement (delivered at a fixed delay). Introducing probabilistic reinforcement, in which each occurrence of a given option, that is, a given discriminative stimulus, is reinforced with some probability less than 1, is, from a timing perspective, another way of introducing an approximately exponential distribution of interreinforcement intervals. That is, it is another way of creating a VI schedule of reinforcement.

In timing theory, *probability* of reinforcement plays no direct role. Put another way, it is not a subjectively meaningful variable. Timing theory assumes that the brain processes probabilistic reinforcement schedules as if the relevant variable was the rate of reinforcement, not its probability. Thus, timing theory predicts that the hyperbolic equation that predicts the results of experiments titrating a fixed-delay option against a VI option will also predict the results of experiments that titrate a fixed-delay option against a probabilistically reinforced option, and this is, indeed, the case (Mazur, 1989; Rachlin, Logue, Gibbon, & Frankel, 1986; Rachlin, Raineri, & Cross, 1991). One attraction of the conceptual framework offered by timing theory is that it unifies the treatment of probability of reinforcement and delay of reinforcement. In a timing framework, both manipulations vary the interreward interval. From a more traditional perspective, they affect different parameters of the associative process, so there is no basis for expecting the results of both manipulations to be quantitatively the same.

Risk Proneness and Risk Aversion

Under opting conditions, partial preference is the result of discrimination failure (sampling error). Reboreda and Kacelnik (1991; see also Kacelnik & Brito e Abreu, 1998) have shown that when partial preference is determined by sampling errors, then scalar memory noise predicts, at least qualitatively, the "irrational" preferences that humans and animals have when confronted with a choice between a certain outcome, on the one hand, and a risky (variable) outcome on the other. When outcomes are negative (aversive), then humans and animals are risk prone: They prefer a risky alternative to a certain one with the same expectation. In contrast, when outcomes are positive (desirable), human and animal subjects are risk averse: they prefer the certain outcome to a risky outcome of the same expectation (see Fig. 6.9A; see Bateson & Kacelnik, 1998 for recent review of the experimental evidence).

The vertical gray bar in Fig. 6.9B gives the discrete probability distribution for an illustrative fixed outcome. The probability of an outcome of the certain (i.e., fixed) magnitude is 1; all other magnitudes have 0 probability. The two vertical black bars show the distribution for an illustrative risky outcome with the same expectation. On any one trial, the subject gets either 50% less or 50% more from a risky choice than it gets from the certain choice. Thus, in the course of repeated trials the subject gets on average

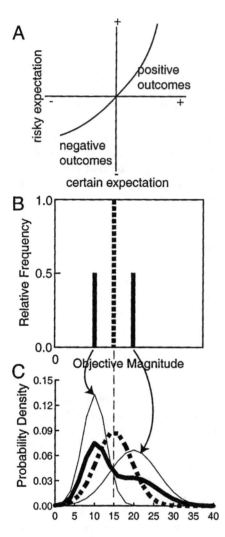

FIG. 6.9. A. Illustrative equipreference function for choices between a risky (variable) outcome and a certain outcome: The expectation of the variable outcome is plotted against the expectation of the fixed outcome to which it is equiprefered. When more is better, subjects tend to prefer a certain outcome over a variable outcome of equal expectation. Thus, to achieve equipreference, the expectation of the risky outcome must be made bigger than the expectation of the certain outcome. When less is better, the risky outcome is preferred to the certain outcome with the same expectation. To achieve equipreference, the expectation of the certain outcome must be bigger (more aversive) than the risky expectation. B. Discrete probability distributions for the magnitude of a certain outcome (dashed bar) and for the magnitudes that compose a risky outcome (solid bars). C. The distributions in memory. The thick dashed curve is for the fixed outcome. The thick solid curve is for the risky outcome. It is the mixture of the two distributions shown by the thin solid curves. Note that the bulk of the mixture distribution lies to the left of the distribution for the fixed outcome, despite the fact that the two distributions have the same expectation.

the same magnitude from the risky choice as from the certain choice. The subject is risk prone if it prefers the risky choice and risk averse if it prefers the certain choice.

In memory, the discrete probability distributions in panel B become probability density distributions, with standard deviations proportional to their means (see Fig. 6.9C). The vertical dashed line from panel B to panel C of Fig. 6.9 indicates the mean (and mode and median) of the distribution for the fixed outcome, which is the bell-shaped thick dashed curve on panel C of Fig. 6.9. The distributions for the two different possible outcomes of the risky choice are the bell-shaped thin solid curves in Fig. 6.9C. Look first at the broader of these two distributions. Note that a substantial fraction of it lies to the left of the dashed line. Now look at the narrower of these two distributions and note that a smaller fraction of it lies to the right of this same line. Thus, the bulk of the *mixture* or *combined* distribution for the risky choice (bumpy heavy curve in Fig. 6.9C) lies to the left of the midpoint of the fixed distribution. As was first pointed our by Gibbon (1977), who analyzed the case of a choice between variable delays and fixed delays, scalar noise in memory has the following consequences for a subject's preference between a certain and a risky option: If smaller is better (e.g., a smaller delay), then the variable (risky) choice will be preferred to the certain choice of equal expectation, because a sample from the distribution represented by the bumpy curve in Fig. 6.9C has a greater than 50% probability of being smaller than a sample from the distribution represented by the bell-shaped dashed curve. For the same reason, however, when bigger is better (e.g., amounts of food), then the certain outcome will be preferred to the risky outcome of equal expectation. Thus, when scalar variability in the decision variables is assumed, sampling error all by itself predicts the irrational patterns of partial preference that are commonly observed in both animal and human subjects.

Risk proneness when the outcomes are aversive and risk aversion when they are desirable are often seen as the consequences of a strategy of some kind (McNamara & Houston, 1992) or of nonlinear utility functions (Kahneman & Tversky, 1979). In the Reboreda and Kacelnik (1991) analysis, they are neither. They are a byproduct of scalar noise in the memory variables on which the choice decision is based (remembered magnitudes, remembered delays, etc.).

It remains to be seen whether this explanation can give quantitatively correct explanations. Kacelnik and Brito e Abreu (1998) showed that a model based on this idea correctly predicted the magnitude of risk aversion when starlings choose between fixed and variable amounts of food, but it did not predict the more extreme risk proneness when the same subjects choose between fixed and variable delays (Bateson & Kacelnik, 1995). In the latter case, the preference may reflect a nonnormative computation of expectations (see section above on harmonic averaging). However, this latter explanation does not have the advantage that a single, empirically very well founded assumption—scalar noise in the decision variables—explains both risk aversion and risk proneness. That is the attraction of this analysis by Kacelnik and his collaborators.

TIME-SCALE INVARIANCE IN FREE OPERANT AVOIDANCE

Our central empirical claim about conditioned behavior—and the claim most pertinent to any inquiry into its neurobiological basis—is that the behavior itself and the underlying processes that mediate it are time-scale invariant. Conditioned behavior depends on the relative durations of experienced intervals, not their absolute duration. We insist on this as a quantitative fact of the first importance. It appears to be true for Pavlovian conditioning with both rewarding and aversive USs. It appears to be equally true for instrumental or operant conditioning, again with both rewarding and punishing reinforcements. One of the earliest published demonstrations of time-scale invariance in conditioned behavior was Gibbon's (1972) analysis of Sidman's (1953) data on the effects of intershock interval and programmed delay on "Sidman avoidance" in the rat.

In the Sidman avoidance paradigm, the rat presses a lever because each press produces a safe interval (the delay, d) within which no shock will occur. However, at the end of this safe interval, shock does occur unless the subject presses again. Thus, there is a penalty for stopping, in that a shock will occur at delay d after the last response, whether a baseline shock was scheduled at that time or not. In the absence of responding, shocks continually recur at intervals of s seconds. Sidman (1953) manipulated s and d. Not cognizant of the importance of relative as opposed to absolute duration, he reported the effects of the durations of these two critical parameters on the frequency of avoidance responses. Gibbon (1972) reanalyzed his data in terms of their relative duration and the relative frequency of responding. In Fig. 6.10, which is reproduced from Gibbon (1972), we plot, for one of Sidman's subjects, the mean interresponse interval (filled symbols) and the resulting mean intershock interval (open symbols), normalized to s in both cases, as a function of the ratio between the baseline intershock interval (s) and the delay (d) produced by a response.

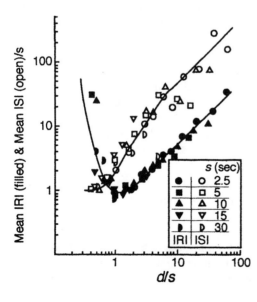

FIG. 6.10. The mean interresponse interval (IRI—filled symbols) and the mean intershock interval (ISI—open symbols) in Sidman avoidance responding are here expressed as proportions of the baseline intershock interval (s) and plotted against the ratio between the delay (d) of shock procured by a lever press and the baseline intershock interval (s), that is, the interval between shocks in the absence of lever pressing. The data are from Rat 46 in Sidman (1953). The curves are the predictions of Scalar Expectancy Theory. This plot of the data is redrawn from Gibbon (1972; Fig. 3, p. 74) by permission of the American Psychological Association.

The range for baseline intershock intervals in Fig. 6.10 covers more than an order of magnitude, from 2.5 to 30 s; the range for delays is even greater. What is obvious in Fig. 6.10, however, is that neither interval is in and of itself important, because the symbols from conditions with very different baseline intershock intervals are tightly intermixed wherever the ratios of the delays to the baseline intervals are the same. What is important is the ratio of the delay to the baseline interval—how big the safe interval is relative to the baseline interval. So long as the shock-free interval procured by a response is at least twice or three times the baseline intershock interval, the subject presses the lever. If the shock-free interval is long relative to the baseline interval—if the $d{:}s$ ratio is high—then the interval between lever presses is also relatively long (solid symbols in Fig. 6.10), that is, it is long relative to the baseline intershock interval. This nicely calibrated and successful avoidance behavior results in experienced intershock intervals that are also relatively long (open symbols). The relative interresponse interval is directly proportional to the relative length of the safety interval from $d{:}s$ ratios as low as 2 up to $d{:}s$ ratios at least as high as 100, and so is the relative reduction in experienced intershock intervals (the factor by which the experienced interval is less than the baseline intervals). Thus, the greater the safe interval, the longer the rat waits before making another response.

Of course, when both the baseline intershock interval and the delay are short, the interresponse intervals are also short, that is, the absolute frequency of responding is high. And when both intervals are long, the absolute frequency of responding is low. A traditional analysis, which conceives of the process in terms of learning *to* respond, would conclude that the CR was strong in the first case and weak in the second. Figure 6.10 makes it clear that this analysis misses a fundamental invariance. In both cases, the animal is measuring the intervals between its responses so as to achieve the same relative reduction in the rate of experienced shock. Thus, it is not a matter of learning *to* respond rapidly or slowly; much less is it a matter of the CR being stronger in one case than in the other. It is a matter of the rat learning *that* the postresponse no-shock interval is longer than the baseline interval by some factor. This knowledge elicits the behavior that we see, just as knowledge of the delay of reinforcement elicits the behavior that we see in a Pavlovian paradigm.

SUMMARY

A coherent quantitative theory of operant choice can be erected on the same foundations as the theory of Pavlovian conditioning. In both cases, probability of reinforcement (whether response reinforcement or stimulus reinforcement) is irrelevant. The behaviorally important variable is the interval between reinforcements in the presence of the conditioned stimulus (the CS, in Pavlovian terminology, or the secondary reinforcer, in operant terminology). The behaviorally important effect of the relevant variable is not the strengthening of associations, or of response tendencies. Rather, experienced intervals are stored in memory, and read from memory when they are needed in the computations that yield decision variables. In operant conditioning as in Pavlovian conditioning, subjects learn *that* certain things are true in their environment and this knowledge elicits the "conditioned" behavior. In other words, it is not the behavior itself that has been conditioned; it is not a matter of learning *to* do something. Rather the effect of experience on behavior is mediated by the creation in the head of the animal of knowledge about the world.

Distinct decision mechanisms mediate distinct kinds of decisions. In Pavlovian conditioning, there are distinct mechanisms for deciding whether to respond, when to respond, and whether to quit responding. In operant choice, there are distinct mechanisms for deciding which of two mutually exclusive options to choose (opting behavior) and for allocating behavior among concurrently exploitable options.

The decision variables in operant choice are subjective incomes (reinforcement expectancies), which are subjective reward magnitudes divided by the subjective interval between rewards. Under concurrent conditions, where both options are continuously present, the time used in computing the income from an option is session time (more precisely, the time when both options are present), not the time specifically devoted to (invested in) an option. In discrete-choice paradigms, where the options are only intermittently available and the choice of one option more or less immediately precludes the choice of the other, the intervals used to compute subjective incomes are the delays between a choice and the delivery of the reward.

Because amount of reward divided by delay of reward goes to infinity as the subjective interval goes to zero, there is a lower bound on subjective intervals. This lower bound—the subjective instant—establishes a scaling constant for subjective time. This leads to the hyperbolic relation between the amount by which a reward is delayed and its subjective value. In other words, subjective value is basically determined by rate of reinforcement, but there is no such thing as an infinite rate of reinforcement because there is an irreducible amount of subjective time, within which delay does not matter. This may be thought of as the amount of time that it takes the subject to begin timing the delay (that is, T_0 in the scalar timing model of Gibbon, Church, & Meck, 1984).

At least two distinct decision mechanisms may be observed in operant choice experiments. One, which we have called the opting mechanism, is the same as the decision mechanism in the analysis of forced-choice data in signal detection theory. It attempts always to choose the option with the greater expectancy. It fails to produce exclusive preference for the subjectively better option only insofar as the memory-sampling distributions for the expectancies (incomes) from the two options overlap. Thus, it is all-or-nothing in principle, but noise-limited in practice. The other decision mechanism allocates behavior among simultaneously available options in such a way as to maximize overall return (under some, but not all possible conditions). This decision mechanism is a first order Markov process; it emits a leaving decision at a rate that is determined by the remembered income(s) for options other than the one that is currently being sampled. Alternatively, it repeatedly samples from the distributions of incomes in memory and leaves the current option whenever the sample for the alternative option is better than the sample for the current option.

In discrete-choice paradigms where the subjects must compute the value of an option that involves more than one delay of reinforcement, they average the income value of each reinforcement. The reinforcement expectancy in these cases is the expected ratio of individual reward magnitudes and their delays rather than the ratio of the expectations. The rationale for this kind of averaging and the conditions that trigger it remain to be elucidated.

Scalar variability in memory predicts risk proneness for choices ranged on an aversive dimension where smaller is better, and risk aversion for choices ranged on an appetitive dimension where bigger is better.

Finally, time-scale invariance appears to be just as salient a property of instrumentally conditioned behavior as it is of classically conditioned behavior.

7

The Challenge for Associative Theory

In the preceding chapters, we have presented timing models that place our understanding of Pavlovian and operant conditioning in a new conceptual framework. The new framework emphasizes the symbolic content of conditioning, the knowledge of intervals and rates gained from the conditioning experience and the diverse decision mechanisms that translate that knowledge into observed behavior. New conceptual frameworks bring facts into prominence that were not featured in the previous framework, often because they fit awkwardly into that framework. In this chapter, we consider the challenge posed to associative theories of conditioning by the facts and issues brought into prominence by the timing framework. Before turning to these challenges, however, we review the fundamental differences between the two frameworks.

DIFFERENT ANSWERS TO BASIC QUESTIONS

That the two conceptual frameworks are fundamentally different is apparent from a consideration of the contrasting answers they offer to the basic questions addressed by the material taught in an introductory course on learning:

- *Why does the conditioned response (CR) appear during conditioning?*
  Standard answer: Because the associative connection gets stronger.
  Timing answer: Because the decision ratio for the *whether-to-respond* decision grows until it exceeds a decision threshold.

- *Why does the CR disappear during extinction?*

  Standard answer: Because there is a loss of net excitatory associative strength. This loss occurs either because the excitatory association itself has been weakened or because a countervailing inhibitory association has been strengthened.

  Timing answer: Because the decision ratio for the *whether-to-stop* decision grows until it exceeds the decision threshold.

- *What is the effect of reinforcement?*

  Standard answer: It strengthens excitatory associations.

  Timing answer: It marks the beginning or the termination of one or more intervals—an interreinforcement interval, a CS–US interval, or both.

- *What is the effect of delay of reinforcement?*

  Standard answer: It reduces the increment in associative strength produced by a reinforcement.

  Timing answer: It lengthens the remembered interreinforcement interval, the remembered CS–US interval, or both.

- *What is the effect of nonreinforcement?*

  Standard answer: The nonreinforcement (the No-US) weakens the excitatory association; or, it strengthens an inhibitory association.

  Timing answer: The timer for the most recent interreinforcement interval continues to accumulate.

- *What happens when nothing happens (during the intertrial interval)?*

  Standard answer: Nothing.

  Timing answer: The timer for the background continues to accumulate.

- *What is the effect of CS onset?*

  Standard answer: It opens the associative window in the mechanism that responds to the temporal pairing of two signals. That is, it begins a trial during which the updating of associative strengths will occur.

  Timing answer: It starts a timer (to time the duration of this presentation) and it causes the cumulative exposure timers to resume cumulating.

- *What is the effect of varying the magnitude of reinforcement?*

  Standard answer: It varies the size of the increment in the excitatory association, so it should increase the rate of conditioning.

  Timing answer: It varies the remembered magnitude of reinforcement, which should have no effect on rate of conditioning so long as the (explicit or implicit) magnitudes of background reinforcers are the same as the magnitudes of CS reinforcers.

- *Why is the latency of the CR proportional to the latency of reinforcement?*

  Standard answer: There is no widely accepted answer to this question in associative theory.

  Timing answer: Because the animal remembers the reinforcement latency and compares a currently elapsing interval to that remembered interval.

- *What happens when more than one CS is present during reinforcement?*

  Standard answer: The CSs compete for a share of a limited increment in associative strength; or, selective attention to one CS denies other CSs access to the associative mechanism (CS processing deficits); or, predicted USs lose the power to reinforce (US processing deficits).

  Timing answer: The rate of reinforcement is partitioned among reinforced CSs in accord with the additivity and predictor-minimization constraints.

- *How does conditioned inhibition arise?*

  Standard answer: The omission of an otherwise expected US (the occurrence of a No-US) strengthens inhibitory associations.

  Timing answer. The additive solution to the rate-estimation problem yields a negative rate of reinforcement.

- *What happens when a CS follows a reinforcer rather than preceding it?*

  Standard answer. Nothing; or, an inhibitory connection between CS and US is formed.

  Timing answer. A negative CS–US interval is recorded, or, equivalently, a positive US–CS interval. (More precisely: Subjective intervals, like objective intervals, are signed.)

- *How does a secondary CS acquire potency?*

  Standard answer. An association forms between the secondary CS and the primary CS, so that activation may be conducted from the secondary CS to the primary CS and hence, to the US via the primary association.

  Timing answer. The signed interval between the secondary and primary CS is summed with the signed interval between the primary CS and the US to obtain the expected interval between the secondary CS and the US.

- *How is CS–US contingency defined?*

  Standard answer. By differences in the conditional probability of reinforcement.

  Timing answer. By the ratio of the rates of reinforcement.

- *What is the fundamental experiential variable in operant conditioning?*

  Standard answer. Probability of reinforcement.

Timing answer. Rate of reinforcement.

- *What is basically going on in conditioning?*

Standard answer: Subjects are learning *to* respond. Experience acts on the processes that translate a given experience into an observable behavior. It does not instill knowledge of prevailing parameters, such as rates of reward, delays of reward, or magnitudes of reward.

Timing answer: Subjects are learning *that* such and such parameters prevail. Responding is elicited by this knowledge.

CONTRASTING BASIC ASSUMPTIONS

Central to the timing framework is the assumption that the nervous system times the durations of the intervals marked off by the events in a conditioning protocol, stores records of these intervals in memory, cumulates successive intervals of exposure to the same CS, and generates CRs through the agency of decision processes that take stored intervals and currently elapsing intervals as their inputs. None of these elements is found in associative analyses of conditioning. There is no provision for the timing of intervals. There is no provision for the summing of intervals. There is no memory process that stores the result of an interval-timing process, and there are no decision processes.

Conversely, none of the elements of associative models is found in timing models. There is no associative bond—no learned, signal-conducting connection—thus also no strengthening of connections through repetition, hence, no associability parameters. There is no notion of a learning *trial*, and the *probability* of reinforcement, whether of stimuli or responses, plays no role. Thus, the two conceptual frameworks have no fundamental elements in common. Timing models of conditioning have more in common with psychophysical models in vision and hearing than with associative models in learning. Like models in psychophysics, they focus on quantitative aspects of the experimental data. Like modern perceptual theories, they contain principles that resolve ambiguities inherent in the input to yield an unambiguous percept (representation) of the state of the world.

Elementary Acquisition Event in Associative Models

The elementary event in the associative conception of acquisition is a change in the strength of a connection. Repetitions of the same learning experience—for example, repetitions of the temporal pairing of a tone and a puff of air directed at the eye—strengthen the connection. Thus, what the associative conception appears to require at the neurobiological level is a mechanism for altering the strength of a synaptic connection between neurons. The immediate and enduring appeal of the associative conception is this neurobiological transparency. A second strong appeal is the straightforwardness of its explanation for the (presumed) gradual increase in the strength of the CR. The strengthening of the CR is naturally seen as a consequence of successive increments in the underlying (synaptic?) connection strengths.

On the other hand, the assumption of a conductive connection whose strength is incremented over successive repetitions places serious obstacles in the way of an associative explanation for the fact that animals learn the durations of intervals, the magnitudes of rewards, the intensities of conditioned and unconditioned stimuli, and other measurable properties of the experimental protocol The size of an increment in associative strength is a function of more than one aspect of the events on a given trial. In most models, the increment in associative strength is, for example, a function of (at least) the intensity or magnitude of the US, also called the reinforcement and the duration of the interval between the onset of the CS and the delivery of the US. It is also a function of the internal state of the animal; the pretrial strength of the association, and the pretrial strengths of other associations to the same US. In many models, it is also a function of the extent to which the animal is attending to the CS, the US, or both. Therefore, the resulting strength of an associative connection confounds several properties of the animal's past experience; among them, the intensity of the USs, the duration of the CS–US interval, and the number and kind of trials the animal has previously experienced. Because of this confounding, no objective property of the animal's conditioning experience is recoverable from the current strengths of the connections forged by that experience. Put more formally, the strength of an associative connection is a many-to-one function of different properties of the conditioning protocol, and many-to-one functions are not invertible; you cannot get from the one back to the many.[1]

Because the basic assumptions about what associations are, how they are strengthened, and how they function are not readily reconcilable with their being used to store the values of variables, it is not surprising that as-

---

[1]It may, however, be possible to get from many back to the many, that is, a manifold of associative connections may—with a very careful choice of connection-forging processes!—be such that one can recover from that manifold the values of the many experiential variables that created that associative manifold. However, the associative processes invoked to explain animal conditioning do not have the properties required to make an associative manifold invertible. It is not clear that it is possible to modify the association-forming process in such a way as to make the associative manifold invertible without eliminating the neurobiological transparency and straightforward explanation of gradual response acquisition that account for much of the appeal of associative models.

sociative models are not built around the assumption that the animals have learned the temporal intervals in the experimental protocol. To be sure, in contemporary associative theorizing, it is commonly assumed that the animal represents properties of the CS, the US, and its own behavior. However, associative theories of conditioning do not address the question of how these stimulus properties are coded into enduring changes in the nervous system. In particular, they do not attempt to describe the representations of stimulus properties or features in associative terms; that is, they do not specify how a measurable property of a stimulus, such as its intensity or magnitude or frequency composition, could be represented by the strengths of associative bonds. Associative theories are theories about the associative bonds that form between mental (or neural) entities. The associated entities may or may not be conceived of as representations, but the theory is about changes in the associations that conduct excitation and inhibition between entities, not the entities themselves.

Elementary Acquisition Event in Timing Models

The elementary event in the timing conception of acquisition is the measuring and recording of an elapsed interval. It is assumed that subjects time all of the salient events in a conditioning protocol and that they attribute reinforcement to external signal sources, such as the CS and the background, quite independently of whether conditioning, extinction, or cue competition of any sort is going to affect their later performance. Learning is the product of an information gathering system that is automatic and does not attribute "value" in the sense used by associative models (= desirability). Each repetition of the same experience (e.g., each trial in an eye blink conditioning experiment) lays down a new record (cf. Logan, 1988). The system also keeps running totals for the cumulative durations of the salient stimuli. Thus, what the timing conception requires at the neurobiological level is a mechanism capable of cumulating and storing the magnitudes (the values in the mathematical sense of the term) of a large number of distinct variables.

It is not difficult to suggest cellular mechanisms capable of storing the values of variables. The genetic code, for example, specifies the values that physiological parameters are to assume at various stages of development. Miall (1996) has proposed network models for accumulation, a central feature in timing models of acquisition, and also for storage and comparison processes. (See also Fiala, Grossberg, & Bullock, 1996; Grossberg & Merrill, 1996, for network timing models.) While these models do not have anything like the complexity of the systems we have proposed, they do illustrate the feasibility in principle of a neural-net kind of representation of accumulated elapsed time. Enduring changes in synaptic strength could be used to record the values of variables, but we do not think it very likely that they are used in this way.

Nonetheless, the timing analysis lacks neurobiological transparency because it is not obvious what currently understood neurobiological mechanisms could create the records, keep track of their location, and retrieve them when they are needed by a decision process. For example, if a change in a synaptic conductance were used to record the value of a variable, then when that value was to be used in a decision process, the strength of the appropriate synaptic connection would have to be "read." That is, the nervous system would have to "fetch" or "get" the value represented by the strength of that synapse. (The terms in quotes are the computer science terms for these operations, which are elementary operations in conventional computation.) The system could read the strength of a synaptic connection by passing a fixed (or known) read signal across it. The strength of the connection would then be coded by the strength of the postsynaptic signal. But in this scheme, the connection no longer functions as a conduction pathway transmitting a varying input signal. If changes in synaptic conductance are used in this way—to store the values of variables for subsequent use in decision processes—they cease to function as paths for through signal flow. They become instead functionally analogous to the memory locations in a conventional computing device or the genes on a chromosome, which no doubt explains why proposals to use "associative" connections in this way are rare to nonexistent.

In sum, what timing models require is a memory functionally analogous to a conventional computer memory, a mechanism for storing and retrieving the values of variables. Although it is not immediately apparent how to create such a memory out of the currently understood elements of neurobiology, such a memory is both physically and biologically possible. The proof of physical possibility is of course computer memory. Genes provide the proof of biological possibility; they store the values of variables for read-out in response to gene-activating stimuli. The genes are repositories of information, not paths for signal flow. Genes are read by gene activating signals, just as computer memories are read by memory-activating signals. Fifty years ago the physico-chemical mechanisms for these genetic operations were deeply mysterious. The mysteriousness of the requisite chemistry was such that more than a few biochemists doubted the validity of the conceptual framework offered by classical genetics; they doubted that there really were such things as genes. What timing models require neurobiologically is a selectively activatable repository for the values of experientially determined variables. The neurobiologically mysteriousness of this requirement is no greater than the biochemical mysteriousness of the requirement for a self-replicating molecule was in the 1950s.

Decision Mechanisms Versus No Decision Mechanisms

Associative models do not have decision mechanisms that take remem-bered values as their inputs and generate CRs as their outputs, whereas decision mechanisms are central to the timing perspective. Miller and Schachtman's (1985) Comparator Hypothesis is an exception to this gener-alization about associative models, which is why it represents a step in the direction of the kind of model we argue for. Timing models of conditioning share with psychophysical models in vision and hearing the explicit, formal specification of decision processes. Associative models, in contrast, have long lacked an explicit specification of the process or mechanism by which the strengths of associations translate into observed behavior (Miller & Matzel, 1989; Wasserman & Miller, 1997). The lack of decision mechanisms in associative models goes hand in hand with the lack of a mechanism for storing and retrieving the values of variables, because decision mecha-nisms take the values of remembered variables as their inputs.

THE CHALLENGES POSED BY EXPERIMENTAL FINDINGS

Partial Reinforcement

The fact that partial reinforcement does not affect the number of reinforce-ments to acquisition nor does it reduce the number that must be omitted to produce extinction is a problem for associative models. None of the for-mally specified associative models we are familiar with can account for this, because they all assume that nonreinforced trials weaken the net excitatory effects of reinforced trials. Therefore, the number of reinforced trials to reach a given level of excitatory effect ought to increase as the schedule of reinforcement gets thinner, but it does not, or does so only slightly.

Also, the net excitatory effect after a given number of reinforcements ought to become weaker as the schedule of reinforcement gets thinner. Therefore, the number of omitted reinforcements required to produce ex-tinction ought to be reduced as the schedule of reinforcement is thinned, but it is not, or only slightly. Gibbon (1981a) showed that, the asymptotic strength of the CS–US association in the Rescorla-Wagner theory is:

$$\frac{p\beta_I}{p\beta_I + (1 - p)\beta_e}, \tag{11}$$

where p is the probability that the CS is reinforced, and β_l and β_e are the learning and extinction rate parameters. When the rates of learning and extinction are equal, then the β's cancel out, and Equation 11 reduces to p. Regardless of the values of the β's, the asymptotic strength of the association declines as the probability of reinforcement declines. Trials (and omitted reinforcements) to extinction should be reduced correspondingly, but, in fact partial reinforcement increases trials to extinction and does not change omitted reinforcements to extinction.

As the extinction rate (β_e) is reduced relative to the learning rate (β_l), the amount by which partial reinforcement reduces asymptotic associative strength is reduced. However, the effect is large for any plausible ratio of extinction rates to learning rates. The extinction rate cannot be made too much slower than the learning rate, because the lower the ratio of the extinction rate to the learning rate, the longer extinction should take relative to learning, which brings us to the second problem.

Extinction

Another problem is the fact that the number of reinforcements that must be omitted in extinction may be the same as, or even substantially less than, the number of reinforcements required in acquisition. In order to avoid catastrophic effects of partial reinforcement on acquisition, associative models generally assume that the rate of extinction is less than the rate of acquisition. In that case, extinction ought to take longer than acquisition, which is not the case. Indeed, by reducing the ratio of the average intertrial interval, I, to the average trial duration, T, to 1.5:1, one can create a protocol in which the number of reinforcements required for acquisition is more than twice the number of omitted reinforcements required for extinction. At this $I{:}T$ ratio, subjects can still be conditioned on a 10:1 partial reinforcement schedule—and with no more reinforcements than are required under continuous reinforcement. We believe that these quantitative facts about the rates of acquisition and extinction pose a serious challenge to associative models of the conditioning process. They challenge the foundational assumption that reinforcement and nonreinforcement have opposing effects on the net excitatory effect of the associations.

It has been pointed out that the basic assumptions of associative conditioning theories about the strengthening and weakening effects of reinforcement and nonreinforcement fail to account for the microstructure of performance on partial reinforcement schedules (the trial-by-trial pattern— Gormezano & Coleman, 1975; Prokasy & Gormezano, 1979; see also Capaldi & Miller, 1988). They also fail to account for the macrostructure, when trials to extinction are considered alongside trials to acquisition. You can adjust the free parameters to predict the rate of acquisition, or to predict the rate of extinction, but it is not clear that it is possible to adjust these parameters so as to predict both rates. It is even less clear that it is possible to adjust the parameters so as to predict the rate of acquisition, the rate of extinction, the lack of an effect of partial reinforcement on reinforcements to acquisition, and the effect of the intertrial interval on reinforcements to acquisition (see immediately below).

Time-Scale Invariance

None of the formally specified associative models we are familiar with accounts for the time-scale invariance of the acquisition process, which we take to be the single most important quantitative fact about conditioning discovered in a century of experimental work. They all assume that delaying reinforcement reduces associability. Indeed, neurobiologically oriented associative theories often take a narrow window of associability as the signature of the associative mechanism (e.g., Gluck & Thompson, 1987; Grossberg & Schmajuk, 1991; Tang et al., 1999; Usherwood, 1993). The problem with the assumption that delaying reinforcement reduces associability is that delaying reinforcement has no effect if the intertrial interval is increased proportionately. This is a manifestation of time-scale invariance: Changing the relevant time intervals by a scaling factor does not affect the results.

Another basic problem for associative theories is that conditioning depends on a contingency between the CS and the US (or the instrumental response and the reinforcement), whereas associative theories assume that conditioning is driven by temporal pairing. Contingency is a global statistical property of the animal's experience. Like all such properties, it is time-scale invariant. It is difficult to see how the operation of a mechanism that is activated by temporal pairing or coincidence detection (Tang et al., 1999) can be time-scale invariant, because the concept of temporal pairing would seem to be a clear example of a non-time-scale invariant concept. The idea in temporal pairing is that there is a critical interval in learning (e.g., Tang et al., 1999); the principle of time-scale invariance says there can be no such critical interval.

The inverse proportionality between reinforcements to acquisition and the trial-to-trial interval also lacks an explanation. The effect of lengthening the intertrial interval on the rate of acquisition is explained qualitatively by the assumption that it gives more scope for the extinction of conditioning to the background (Durlach, 1989; Rescorla & Durlach, 1987). However, (Gibbon, 1981a) showed that the Rescorla-Wagner theory predicted only a weak effect of intertrial interval on reinforcements to acquisition, while predicting a strong effect of partial reinforcement—the opposite of what is observed empirically.

We believe that other associative models would make the same predictions regarding the relative potencies of these two basic variables if they were modified so as to make predictions regarding the effect of the intertrial interval. It is hard to say what most associative models, as they now stand, would predict about the relative effects of varying partial reinforcement and the intertrial interval on the rates of conditioning and extinction, because they cannot predict the effect of the intertrial interval at all without making use of the assumption of multiple background "trials" during one intertrial interval. This assumption brings up the "trial problem" in associative models.

The Trial Problem

The notion of a trial is a fundamental but insufficiently scrutinized notion at the heart of most associative models. A trial is the discrete interval of time during which the events occur that cause the updating of an associative connection. In Pavlovian conditioning, if a CS and a US both occur during a trial, it is a reinforced trial; if a CS occurs but not a US, it is an unreinforced trial. In instrumental conditioning, a trial is an interval during which there is an input (a stimulus), an output (a response), and finally, an error-correcting feedback (reinforcement or nonreinforcement). This latter conception of a trial also applies to the many contemporary associative network models that use an error-correcting algorithm to update associative strengths (supervised learning algorithms). The notion of a trial is intimately linked to the notion that it is the probability of reinforcement that drives learning, because probabilities cannot be defined in the absence of trials (intervals of a specified, finite duration; see Granger & Schlimmer, 1986).

We discern four different traditions governing the identification of the theoretician's trial with the elements of a conditioning protocol. In one conception, which one might call the neurobiological conception of Pavlovian conditioning, the beginning of a trial corresponds to the onset of a CS and the termination of a trial corresponds to the closing of the window of associability. The onset of a CS opens the window of associability; if a reinforcement occurs while the window remains open, it is a reinforced trial; if a reinforcement does not occur while the window is open, it is an unreinforced trial. Another trial does not begin until there is another CS onset.

In the second, more pragmatic conception of a Pavlovian trial, a trial begins when a CS comes on and it terminates when the CS goes off (or soon thereafter). If a reinforcement occurs while the CS is on (or soon thereafter), it is a reinforced trial, if it does not, it is an unreinforced trial.

Third, in the instrumental or operant tradition, a trial begins when the animal makes a response. The response opens a window of associability. If reinforcement is delivered while the window is open, the association between the response and the stimuli present when it was made is strengthened. If reinforcement does not occur soon after the response is made, it is an unreinforced trial.

Finally, in some analyses (e.g., Rescorla & Wagner, 1972), experientially undemarcated trials of a duration specified by the theorist are assumed to follow each other without interruption, that is, the theoretical analysis divides continuous experience up into a sequence of mutually exclusive and exhaustive discreet intervals. This assumption about trials is implicit in almost all discussions of the effects of background conditioning, but only in the rare attempts to model conditioning quantitatively is this assumption made explicit.

The trouble with the first conception is that it is known to be empirically indefensible. It has not been possible to define by experiment either when the window of association opens or how long it stays open (see Rescorla, 1972, for a review of such efforts). That is, it has never been possible to define temporal pairing in the simple way that this traditional conception suggests that it should be defined. Indeed, the time-scale invariance of the acquisition process would appear to be irreconcilable with any such definition.

The trouble with the more pragmatic notion of a Pavlovian trial is that it cannot be applied in the case of background conditioning, or in any of the conditioning protocols in which there may be many reinforcements during a sustained CS presentation. Such protocols are common in operant paradigms, where a stimulus present at the time of reinforcement is called a secondary reinforcer, or a discriminative stimulus, or both. The stimuli reinforced in operant paradigms (the stimuli projected onto the keys that the pigeons peck) are often continuously present, as for example in concurrent schedules of reinforcement. Background conditioning—and, more generally, conditioning to continuously present multiply reinforced stimuli—is an empirically well-established phenomenon: Reinforcements that occur while an aplysia, a pigeon, or a rat is in an experimental chamber establish a CR to the chamber (Baker & Mackintosh, 1977; Balsam, 1985; Balsam & Schwartz, 1981; Colwill, Absher, & Roberts, 1988; Rescorla, 1968, 1972). The more frequent the reinforcer, the stronger the conditioning (Mustaca, Gabelli, Papine, & Balsam, 1991).

When the pragmatic conception of a trial is applied to a background conditioning protocol, each experimental session constitutes one trial, because the CS (the background) "comes on" at the beginning of the session, when the subject is placed in the apparatus, and terminates with the end of the session, when it is removed. How to deal with the effects of reinforcer frequency is then problematic. To get round this problem, Rescorla and Wagner (1972) posited a "trial clock" that carved the intertrial interval up into purely subjective trials. This permitted them to treat the intertrial intervals, when the background alone was present, as composed of sequences of multiple internally timed event-independent trials (autotrials, for short), with the association between the background and the US strengthened or weakened accordingly as a reinforcer did or did not happen to occur during such a "trial."

Rescorla and Wagner's (1972) immensely influential analysis of the effect of background conditioning on conditioning to a transient CS depended on this autotrial assumption—the fourth approach to trial definition—just as strongly as on the much better known assumption that associations to a given US compete for an asymptotically limited total associative strength. But the authors themselves seem to have regarded the autotrials assumption as a temporary theoretical expedient. There has been no attempt to explore its consequences, despite the fact that this approach to defining trials has been very widely used by other theorists; indeed, it is all but universal in connectionist models. We believe that such an attempt would uncover unfortunate implications.

The problem is that in many cases, it appears necessary to assume that autotrials are very short (on the order of a second or less). If they are allowed to be as long as Rescorla and Wagner assumed them to be for the purposes of their analysis (2 minutes) then, in many conditioning protocols, one again encounters the problem that a single trial encompasses more than one presentation of both the CS and the US. And, two CSs that did not in fact coincide are counted as coinciding because they both occurred during one autotrial. However, if autotrials are assumed to be very short, then many protocols have very large numbers of unreinforced autotrials. Unreinforced trials either weaken excitatory associations (as in the Rescorla-Wagner theory), or strengthen inhibitory associations, which negate the behavioral effects of excitatory associations, or reduce attention to the CS. In any event, the numerous unreinforced trials introduced into the analysis by the (short) autotrials assumption would seem to make the build up of any appreciable net excitatory effect impossible. The effects of rare reinforced autotrials are swamped by the effects of the frequent unreinforced autotrials. One is forced to assume that the effects of nonreinforcement are extremely weak relative to the effects of reinforcement, but then it becomes difficult to explain the results of experiments on extinction and conditioned inhibition, which imply that conditioned inhibition can develop rapidly (Nelson & Bouton, 1997) and that extinction can occur more rapidly than acquisition.

From informal conversations with colleagues interested in associative models of learning, we think it is commonly imagined that the notion of a trial and the notion of probability of reinforcement, which is fundamentally dependent on the concept of a discrete trial—while on their surface clearly untenable—are not really problematic. When we challenged them about the plausibility of imagining that continuous experience is somehow carved into discrete trials, thereby making it possible to define probabilities of reinforcement, we have often heard something like the following. Of course, it is not reasonable to imagine that the animal's ongoing experience of the world is really carved into discrete trials, but the theoretical analysis in terms of discrete trials of finite duration can easily be made more realistic simply by imagining that the "trials" are made shorter and shorter until their duration is negligible, at which point experience is effectively continuous.

This will not work. What it overlooks is that as the durations of the intervals (trials) within which the probabilities of events are defined go to zero, so do the probabilities. Most importantly, as the durations of trials become negligibly small, so do all differences in probability, and it is the differences in probability that are important in associative modeling. This is just a somewhat more formal way of making the point we made in the preceding paragraph, namely that as trials are made shorter and shorter, unreinforced trials become so numerous that their effects swamp the effects of the ever rarer reinforced trials.

The instrumental conception of a trial has similar problems. There are no data that define a privileged interval following a response, during which a reinforcement must occur if the response is to become conditioned. One can delay reinforcement for long intervals provided that intertrial intervals are made correspondingly long. Indeed, the phenomenon of autoshaping, as we have already noted, calls into question the distinction between the Pavlovian and operant or instrumental paradigms. It is not clear that conditioning in any paradigm actually depends on the animal's making a response, except insofar as the failure to make a response may prevent its observing a crucial fact about the world. Conditioning in operant paradigms, as in Pavlovian paradigms, appears to be driven by the temporal relations between events, including events initiated by the subject, such as key pecks, lever presses, and chain pulls. Insofar as an operant response is irrelevant in operant conditioning—or relevant only insofar as it constitutes a distinguishable kind of event—then the operant conception of a trial (response-initiated trials) becomes inapplicable.

If the trial notion is theoretically indispensable but operationally undefinable—that is, if one cannot say when a given segment of a protocol constitutes a trial—then one must question whether associative theories can be validly applied to the phenomena they seek to explain. Certainly, if associative models are to be used successfully as a guide to mechanisms to be looked for at the neurobiological level of analysis, they are going to have to come to terms with the trial problem. There is no room in a materialist neurobiology for a *deus ex machina*, who decides on a case by case ad hoc basis what constitutes a trial. At the moment, associative theorists are playing the role of this god outside the machine. They decide what constitutes a trial, because their models have no principles specifying what constitutes a trial.

One might object that the notion of a stimulus, for example, is indispensable in any analysis of conditioning but difficult to define rigorously. However, there is no problem in practice in identifying elements that function as stimuli in a very broad range of conditioning situations. So far as we are aware, the notion of what constitutes a stimulus onset or offset in one protocol does not become problematic when one turns one's attention to the analysis of a different protocol involving the same stimuli, the same reinforcers, the same responses, and the same subjects. This is emphatically not the case for the notion of a trial.

The Contrasting Effects of Reinforcement Magnitude on Acquisition and Preference

An animal's preference for one concurrent VI schedule of reinforcement over another is proportional to the relative magnitudes of the reinforcements (Catania, 1963; Keller & Gollub, 1977; Leon & Gallistel, 1998). The natural associative interpretation of this is that bigger reinforcements produce bigger increments in associative strength and therefore, a bigger asymptotic associative strength. In the Rescorla-Wagner theory, for example, the parameter lambda, which is the asymptotic net associative strength that a US can support, is generally taken to be a function of the magnitude of reinforcement. That assumption has the just specified consequence, at least qualitatively (greater preference for bigger rewards). If bigger reinforcements increase the size of the increments in associative strength, they ought to increase the rate of acquisition, but they do not. It is difficult to see how an associative model is going to explain the findings of Balsam and Payne (1979). They found that the rate of conditioning in pigeon auto-shaping was virtually unchanged when the duration of the pigeon's access to the grain hopper was increased 15 fold, from the usual 5 seconds of access to a lengthy 60 seconds. On the other hand, the rate of acquisition was dramatically increased by reducing the duration of the pigeon's access to the food hopper for each reinforcement by a factor of 15 (a very large reduction in the magnitude of reinforcement) and adding the time thus saved to the intertrial interval, the interval during which in most associative theories nothing of any relevance to conditioning happens. It is difficult to see how to account for these results while also accounting for the strong effect of reinforcement magnitude on preference.

The No-US Problem

Extinction and conditioned inhibition require an associative change in response to the failure of a US to occur. For a CS to become an inhibitor it must signal the nonoccurrence of an otherwise expected stimulus (LoLordo

& Fairless, 1985; Rescorla, 1988). It is unclear how to conceptualize this within an associative context. Both Pavlov (1928) and Hull (1943) spent pages wrestling with the question of how the nonoccurrence of a stimulus could be the cause of something. We do not think the question has been solved in the decades since they wrestled with it. For a relatively recent discussion of expectancy in conditioning, see Dickinson (1989), who refers to this as the No-US problem.

There is nothing inherently puzzling about a process set in motion by the failure of something to occur. In a device like a computer, which is capable of comparing input values against internally generated or stored values (that is, against an expectation in the sense that term is used in this paper), the failure of an input to occur generates a signal from the comparison process. This signal is proportional to the difference or ratio between the input magnitude (zero, in the case of failure) and the comparison magnitude (the expectation). The discrepancy signal initiates whatever events are to be a consequence of the failure. This is the nature of our explanation of extinction in which the decision to stop responding is based on the ratio between a currently elapsing unreinforced interval and an expected inter-reinforcement interval. Indeed, an expected interval between reinforcements is the denominator in each of the decision ratios that appear in the timing analysis of acquisition, extinction, and response timing.

The basic problem is that, in associative theory, the nonoccurrence of reinforcement, that is, the occurrence of a No-US, must set in motion the mechanism that responds to nonreinforcement. Even if one adds to an associative model the machinery necessary to have an expectation (as is implicitly done in the Rescorla & Wagner, 1972, model and many other contemporary associative models), it is still unclear how to make the associative analysis go through, because in many conditioning paradigms there is no particular moment at which a reinforcement is to be expected. That is, not only does the No-US have no other physical attributes, it also has no location in time. Yet, the changes it is supposed to set in motion must have a location in time, because all physical changes do. Acquisition and extinction proceed normally when the reinforcements are delivered by random rate scheduling mechanisms. Under these conditions, reinforcement is no more likely at any one moment than at any other. There is no basis for expecting the reinforcement to occur at any one time, only a basis for expecting it to occur within some interval. How can the changes that underlie extinction and inhibition be set in motion by the failure of an expected reinforcement to occur if that reinforcement is no more likely at any one moment than at any other? It would seem that either the failure must be deemed to happen at every moment, or it must be deemed never to happen. In either case, it is unclear how to make a physically realizable, real-time model of extinction and inhibitory conditioning within the associative conceptual framework.

The paradox concerning when a No-US may be deemed to have occurred arises only when one considers the problem in a real-time context, where time is continuous, rather than broken into discrete intervals, that is, into trials. When time is treated as a sequence of discrete trials, then one can imagine that the occurrence of reinforcement on any trial creates an expectation of reinforcement on every trial. The disappointment of this expectation on unreinforced trials sets in motion the changes in associative strength that are assumed to be a consequence of nonreinforcement (of No-USs). This is the implicit assumption in the Rescorla and Wagner (1972) model and many other contemporary associative models, indeed, in all connectionist models that we know of. The strength of the excitatory association is made to be the expectation. It is implicitly taken to represent the magnitude of the expected reinforcement. The discrepancy (arithmetic difference) between this expectation and the observed magnitude of reinforcement (0) is what causes the changes due to nonreinforcement. Because there is only a finite number of trials, this does not lead to an infinite number of nonreinforcements in any finite amount of time. However, for this approach to work, that is, for it to be physically realizable, one needs to resort to the autotrials assumption. One has to assume that the nervous system itself breaks continuous experience into trials. As we have already seen, this assumption is itself problematic, because there does not seem to be a way of specifying a priori (i.e., without reference to a particular experimental protocol) how long an autotrial is. Thus, the introduction of trials into the analysis does not avoid the paradox that arises when one tries to specify whether a No-US has occurred within any given interval; it just hides it.

The paradoxes surrounding the concept of a No-US do not arise in the Rate Estimation Theory of extinction and inhibitory conditioning. When nothing happens (when there is no reinforcement) the timers timing intervals delimited by reinforcement simply go on accumulating. The failure of reinforcement to occur at some particular moment does not have to initiate any events within the nervous system in this model. Events are initiated when the ratio of the accumulated interval without reinforcement to the expected interval between reinforcements becomes too great (exceeds the decision threshold). This gives a physically realizable model of what occurs during extinction and the development of conditioned inhibition, a mechanism that can operate in continuous real time, as the brain must do.

Directionality

In associative models, a special class of stimuli, reinforcing stimuli, set the associative mechanism in motion and confer directionality on the associative process. If there is no stimulus that can be identified as a reinforcing stimulus, then there is no way of saying whether one is dealing with forward or backward conditioning. This makes the phenomenon of sensory preconditioning an awkward phenomenon for associative theories to come to terms with. On the face of it—if one does not believe that there is a special class of stimuli called reinforcing stimuli—then sensory preconditioning is simply conditioning: Two stimuli, say, a tone and a light, are temporally paired and they become associated. The problem arises because almost all theories of the associative process assume that it matters which stimulus comes first, the CS or the US. If the CS comes first, it is forward conditioning. If the US comes first, it is backward conditioning. The associative mechanism itself is assumed to be sensitive to the temporal order. Different orderings of the stimuli being associated must produce different associative effects. If they did not, then it would not matter whether Pavlov rang the bell before or after presenting food to his dogs, which we know to be false. But when it is two neutral CSs that are paired, there is no way to specify whether one has to do with forward or backward conditioning.

There is no problem of directionality from a timing perspective, because, it starts with the assumptions that the system can add, subtract, and divide temporal intervals, and that it learns both the sign and the magnitudes of the intervals between events. From a timing perspective, reinforcers play no privileged role in learning per se. Like other stimuli, their onsets and offsets may mark either or both ends of a timed interval. The memory of the reinforcement plays a privileged role only in determining whether a decision mechanism is used to determine a response. Neutral stimuli—stimuli that do not elicit stimulus-specific unconditioned responses—do not evoke CRs because they are not intrinsically important to any behavior system. In order for a behavior-determining decision to be made, a behavior system must operate (cf. Fanselow, 1989; Timberlake & Lucas, 1989). That is, the animal must be motivated to make use of the conditioned stimuli in the control of its behavior. Reinforcers are simply motivationally significant stimuli; stimuli whose occurrence motivates behavior that anticipates that occurrence.

Secondary Conditioning

In chap. 5, we reviewed recent findings from Ralph Miller's lab (Barnet & Miller, 1996; Cole, Barnet, & Miller, 1995a, 1995b) on trace conditioning versus delay conditioning, backward versus forward conditioning, inhibitory conditioning, and secondary conditioning. These findings pose strong challenges to the traditional associative conception of all of these phenomena. They show that knowledge of the temporal relations among stimuli are paramount, not the supposed effects of different stimulus arrangements on the strength of the resulting association. By manipulating temporal relations, the backward conditioning may be made to appear stronger than forward conditioning in one test of what has been learned, whereas another test of the same learning gives the traditional result that forward conditioning is better than backward conditioning.

The challenge for associative theory posed by the results from Miller's lab is to explain the reversals in the apparent relative strengths of primary CS–US associations when their strengths are tested directly and indirectly (Barnet & Miller, 1996; Cole, Barnet, & Miller, 1995a, 1995b). In the direct tests, when the strength of the CR to the primary CS is measured, backwardly conditioned and trace conditioned CSs appear to have considerably weaker associations with the US than forwardly conditioned and delay conditioned CSs. But in the indirect tests, when the strength of the CR to CSs that have been linked to the primary CSs through identical secondary conditioning is measured, the backwardly conditioned and trace conditioned primary CSs appear to have much stronger associations with the US than the forwardly conditioned and delay conditioned primary CSs. These results are perplexing from an associative point of view, because they seem to require the kind of assumption that is the foundation of the timing perspective, namely, that in the course of conditioning, the subject acquires knowledge of the temporal relations between events, and that it is this knowledge and inferences drawn from it that determine the CR.

These experiments also show that animal subjects in conditioning experiments remember the evidence leading to their conclusions about which CSs predict which rates of reinforcement, so that they may revise these conclusions after a disambiguating later experience. The best documented instance of this is the retroactive reversal of overshadowing (see Baker & Mercier, 1989 for review). In the overshadowing paradigm, two CSs are always presented and reinforced together during original training, so it is inherently ambiguous which stimulus predicts what rate of reinforcement. Animal subjects typically resolve this ambiguity by crediting the reinforcements to only one of the two CSs (e.g., Reynolds, 1961). The CS that gets credited is called the overshadowing CS. When, however, the ambiguity is removed by later training in which the overshadowing CS is presented alone and not reinforced, the animal appears to credit the previously overshadowed CS with the rate of reinforcement originally credited to the overshadowing CS. The lack of a memory for the path of an associative connection prohibits a clear explanation for retroactive effects of this kind.

Reinstatement

Associative models conceive of extinction in one of two ways: (a) as the weakening of an association (e.g., Pearce, 1994; Rescorla & Wagner, 1972), or (b) as the development of an opposing association (or negating process of some kind) whose effects cancel the effects of the excitatory association.

The first assumption is almost universally adhered to in connectionist models. However, it is now widely recognized by experimentalists to be irreconcilable with a large literature demonstrating that conditioning is forever: No subsequent experience can expunge the memories (associations/connections) implanted (strengthened) by earlier conditioning (Bouton, 1991, 1993; Bouton & Ricker, 1994; Brooks, Hale, Nelson, & Bouton, 1995; Kaplan & Hearst, 1985; Mazur, 1996; Rescorla, 1992, 1993, 1998; Rescorla & Heth, 1975). To be sure, subsequent experience can lead to the disappearance of the CR, but a variety of reinstatement procedures show that the "associations" (the memories implanted during earlier conditioning) remain when the CR has disappeared. The simplest of the reinstatement procedures is to wait awhile after extinction before testing for the presence of the CR. The response comes back (e.g., Rescorla, 1996), a phenomenon that Pavlov (1928) dubbed spontaneous recovery. Changing the spatial context (the background, that is, the experimental chamber) also brings the response back (Bouton & Ricker, 1994).

Bringing back the CR after its extinction by changing the temporal or spatial context, or both, is called reinstatement. The finding that it is almost always possible to reinstate an extinguished (or even counterconditioned) response has led specialists in conditioning to favor the view that extinction involves the development of an association with an opposing (or cancelling) effect rather than the weakening of the originally conditioned association—a view favored by Pavlov himself. It is not, however, clear how this solves the problem. The problem is to explain why reinstatement procedures make old excitatory associations prevail over newer inhibitory (or cancelling) associations.

From the perspective of the analysis of extinction presented in chap. 4, a precondition for extinction is that the animal not forget the path to its present estimates of the state of the world. In this analysis, extinction is a consequence of a decision mechanism designed to detect a change in the rate of reinforcement attributed to the CS, that is, to decide whether recent experience is inconsistent with earlier experience. This requires that recent experience be compared to earlier experience. A precondition for that comparison is that recent experience be kept distinct from more remote experience in memory. To detect a change, the system must *not* represent its experience solely by means of a running average, which is the universal assumption in associative models of conditioning. It cannot use a simple running average of its experience to determine its behavior, because a segment of the recent past must be compared to the earlier past. Thus, although there are no well worked out principles for explaining reinstatement from a timing perspective, it is fair to say that the phenomenon is not, on its face, perplexing from a timing perspective. The principle seems to be that when the animal detects a change in the rate of reinforcement predicted by a CS, it looks back through its experience to find what rate that stimulus predicted in the more distant past.

SUMMARY

The experimental results from the behaviorist program of research on learning call into question the central assumptions of this program. The assumption that more frequently reinforced responses are stronger, for example, is apparently false. So is the assumption that reinforcement strengthens behavior and nonreinforcement weakens it. So is the assumption that temporal pairing drives the associative process. So is the assumption that forward temporal pairing produces better learning than backward temporal pairing. So is the assumption that nonreinforcement produces inhibitory associations. When looked at from a timing perspective and in the light of the experimental findings of the last 30 years, much of what is taught in the standard course in animal learning requires reinterpretations so far reaching as to make the new interpretations more or less incommensurable with the standard interpretation.

These new interpretations are powerful. They bring clarity and rigor to conceptual problems that have caused confusion and paradox for a century. They give, for example, a new, rigorous definition of contingency and specify a process by which contingency may be perceived. They solve the problem of nonreinforcement, the problem of the mysterious "No-US" that causes learning to occur despite its lack of any physical properties. They explain why reinforcement magnitude has no effect on the rate of acquisition but a strong effect on preference. They explain the mysterious reversals in the apparent strengths and signs of associative connections when the strengths of primary connections are assessed by means of secondarily conditioned CSs. These new interpretations make quantitative predictions about old phenomena such as the effects of partial reinforcement, delay of reinforcement, and trial spacing. And they make new predictions; a number of them have been pointed out in the preceding chapters. Finally, they bring to the fore far reaching empirical principles, such as the principle of time-scale invariance, a principle of such far-reaching importance that it should motivate an extensive program of experimental testing, designed to reveal the limits of its application and why those limits arise.

The timing framework brings to the study of conditioning a fundamentally different conceptual framework. One hopes that the challenge posed to the traditional framework by this new framework will lead to vigorous new programs of research, as has usually been the case when a new and clearly powerful conceptual framework arises to challenge a long entrenched way of thinking.

One hopes also that neurobiologists will begin to ponder the implications of this new framework for the attempts to find the cellular and molecular bases of learning and memory. At present, these attempts are based entirely on the associative framework. Neurobiologists have committed themselves to the hypothesis that the formation of associations is the fundamental event in higher learning, that memories are simply associations, and that changes in associative strength must be mediated by changes in synaptic conductance. They have ignored the extensive evidence that animals learn the parameters of their environment, and so they have not attempted to imagine a neurobiological mechanism for storing the values of variables, the neurobiological analog of the memory in a conventional computer, much less have they designed experiments to get at this mechanism. We hope that they will not continue to ignore this fundamental question: How does the nervous system record and retrieve the value of a variable?

References

Anderson, N. H. (1969). Variation of CS–US interval in long-term avoidance conditioning in the rat with wheel turn and with shuttle tasks. *Journal of Comparative and Physiological Psychology, 68*, 100–106.

Annau, Z., & Kamin, L. (1961). The conditioned emotional response as a function of intensity of the US. *Journal of Comparative and Physiological Psychology, 54*, 428–432.

Aronson, L., Balsam, P., et al. (1991). *Context value modulates levels of response recovery after random control training.* Annual Meeting of the Psychonomics Society, San Francisco.

Autor, S. M. (1969). The strength of conditioned reinforcers as a function of frequency and probability of reinforcement. In D. P. Hendry (Ed.), *Conditioned reinforcement* (pp. 127–162). Homewood, IL: Dorsey Press.

Baker, A. G., & Mackintosh, N. J. (1977). Excitatory and inhibitory conditioning following uncorrelated presentations of the CS and US. *Animal Learning and Behavior, 5*, 315–319.

Baker, A. G., & Mercier, P. (1989). Attention, retrospective processing and cognitive representations. In S. B. Klein & R. R. Mowrer (Eds.), *Contemporary learning theories: Pavlovian conditioning and the status of traditional learning theory* (pp. 85–116). Hillsdale, NJ: Lawrence Erlbaum Associates.

Balleine, B. W., Garner, C., Ganzalez, F., & Dickinson, A. (1995). Motivational control of heterogeneous instrumental chains. *Journal of Experimental Psychology: Animal Behavior Processes, 21*, 203–217.

Balsam, P. (1984). Relative time in trace conditioning. In J. Gibbon & L. Allan (Eds.), *Timing and time perception*. New York: New York Academy of Sciences, 243, 211–227.

Balsam, P. (1985). The functions of context in learning and performance. In P. Balsam & A. Tomie (Eds.), *Context and learning* (pp. 1–21). Hillsdale, NJ: Lawrence Erlbaum Associates.

Balsam, P. D., & Payne, D. (1979). Intertrial interval and unconditioned stimulus durations in autoshaping. *Animal Learning and Behavior, 7*, 477–482.

Balsam, P. D., & Schwartz, A. L. (1981). Rapid contextual conditioning in autoshaping. *Journal of Experimental Psychology: Animal Behavior Processes, 7*, 382–393.

Barela, P. B. (1999). Theoretical mechanisms underlying the trial-spacing effect in Pavlovian fear conditioning. *Journal of Experimental Psychology: Animal Behavior Processes, 25*, 177–193.

Barnet, R. C., Arnold, H. M., & Miller, R. R. (1991). Simultaneous conditioning demonstrated in second-order conditioning: Evidence for similar associative structure in forward and simultaneous conditioning. *Learning and Motivation, 22,* 253–268.

Barnet, R. C., Cole, R. P., & Miller, R. R. (1997). Temporal integration in second-order conditioning and sensory preconditioning. *Animal Learning and Behavior, 25*(2), 221–233.

Barnet, R. C., Grahame, N. J., & Miller, R. R. (1991). Comparing the magnitudes of second-order conditioning and sensory pre-conditioning. *Bulletin of the Psychonomic Society, 29,* 133–135.

Barnet, R. C., Grahame, N. J., & Miller, R. R. (1993a). Local context and the comparator hypothesis. *Animal Learning and Behavior, 21,* 1–13.

Barnet, R. C., Grahame, N. J., & Miller, R. R. (1993b). Temporal encoding as a determinant of blocking. *Journal of Experimental Psychology: Animal Behavior Processes, 19,* 327–341.

Barnet, R. C., & Miller, R. R. (1996). Second order excitation mediated by a backward conditioned inhibitor. *Journal of Experimental Psychology: Animal Behavior Processes, 22*(3), 279–296.

Bateson, M., & Kacelnik, A. (1995). Preferences for fixed and variable food sources: Variability in amount and delay. *Journal of the Experimental Analysis of Behavior, 63,* 313–329.

Bateson, M., & Kacelnik, A. (1996). Rate currencies and the foraging starling: The fallacy of the averages revisited. *Behavioral Ecology, 7,* 341–352.

Bateson, M., & Kacelnik, A. (1998). Risk-sensitive foraging: Decision making in variable environments. *Cognitive ecology: The evolutionary ecology of information processing and decision making.* Illinois: University of Chicago Press.

Baum, W. M. (1981). Optimization and the matching law as accounts of instrumental behavior. *Journal of the Experimental Analysis of Behavior, 36,* 387–403.

Baum, W. M. (1992). In search of the feedback function for variable-interval schedules. *Journal of the Experimental Analysis of Behavior, 57,* 365–375.

Baum, W. M., & Rachlin, H. C. (1969). Choice as time allocation. *Journal of the Experimental Analysis of Behavior, 12,* 861–874.

Belke, T. W. (1992). Stimulus preference and the transitivity of preference. *Animal Learning and Behavior, 20,* 401–406.

Bevins, R. A., & Ayres, J. J. B. (1995). One-trial context fear conditioning as a function of the interstimulus interval. *Animal Learning and Behavior, 23*(4), 400–410.

Bitterman, M. E. (1965). Phyletic differences in learning. *American Psychologist, 20,* 396–410.

Bolles, R. C., Collier, A. C., Bouton, M. E., & Marlin, N. A. (1978). Some tricks for ameliorating the trace-conditioning deficit. *Bulletin of the Psychonomic Society, 11,* 403–406.

Bouton, M. B. (1991). Context and retrieval in extinction and in other examples of interference in simple associative learning. In L. Dachowski & C. R. Flaherty (Eds.), *Current topics in animal learning* (pp. 25–53). Hillsdale, NJ: Lawrence Erlbaum Associates.

Bouton, M. E. (1993). Context, ambiguity, and classical conditioning. *Current Directions in Psychological Science, 3,* 49–53.

Bouton, M. E., & Ricker, S. T. (1994). Renewal of extinguished responding in a second context. *Animal Learning and Behavior, 22*(3), 317–324.

Brelsford, J., & Theios, J. (1965). Single session conditioning of the nictitating membrane in the rabbit: Effect of intertrial interval. *Psychonomic Science, 2,* 81–82.

Brooks, D. C., Hale, B., Nelson, J. B., & Bouton, M. E. (1995). Reinstatement after counterconditioning. *Animal Learning and Behavior, 23*(4), 383–390.

Brown, P. L., & Jenkins, H. M. (1968). Autoshaping of the pigeon's key-peck. *Journal of the Experimental Analysis of Behavior, 11,* 1–8.

Brunner, D., Fairhurst, S., Stolovitsky, G., & Gibbon, J. (1997). Mnemonics for variability: Remembering food delay. *Journal of Experimental Psychology: Animal Behavior Processes, 23*(1), 68–83.

Brunner, D., & Gibbon, J. (1995). Value of food aggregates: Parallel versus serial discounting. *Animal Behaviour, 50,* 1627–1634.

Brunner, D., Gibbon, J., & Fairhurst, S. (1994). Choice between fixed and variable delays with different reward amounts. *Journal of Experimental Psychology: Animal Behavior Processes, 20,* 331–346.

Brunswik, E. (1939). Probability as a determiner of rat behavior. *Journal of Experimental Psychology, 25,* 175–197.

Capaldi, E. J., & Miller, D. J. (1988). Counting in rats: Its functional significance and the independent cognitive processes which comprise it. *Journal of Experimental Psychology: Animal Behavior Processes, 14,* 3–17.

Catania, A. C. (1963). Concurrent performances: A baseline for the study of reinforcement magnitude. *Journal of the Experimental Analysis of Behavior, 6,* 299–300.

Church, R. M., Broadbent, H. A., & Gibbon, J. (1992). Biological and psychological description of an internal clock. In I. Gormezano & E. Wasserman (Eds.), *Learning and memory: The behavioral and biological substrates* (pp. 105–128). Hillsdale, NJ: Lawrence Erlbaum Associates.

Church, R. M., & Deluty, M. Z. (1977). Bisection of temporal intervals. *Journal of Experimental Psychology: Animal Behavior Processes, 3,* 216–228.

Church, R. M., Meck, W. H., & Gibbon, J. (1994). Application of scalar timing theory to individual trials. *Journal of Experimental Psychology: Animal Behavior Processes, 20*(2), 135–155.

Clayton, N. S., & Dickinson, A. (1998). Episodic-like memory during cache recovery by scrub jays. *Nature, 395,* 272–274.

Clayton, N. S., & Dickinson, A. (1999). Memory for the content of caches by scrub jays (Aphelocoma coerulescens). *Journal of Experimental Psychology: Animal Behavior Processes, 25*(1), 82–91.

Cole, R. P., Barnet, R. C., & Miller, R. R. (1995a). Effect of relative stimulus validity: Learning or performance deficit? *Journal of Experimental Psychology: Animal Behavior Processes, 21,* 293–303.

Cole, R. P., Barnet, R. C., & Miller, R. R. (1995b). Temporal encoding in trace conditioning. *Animal Learning and Behavior, 23*(2), 144–153.

Colwill, R. M., Absher, R. A., & Roberts, M. L. (1988). Context-US learning in *Aplysia californica. Journal of Neuroscience, 8*(12), 4434–4439.

Colwill, R. M., & Rescorla, R. A. (1990). Effect of reinforcer devaluation on discriminative control of instrumental behavior. *Journal of Experimental Psychology: Animal Behavior Processes, 16,* 40–47.

Commons, M. L., Herrnstein, R. J., & Rachlin, H. (Eds.). (1982). *Quantitative analyses of behavior: Vol. 2. Matching and maximizing accounts.* Cambridge, MA: Ballinger.

Cooper, L. D., Aronson, L., Balsam, P. D., & Gibbon, J. (1990). Duration of signals for intertrial reinforcement and nonreinforcement in random control procedures. *Journal of Experimental Psychology: Animal Behavior Processes, 16,* 14–26.

Davis, D. G., Staddon, J. E., Machado, A., & Palmer, R. G. (1993). The process of recurrent choice. *Psychological Review, 100,* 320–341.

Davison, M., & McCarthy, D. (1988). *The matching law: A research review.* Hillsdale, NJ: Lawrence Erlbaum Associates.

Davison, M. C. (1969). Preference for mixed-interval versus fixed-interval schedules. *Journal of the Experimental Analysis of Behavior, 12,* 247–252.

Desmond, J. E., & Moore, J. W. (1991). Altering the synchrony of stimulus trace processes: Tests of neural-network model. *Biological Cybernetics, 65,* 161–169.

Devenport, L. D., & Devenport, J. A. (1994). Time-dependent averaging of foraging information in least chipmunks and golden-mantled squirrels. *Animal Behaviour, 47,* 787–802.

Devenport, L., Hill, T., Wilson, M., & Ogden, E. (1997). Tracking and averaging in variable environments: A transition rule. *Journal of Experimental Psychology: Animal Behavior Processes, 23*(4), 450–460.

Dews, P. B. (1970). The theory of fixed-interval responding. In W. N. Schoenfeld (Ed.), *The theory of reinforcement schedules* (pp. 43–61). New York: Appleton-Century-Crofts.

Dickinson, A. (1989). Expectancy theory in animal conditioning. In S. B. Klein & R. R. Mowrer (Eds.), *Contemporary learning theories: Pavlovian conditioning and the status of traditional learning theory* (pp. 279–308). Hillsdale, NJ: Lawrence Erlbaum Associates.

Dickinson, A., & Balleine, B. (1994). Motivational control of goal-directed action. *Animal Learning and Behavior, 22*(1), 1–18.

Dickinson, A., & Burke, J. (1996). Within-compound associations mediate the retrospective revaluation of causality judgments. *Quarterly Journal of Experimental Psychology. B, Comparative and Physiological Psychology, 49*, 60–80.

Dickinson, A., Hall, G., & Mackintosh, N. J. (1976). Surprise and the attenuation of blocking. *Journal of Experimental Psychology: Animal Behavior Processes, 2*, 213–222.

Dreyfus, L. R. (1991). Local shifts in relative reinforcement rate and time allocation on concurrent schedules. *Journal of Experimental Psychology: Animal Behavior Processes, 17*, 486–502.

Durlach, P. J. (1983). Effect of signaling intertrial unconditioned stimuli in autoshaping. *Journal of Experimental Psychology: Animal Behavior Processes, 9*, 374–389.

Durlach, P. J. (1986). Explicitly unpaired procedure as a response elimination technique in autoshaping. *Journal of Experimental Psychology: Animal Behavior Processes, 12*, 172–185.

Durlach, P. J. (1989). Role of signals for unconditioned stimulus absence in the sensitivity of autoshaping to contingency. *Journal of Experimental Psychology: Animal Behavior Processes, 15*, 202–211.

Estes, W. (1964). Probability learning. In A. W. Melton (Ed.), *Categories of human learning* (pp. 89–128). New York: Academic.

Fanselow, M. S. (1986). Associative vs topographical accounts of the immediate-shock freezing deficit in rats: Implications for the response selection rules governing species specific defense reactions. *Learning and Motivation, 17*, 16–39.

Fanselow, M. S. (1989). The adaptive function of conditioned defensive behavior: An ecological approach to Pavlovian stimulus-substitution theory. In R. J. Blanchard, P. F. Brain, D. C. Blanchard, & S. Parmigiani (Eds.), *Ethoexperimental approaches to the study of behavior* (MATO ASI Series D., Vol. 48, pp. 151–166). Boston: Kluver.

Fanselow, M. S. (1990). Factors governing one-trial contextual conditioning. *Animal Learning and Behavior, 18*, 264–270.

Fanselow, M. S., DeCola, J. P., & Young, S. L. (1993). Mechanisms responsible for reduced contextual conditioning with massed unsignaled unconditional stimuli. *Journal of Experimental Psychology: Animal Behavior Processes, 19*, 121–137.

Fanselow, M. S., & Stote, D. (1995, November). *Temporal vs. associative accounts of the immediate shock deficit in contextual fear.* Paper presented at the Annual Meeting of the Psychonomics Society, Los Angeles.

Fantino, E. (1969). Conditioned reinforcement, choice, and the psychological distance to reward. In D. P. Hendry (Ed.), *Conditioned reinforcement* (pp. 163–191). Homewood, IL: Dorsey Press.

Fiala, J. C., Grossberg, S., & Bullock, D. (1996). Metabotropic glutamate receptor activation in cerebellar Purkinje cells as substrate for adaptive timing of the classically conditioned eye-blink response. *Journal of Neuroscience, 16*(11), 3760–3774.

Fischer, G. (1972). Maximizing and role of correction method in probability learning in chicks. *Journal of Comparative and Physiological Psychology, 80*, 49–53.

Foree, D. D., & LoLordo, V. M. (1973). Attention in the pigeon: Differential effects of food-getting versus shock-avoidance procedures. *Journal of Comparative and Physiological Psychology 85*, 551–558.

Gallistel, C. R. (1990). *The organization of learning.* Cambridge, MA: Bradford Books/MIT Press.

Gallistel, C. R. (1992b). Classical conditioning as an adaptive specialization: A computational model. In D. L. Medin (Ed.), *The psychology of learning and motivation: Advances in research and theory* (Vol. 28, pp. 35–67). New York: Academic Press.

Gallistel, C. R. (1999). The Replacement of General-Purpose Learning Models with Adaptively Specialized Learning Modules. In M. S. Gazzaniga (Ed.), *The cognitive neurosciences* (2nd ed.). Cambridge, MA: MIT Press.

Gallistel, C. R., & Gibbon, J. (2000). Time, rate and conditioning. *Psychological Review, 107*, 289–344.

Gallistel, C. R., Mark, T. A., King, A., & Latham, P. E. (2001). The rat approximates an ideal detector of changes in rates of reward: Implications for the law of effect. *Journal of Experimental Psychology: Animal Behavior Processes, 27*, 354–372.

Ganesan, R., & Pearce, J. M. (1988). Effect of changing the unconditioned stimulus on appetitive blocking. *Journal of Experimental Psychology: Animal Behavior Processes, 14*, 280–291.

Gibbon, J. (1971). Scalar timing and semi-Markov chains in free-operant avoidance. *Journal of Mathematical Psychology, 8*, 109–138.

Gibbon, J. (1972). Timing and discrimination of shock density in avoidance. *Psychological Review, 79*, 68–92.

Gibbon, J. (1977). Scalar expectancy theory and Weber's Law in animal timing. *Psychological Review, 84*, 279–335.

Gibbon, J. (1981a). The contingency problem in autoshaping. In C. M. Locurto, H. S. Terrace, & J. Gibbon (Eds.), *Autoshaping and conditioning theory* (pp. 285–308). New York: Academic.

Gibbon, J. (1992). Ubiquity of scalar timing with a Poisson clock. *Journal of Mathematical Psychology, 36*, 283–293.

Gibbon, J. (1995). Dynamics of time matching: Arousal makes better seem worse. *Psychonomic Bulletin and Review, 2*(2), 208–215.

Gibbon, J., Baldock, M. D., Locurto, C. M., Gold, L., & Terrace, H. S. (1977). Trial and intertrial durations in autoshaping. *Journal of Experimental Psychology: Animal Behavior Processes, 3*, 264–284.

Gibbon, J., & Balsam, P. (1981). Spreading associations in time. In C. M. Locurto, H. S. Terrace, & J. Gibbon (Eds.), *Autoshaping and conditioning theory* (pp. 219–253). New York: Academic Press.

Gibbon, J., & Church, R. M. (1981). Time left: Linear versus logarithmic subjective time. *Journal of Experimental Psychology: Animal Behavior Processes, 7*(2), 87–107.

Gibbon, J., Church, R. M., Fairhurst, S., & Kacelnik, A. (1988). Scalar expectancy theory and choice between delayed rewards. *Psychological Review, 95*, 102–114.

Gibbon, J., Church, R. M., & Meck, W. H. (1984). Scalar timing in memory. In J. Gibbon & L. Allan (Eds.), *Timing and time perception* (Vol. 423, pp. 52–77). New York: New York Academy of Sciences.

Gibbon, J., & Fairhurst, S. (1994). Ratio versus difference comparators in choice. *Journal of the Experimental Analysis of Behavior, 62*, 409–434.

Gibbon, J., Farrell, L., Locurto, C. M., Duncan, H. J., & Terrace, H. S. (1980). Partial reinforcement in autoshaping with pigeons. *Animal Learning and Behavior, 8*, 45–59.

Gluck, M. A., & Thompson, R. F. (1987). Modeling the neural substrates of associative learning and memory: A computational approach. *Psychological Review, 94*(2), 176–191.

Goddard, M. J., & Jenkins, H. M. (1987). Effect of signaling extra unconditioned stimuli on autoshaping. *Animal Learning and Behavior, 15*(1), 40–46.

Godin, J.-G. J., & Keenleyside, M. H. A. (1984). Foraging on patchily distributed prey by a cichlid fish (Teleosti, Cichlidae): A test of the ideal free distribution theory. *Animal Behaviour, 32*, 120–131.

Gormezano, I., & Coleman, S. R. (1975). Effects of partial reinforcement on conditioning, conditional probabilities, asymptotic performance, and extinction of the rabbit's nictitating membrane response. *Pavlovian Journal of Biological Science, 10*, 13–22.

Grahame, N. J., Barnet, R. C., & Miller, R. R. (1992). Pavlovian inhibition cannot be obtained by posttraining A-US pairings: Further evidence for the empirical asymmetry of the comparator hypothesis. *Bulletin of the Psychonomic Society, 30*, 399–402.

Granger, R. H. J., & Schlimmer, J. C. (1986). The computation of contingency in classical conditioning. In G. H. Bower (Ed.), *The psychology of learning and motivation: Vol. 20* (pp. 137–192). New York: Academic.

Grossberg, S., & Merrill, J. W. L. (1996). The hippocampus and cerebellum in adaptively timed learning, recognition, and movement. *Journal of Cognitive Neuroscience, 8*, 257–277.

Grossberg, S., & Schmajuk, N. A. (1991). Neural dynamics of adaptive timing and temporal discrimination during associative learning. In G. A. Carpenter & S. Grossberg (Eds.), *Pattern recognition by self-organizing neural networks* (pp. 637–674). Cambridge, MA: MIT Press.

Hallam, S. C., Matzel, L. D., Sloat, J. S., & Miller, R. R. (1990). Excitation and inhibition as a function of post-training extinction of the excitatory cue used in Pavlovian inhibition training. *Learning and Motivation, 21*, 59–84.

Harper, D. G. C. (1982). Competitive foraging in mallards: Ideal free ducks. *Animal Behaviour, 30*, 575–584.

Hawkins, R. D., Abrams, T. W., Carew, T. J., & Kandel, E. R. (1983). A cellular mechanism of classical conditioning in *Aplysia*: Activity-dependent amplification of presynaptic facilitation. *Science, 219*, 400–404.

Herrnstein, R. J. (1961). Relative and absolute strength of response as a function of frequency of reinforcement. *Journal of the Experimental Analysis of Behavior, 4*, 267–272.

Herrnstein, R. J. (1964). Secondary reinforcement and rate of primary reinforcement. *Journal of the Experimental Analysis of Behavior, 7*, 27–36.

Herrnstein, R. J., & Loveland, D. H. (1975). Maximizing and matching on concurrent ratio schedules. *Journal of the Experimental Analysis of Behavior, 24*, 107–116.

Herrnstein, R. J., & Prelec, D. (1991). Melioration: A theory of distributed choice. *Journal of Economic Perspectives, 5*, 137–156.

Herrnstein, R. J., & Vaughan, W. J. (1980). Melioration and behavioral allocation. In J. E. R. Staddon (Ed.), *Limits to action: The allocation of individual behavior* (pp. 143–176). New York: Academic Press.

Heyman, G. M. (1979). A Markov model description of changeover probabilities on concurrent variable-interval schedules. *Journal of the Experimental Analysis of Behavior, 31*, 41–51.

Heyman, G. M. (1982). Is time allocation unconditioned behavior? In M. Commons, R. Herrnstein, & H. Rachlin (Eds.), *Quantitative analyses of behavior, Vol. 2: Matching and maximizing accounts* (pp. 459–490). Cambridge, MA: Ballinger Press.

Holland, P. C. (1990). Event representation in Pavlovian conditioning: Image and action. *Cognition, 37*, 105–131.

Holmes, J. D., & Gormezano, I. (1970). Classical appetitive conditioning of the rabbit's jaw movement response under partial and continuous reinforcement schedules. *Learning and Motivation, 1*, 110–120.

Honig, W. K. (1981). Working memory and the temporal map. In N. E. Spear & R. R. Miller (Eds.), *Information processing in animals: Memory mechanisms* (pp. 167–197). Hillsdale, NJ: Lawrence Erlbaum Associates.

Hornik, K., Stinchcombe, M., & White, H. (1989). Multilayer feedforward networks are universal approximators. *Neural Networks, 2*, 359–366.

Hull, C. L. (1929). A functional interpretation of the conditioned reflex. *Psychological Review, 36*, 498–511.

Hull, C. L. (1943). *Principles of behavior*. New York: Appleton-Century-Crofts.

Hyman, A. (1969). Two temporal parameters of free-operant discriminated avoidance in the rhesus monkey. *Journal of the Experimental Analysis of Behavior, 12*, 641–648.

Kacelnik, A., & Brito e Abreu, F. (1998). Risky choice and Weber's law. *Journal of Theoretical Biology, 194*(2), 289–298.

Kamin, L. J. (1954). Traumatic avoidance learning: The effects of CS–US interval with a trace-conditioning procedure. *Journal of Comparative and Physiological Psychology, 47*, 65–72.

Kamin, L. J. (1967). "Attention-like" processes in classical conditioning. In M. R. Jones (Ed.), *Miami symposium on the prediction of behavior: Aversive stimulation* (pp. 9–33). Miami: University of Miami Press.

Kamin, L. J. (1969). Predictability, surprise, attention, and conditioning. In B. A. Campbell & R. M. Church (Eds.), *Punishment and aversive behavior* (pp. 276–296). New York: Appleton-Century-Crofts.

Kamin, L. J., & Gaioni, S. J. (1974). Compound conditioned emotional response conditioning with differentially salient elements in rats. *Journal of Comparative and Physiological Psychology, 87,* 591–597.

Kaplan, P. (1984). Importance of relative temporal parameters in trace autoshaping: From excitation to inhibition. *Journal of Experimental Psychology: Animal Behavior Processes, 10,* 113–126.

Kaplan, P., & Hearst, E. (1985). Contextual control and excitatory vs. inhibitory learning: Studies of extinction, reinstatement, and interference. In P. D. Balsam & A. Tomie (Eds.), *Context and learning* (pp. 195–224). Hillsdale, NJ: Lawrence Erlbaum Associates.

Kaufman, M. A., & Bolles, R. C. (1981). A nonassociative aspect of overshadowing. *Bulletin of the Psychonomic Society, 18,* 318–320.

Kehoe, E. J., & Gormezano, I. (1974). Effects of trials per session on conditioning of the rabbit's nictitating membrane response. *Bulletin of the Psychonomic Society, 4,* 434–436.

Kehoe, E. J., Graham-Clarke, P., & Schreurs, B. G. (1989). Temporal patterns of the rabbit's nictitating membrane response to compound and component stimuli under mixed CS–US intervals. *Behavioral Neuroscience, 103,* 283–295.

Keller, J. V., & Gollub, L. R. (1977). Duration and rate of reinforcement as determinants of concurrent responding. *Journal of the Experimental Analysis of Behavior, 28,* 145–153.

Killeen, P. (1968). On the measurement of reinforcement frequency in the study of preference. *Journal of the Experimental Analysis of Behavior, 11,* 263–269.

Killeen, P. (1975). On the temporal control of behavior. *Psychological Review, 82,* 89–115.

Killeen, P. R. (1982). Incentive theory: II. Models for choice. *Journal of the Experimental Analysis of Behavior, 38,* 217–232.

Killeen, P. R., & Fetterman, J. G. (1988). A behavioral theory of timing. *Psychological Review, 94,* 455–468.

Killeen, P. R., & Weiss, N. A. (1987). Optimal timing and the Weber function. *Psychological Review, 94,* 455–468.

Kremer, E. F. (1978). The Rescorla-Wagner model: Losses in associative strength in compound conditioned stimuli. *Journal of Experimental Psychology: Animal Behavior Processes, 4,* 22–36.

LaBarbera, J. D., & Church, R. M. (1974). Magnitude of fear as a function of the expected time to an aversive event. *Animal Learning and Behavior, 2,* 199–202.

Lattal, K. M., & Nakajima, S. (1998). Overexpectation in appetitive Pavlovian and instrumental conditioning. *Animal Learning and Behavior, 26*(3), 351–360.

Leon, M. I., & Gallistel, C. R. (1998). Self-stimulating rats combine subjective reward magnitude and subjective reward rate multiplicatively. *Journal of Experimental Psychology: Animal Behavior Processes, 24*(3), 265–277.

Levinthal, C. F., Tartell, R. H., Margolin, C. M., & Fishman, H. (1985). The CS–US interval (ISI) function in rabbit nictitating membrane response conditioning with very long intertrial intervals. *Animal Learning and Behavior, 13*(3), 228–232.

Libby, M. E., & Church, R. M. (1974). Timing of avoidance responses by rats. *Journal of the Experimental Analysis of Behavior, 22,* 513–517.

Logan, G. D. (1988). Toward an instance theory of automatization. *Psychological Review, 95,* 492–527.

Logue, A. W., & Chavarro, A. (1987). Effect on choice of absolute and relative values of reinforcer delay, amount, and frequency. *Journal of Experimental Psychology: Animal Behavior Processes, 13,* 280–291.

LoLordo, V. M., & Fairless, J. L. (1985). Pavlovian conditioned inhibition: The literature since 1969. In R. R. Miller & N. E. Spear (Eds.), *Information processing in animals* (pp. 117–163). Hillsdale, NJ: Lawrence Erlbaum Associates.

Lolordo, V. M., Jacobs, W. J., & Foree, D. D. (1982). Failure to block control by a relevant stimulus. *Animal Learning and Behavior, 10*, 183–193.

Low, L. A., & Low, H. I. (1962). Effects of CS–US interval length upon avoidance responding. *Journal of Comparative and Physiological Psychology, 55*, 1059–1061.

Mackintosh, N. J. (1971). An analysis of overshadowing and blocking. *Quarterly Journal of Experimental Psychology, 23*, 118–125.

Mackintosh, N. J. (1974). *The psychology of animal learning.* New York: Academic.

Mackintosh, N. J. (1975). A theory of attention: Variations in the associability of stimuli with reinforcement. *Psychological Review, 82*, 276–298.

Mackintosh, N. J. (1976). Overshadowing and stimulus intensity. *Animal Learning and Behavior, 4*, 186–192.

Mackintosh, N. J., & Reese, B. (1970). One-trial overshadowing. *Quarterly Journal of Experimental Psychology, 31*, 519–526.

Mark, T. A. (1997). *The microstructure of choice.* Unpublished doctoral dissertation, University of California, Los Angeles.

Mark, T. A., & Gallistel, C. R. (1994). The kinetics of matching. *Journal of Experimental Psychology: Animal Behavior Processes, 20*, 79–95.

Matzel, L. D., Held, F. P., & Miller, R. R. (1988). Information and expression of simultaneous and backward associations: Implications for contiguity theory. *Learning and Motivation, 19*, 317–344.

Matzel, L. D., Schachtman, T. R., & Miller, R. R. (1985). Recovery of overshadowed association achieved by extinction of the overshadowing stimulus. *Learning and Motivation, 16*, 398–412.

Mazur, J. E. (1984). Tests of an equivalence rule for fixed and variable delays. *Journal of Experimental Psychology: Animal Behavior Processes, 10*, 426–436.

Mazur, J. E. (1986). Fixed and variable ratios and delays: Further test of an equivalence rule. *Journal of Experimental Psychology: Animal Behavior Processes, 12*, 116–124.

Mazur, J. E. (1989). Theories of probabilistic reinforcement. *Journal of the Experimental Analysis of Behavior, 51*, 87–99.

Mazur, J. E. (1991). Choice with probabilistic reinforcement: Effects of delay and conditioned reinforcers. *Journal of the Experimental Analysis of Behavior, 55*, 63–77.

Mazur, J. E. (1995). Development of preference and spontaneous recovery in choice behavior with concurrent variable-interval schedules. *Animal Learning and Behavior, 23*(1), 93–103.

Mazur, J. E. (1996). Past experience, recency, and spontaneous recovery in choice behavior. *Animal Learning & Behavior, 24*(1), 1–10.

Mazur, J. E. (1997). Choice, delay, probability, and conditioned reinforcement. *Animal Learning and Behavior, 25*(2), 131–147.

McDiarmid, C. G., & Rilling, M. E. (1965). Reinforcement delay and reinforcement rate as determinants of schedule preference. *Psychonomic Science, 2*, 195–196.

McNamara, J. M., & Houston, A. I. (1992). Risk-sensitive foraging: A review of the theory. *Bulletin of Mathematical Biology, 54*, 355–378.

Meck, W. H., Church, R. M., & Gibbon, J. (1985). Temporal integration in duration and number discrimination. *Journal of Experimental Psychology: Animal Behavior Processes, 11*, 591–597.

Miall, C. (1996). Models of neural timing. In M. Pastor & A. Artieda (Eds.), *Time, internal clocks and movement. Advances in psychology: Vol. 115* (pp. 69–94). Amsterdam: North-Holland/Elsevier Science.

Miller, R. R., & Barnet, R. C. (1993). The role of time in elementary associations. *Current Directions in Psychological Science, 2*, 106–111.

Miller, R. R., Barnet, R. C., & Grahame, N. J. (1992). Responding to a conditioned stimulus depends on the current associative status of other cues that were present during training of that specific stimulus. *Journal of Experimental Psychology: Animal Behavior Processes, 18*, 251–264.

Miller, R. R., & Grahame, N. J. (1991). Expression of learning. In L. Dachowski & C. F. Flaherty (Eds.), *Current topics in animal learning* (pp. 95–117). Hillsdale, NJ: Lawrence Erlbaum Associates.

Miller, R. R., & Matzel, L. D. (1989). Contingency and relative associative strength. In S. B. Klein & R. R. Mowrer (Eds.), *Contemporary learning theories: Pavlovian conditioning and the status of traditional learning theory* (pp. 61–84). Hillsdale, NJ: Lawrence Erlbaum Associates.

Miller, R. R., & Schachtman, T. R. (1985). Conditioning context as an associative baseline: Implications for response generation and the nature of conditioned inhibition. In R. R. Miller & N. S. Spear (Eds.), *Information processing in animals: Conditioned inhibition* (pp. 51–88). Hillsdale, NJ: Lawrence Erlbaum Associates.

Montague, P. R., & Sejnowski, T. J. (1994). The predictive brain: Temporal coincidence and temporal order in synaptic learning mechanisms. *Learning & Memory, 1*, 1–33.

Mustaca, A. E., Gabelli, F., Papine, M. R., & Balsam, P. (1991). The effects of varying the interreinforcement interval on appetitive contextual conditioning. *Animal Learning and Behavior, 19*, 125–138.

Myerson, J., & Miezin, F. M. (1980). The kinetics of choice: An operant systems analysis. *Psychological Review, 87*, 160–174.

Nelson, J. B., & Bouton, M. E. (1997). The effects of a context switch following serial and simultaneous feature-negative discriminations. *Learning & Motivation, 28*, 56–84.

Nevin, J. A. (1982). Some persistent issues in the study of matching and maximizing. In M. L. Commons, R. J. Herrnstein, & H. Rachlin (Eds.), *Quantitative analyses of behavior: Vol. 2: Matching and maximizing accounts* (pp. 153–165). Cambridge, MA: Ballinger.

Pavlov, I. V. (1928). *Lectures on conditioned reflexes: The higher nervous activity of animals* (H. Gantt, Trans.). London: Lawrence & Wishart.

Pearce, J. M. (1994). Similarity and discrimination: A selective review and a connectionist model. *Psychological Review, 101*, 587–607.

Pearce, J. M., & Hall, G. (1980). A model for Pavlovian learning: Variation in the effectiveness of conditioned but not of unconditioned stimuli. *Psychological Review, 87*, 532–552.

Penny, T. B., Allan, L. G., Meck, W. H., & Gibbon, J. (1998). Memory mixing in duration bisection. In D. A. Rosenbaum, C. E. Collier, et al. (Eds.), *Timing of behavior: Neural, psychological, and computational perspectives* (pp. 165–193). Cambridge, MA: MIT Press.

Pliskoff, S. S. (1971). Effects of symmetrical and asymmetrical changeover delays on concurrent performances. *Journal of the Experimental Analysis of Behavior, 16*, 249–256.

Prokasy, W. F., & Gormezano, I. (1979). The effect of US omission in classical aversive and appetitive conditioning of rabbits. *Animal Learning and Behavior, 7*, 80–88.

Pubols, B. H. (1962). Constant versus variable delay of reinforcement. *Journal of Comparative and Physiological Psychology, 55*, 52–56.

Rachlin, H. (1974). Self-control. *Behaviorism, 2*, 94–107.

Rachlin, H. (1978). A molar theory of reinforcement schedules. *Journal of the Experimental Analysis of Behavior, 30*, 345–360.

Rachlin, H. (1995). Self-control: Beyond commitment. *Behavioral and Brain Sciences, 18*, 109–121.

Rachlin, H., Logue, A. W., Gibbon, J., & Frankel, M. (1986). Cognition and behavior in studies of choice. *Psychological Review, 93*, 33–45.

Rachlin, H., Raineri, A., & Cross, D. (1991). Subjective probability and delay. *Journal of the Experimental Analysis of Behavior, 55*, 233–244.

Reboreda, J. C., & Kacelnik, A. (1991). Risk sensitivity in starlings: Variability in food amount and food delay. *Behavioral Ecology, 2*, 301–308.

Rescorla, R. A. (1967). Inhibition of delay in Pavlovian fear conditioning. *Journal of Comparative and Physiological Psychology, 64*, 114–120.

Rescorla, R. A. (1968). Probability of shock in the presence and absence of CS in fear conditioning. *Journal of Comparative and Physiological Psychology, 66*(1), 1–5.

Rescorla, R. A. (1969). Pavlovian conditioned inhibition. *Psychological Bulletin, 72*, 77–94.

Rescorla, R. A. (1972). Informational variables in Pavlovian conditioning. In G. H. Bower (Ed.), *The psychology of learning and motivation: Vol. 6* (pp. 1–46). New York: Academic Press.

Rescorla, R. A. (1988). Behavioral studies of Pavlovian conditioning. *Annual Review of Neuroscience, 11,* 329–352.

Rescorla, R. A. (1990). Instrumental responses become associated with reinforcers that differ in one feature. *Animal Learning and Behavior, 18*(2), 206–211.

Rescorla, R. A. (1991). Associations of multiple outcomes with an instrumental response. *Journal of Experimental Psychology: Animal Behavior Processes, 17,* 465–474.

Rescorla, R. A. (1992). Response-independent outcome presentation can leave instrumental R-O associations intact. *Animal Learning and Behavior, 20*(2), 104–111.

Rescorla, R. A. (1993). The preservation of response-outcome associations through extinction. *Animal Learning and Behavior, 21*(3), 238–245.

Rescorla, R. A. (1996). Spontaneous recovery after training with multiple outcomes. *Animal Learning and Behavior, 24,* 11–18.

Rescorla, R. A. (1998). Instrumental learning: Nature and persistence. In M. Sabourin, F. I. M. Craik, & M. Roberts (Eds.), *Proceedings of the XXVI International Congress of Psychology: Vol. 2. Advances in psychological science: Biological and cognitive aspects* (pp. 239–258). London: Psychology Press.

Rescorla, R. A., & Colwill, R. M. (1989). Associations with anticipated and obtained outcomes in instrumental conditioning. *Animal Learning and Behavior, 17,* 291–303.

Rescorla, R. A., & Cunningham, C. L. (1978). Within-compound flavor association. *Journal of Experimental Psychology: Animal Behavior Processes, 4,* 267–275.

Rescorla, R. A., & Durlach, P. J. (1987). The role of context in intertrial interval effects in autoshaping. *Quarterly Journal of Experimental Psychology, 39B,* 35–48.

Rescorla, R. A., & Heth, C. D. (1975). Reinstatement of fear to an extinguished conditioned stimulus. *Journal of Experimental Psychology: Animal Behavior Processes, 104,* 88–106.

Rescorla, R. A., & Wagner, A. R. (1972). A theory of Pavlovian conditioning: Variations in the effectiveness of reinforcement and nonreinforcement. In A. H. Black & W. F. Prokasy (Eds.), *Classical conditioning II* (pp. 64–99). New York: Appleton-Century-Crofts.

Reynolds, G. S. (1961). Attention in the pigeon. *Journal of the Experimental Analysis of Behavior, 4,* 203–208.

Ricker, S. T., & Bouton, M. E. (1996). Reacquisition following extinction in appetitive conditioning. *Animal Learning and Behavior, 24*(4), 423–436.

Roberts, S., & Church, R. M. (1978). Control of an internal clock. *Journal of Experimental Psychology: Animal Behavior Processes, 4,* 318–337.

Schneider, B. (1969). A two-state analysis of fixed-interval responding in the pigeon. *Journal of the Experimental Analysis of Behavior, 12,* 667–687.

Schneiderman, N., & Gormezano, I. (1964). Conditioning of the nictitating membrane of the rabbit as a function of CS-US interval. *Journal of Comparative and Physiological Psychology, 57,* 188–195.

Schull, R. L., Mellon, R., & Sharp, J. A. (1990). Delay and number of food reinforcers: Effects on choice and latencies. *Journal of the Experimental Analysis of Behavior, 53,* 235–246.

Sheafor, P. J., & Gormezano, I. (1972). Conditioning the rabbit's (*Oryctolagus cuniculus*) jaw-movement response. *Journal of Comparative and Physiological Psychology, 81,* 449–456.

Shimp, C. P. (1969). Optimal behavior in free-operant experiments. *Psychological Review, 76,* 97–112.

Sidman, M. (1953). Two temporal parameters of the maintenance of avoidance behavior by the white rat. *Journal of Comparative and Physiological Psychology, 46,* 253–261.

Staddon, J. E. R., & Motheral, S. (1979). On matching and maximizing in operant choice experiments. *Psychological Review, 85,* 436–444.

Sutton, R. S., & Barto, A. G. (1981). Toward a modern theory of adaptive networks: Expectation and prediction. *Psychological Review, 88,* 135–170.

Sutton, R. S., & Barto, A. G. (1990). Time-derivative models of Pavlovian reinforcement. In M. Gabriel & J. Moore (Eds.), *Learning and computational neuroscience: Foundations of adaptive networks* (pp. 497–537). Cambridge, MA: Bradford/MIT Press.

Tang, Y. -P., Shimizu, E., Dube, G. R., Rampon, C., Kerchner, G. A., Zhuo, M., Liu, G., & Tsien, J. Z. (1999). Genetic enhancement of learning and memory in mice. *Nature, 401*, 63–69.

Timberlake, W., & Lucas, G. A. (1989). Behavior systems and learning: From misbehavior to general principles. In S. B. Klein & R. R. Mowrer (Eds.), *Contemporary learning theories: Instrumental conditioning theory and the impact of biological constraints on learning* (pp. 237–275). Hillsdale, NJ: Lawrence Erlbaum Associates.

Usherwood, P. N. R. (1993). Memories are made of this. *Trends in Neurosciences, 16*(11), 427–429.

Van Hamme, L. J., & Wasserman, E. A. (1994). Cue competition in causality judgments: The role of nonpresentation of compound stimulus elements. *Learning & Motivation, 25*, 127–151.

Wade, N. (1999, September 7). Of smart mice and even smarter man. *New York Times*, pp. D1–D2.

Wagner, A. R. (1981). SOP: A model of automatic memory processing in animal behavior. In N. E. Spear & R. R. Miller (Eds.), *Information processing in animals: Memory mechanisms* (pp. 5–47). Hillsdale, NJ: Lawrence Erlbaum Associates.

Wagner, A. R., Logan, F. A., Haberlandt, K., & Price, T. (1968). Stimulus selection in animal discrimination learning. *Journal of Experimental Psychology, 76*(2), 171–180.

Wasserman, E. A., Franklin, S. R., & Hearst, E. (1974). Pavlovian appetitive contingencies and approach versus withdrawal to conditioned stimuli in pigeons. *Journal of Comparative and Physiological Psychology, 86*, 616–627.

Wasserman, E. A., & Miller, R. R. (1997). What's elementary about associative learning? *Annual Review of Psychology, 48*, 573–607.

White, N. E., Kehoe, E. J., Choi, J. -S., & Moore, J. W. (2000). Coefficients of variation in timing of the classically conditioned eyeblink in rabbits. *Psychobiology, 28*(4), 520–524.

Williams, B. A. (1981). Invariance in reinforcements to acquisition, with implications for the theory of inhibition. *Behaviour Analysis Letters, 1*, 73–80.

Williams, B. A., & Royalty, P. (1989). A test of the melioration theory of matching. *Journal of Experimental Psychology: Animal Behavior Processes, 15*(2), 99–113.

Author Index

Subject Index

A

Acquisition
  cause of, 156
  elementary event in associative, 159
  function, location & asymptote, 35
  of a timed response, 49ff
  rate of, 28, 30, 31, 34, 35, 37, 43
  variability, 44
Allocating mechanism, 125ff
Arithmetic mean
  evidence for in acquisition, 147
  vs. geometric, 21
  vs. harmonic, 143
Artificial Intelligence (AI), Preface vii
Associations
  and conditioning paradigms, 1
  and stimulus encoding, 2
  asymptotic strength in R-W theory, 163
  directionality of, 172f
  in R-W model, 65
  do not have symbolic content, 2, 160
  functions of many variables, 160
  neurobiological search for, Preface viii
  neurobiological transparency of, 160
  not foundation of conditioning, 1
  strengthened by repetitive experience, 1
  weaker produce slower responses, 20
  within compound, 71

Associative framework
  basic assumptions, 159ff
  challenge to, Chap. 7
  foundation of neurobiology of memory, 177
Autoshaping, 25f
Aversive conditioned responses, 15
Avoidance responses
  timing of, 15f, 153

B

Background conditioning
  see Conditioning, background
Bayes theorem, 93
Behaviorism, Preface vii
Bisection paradigm, 21
Blocking, 58, 65
  retroactive, 73ff

C

CER
  see Conditioned emotional response
Choice
  see Operant choice
Cognitivism, Preface vii
Coincidence detection
  see Temporal pairing
Comparator hypothesis, 39
Computation, Preface vii, ix, 23, 36, 44, 45, 100, 143, 146, 151, 162
Concurrent Variable Interval Schedules, 87ff
Conditioned emotional response, 18
Conditioned eye blink, 20

35177365